Queering the Color Line

Edited by Michèle Aina Barale, Jonathan Goldberg,
Michael Moon, and Eve Kosofsky Sedgwick

QUEERING

the

COLOR LINE

Race and the Invention of Homosexuality
in American Culture

SIOBHAN B. SOMERVILLE

Duke University Press
Durham and London, 2000

© 2000 Duke University Press
All rights reserved
Printed in the United States of America on acid-free paper ∞
Designed by Rebecca Filene Broun
Typeset in Bembo by Tseng Information Systems, Inc.
Library of Congress Cataloging-in-Publication Data
appear on the last printed page of this book.
2nd printing, 2001

For my parents

Contents

Acknowledgments

Writing this book would not have been possible without the collective help of many individuals and institutions, which I would like to gratefully acknowledge here. First, I owe great thanks to Hazel Carby, whose encouraging response to my initial ideas for this project inspired me to pursue it. Her scholarship, teaching, political vision, and unflagging support have enlivened and sustained my work. I am also indebted to David Rodowick for his interest in the project in its early stages and for his continuing encouragement. For their lasting influence on my thinking, I also thank Harriet Chessman, Margaret Homans, Charles Musser, Robert Stepto, and Jennifer Wicke. Cathy Davidson's support made an important difference in this project's completion; for her generosity and good advice, I am grateful.

I benefited enormously from the suggestions of Michael Moon and Robyn Wiegman, who read the manuscript in its entirety; I could not have asked for more discerning and generous readers. Their insights have been invaluable for shaping a stronger book than I could have envisioned on my own.

For reading individual chapter drafts and for their friendship, I thank Elizabeth Abrams, Lauren Chattman, Susan Edmunds, Judy Frank, Heather Hendershot, and Laura Saltz. I am also grateful to members of the Lesbian and Gay Studies Workshop at the University of Chicago for reading and commenting on an earlier draft of chapter 5. Stuart Clarke, David Edwards, Jacob Meskin, Mark Reinhardt, and Angela Zito, members of a faculty seminar at Williams College, provided helpful comments on a very early version of chapter 1. For their collective intellectual generosity and culinary gifts, I am grateful to Jeanne Bergman, Cassandra Cleghorn, Bridget Conrad, Carrie Waara, and Kimberly Wallace-Sanders.

I also thank my colleagues at Purdue University for their interest in this project, especially those currently and formerly in the Women's

Studies Program and the English Department. Diane Rubenstein deserves special thanks for being such a remarkable friend and colleague. During my work on this project, I was also fortunate to have a visiting appointment in the English Department at Duke University and a fellowship in the Women's Studies Program at the University of California, Santa Barbara. I am grateful to the many colleagues who made me feel welcome at those institutions. I would also like to acknowledge my students, especially those who took "Love American Style," for their thoughtful engagement with many of the texts and ideas that are central to this book.

Librarians and other staff of a number of archival collections facilitated my research. In particular, Madeline Matz of the Motion Picture, Broadcasting and Recorded Sound Division of the Library of Congress provided crucial assistance. I also thank the staff of the Beinecke Rare Book and Manuscript Library at Yale University; the Billy Rose Theatre Collection at the New York Public Library for the Performing Arts; the Schomberg Center for Research in Black Culture; the Film Department of the International Museum of Photography at George Eastman House; the Film Studies Center at the Museum of Modern Art; the Department of Special Collections, University Research Library, University of California, Los Angeles; the Margaret Herrick Library at the Academy of Motion Picture Arts and Sciences; and the Department of Special Collections, Davidson Library, University of California, Santa Barbara. For permission to reprint a sketch by Miguel Covarrubias, I thank Bruce Kellner and the Van Vechten Trust. For providing this image, I thank the Yale Collection of American Literature, Beinecke, Rare Book and Manuscript Library, Yale University.

Funding from several sources supported my research and writing at various stages. For fellowships, I thank the Mrs. Giles D. Whiting Foundation; the United States Department of Education; the University of California at Santa Barbara; and Yale University. Faculty incentive grants from the School of Liberal Arts and research funds from the Department of English at Purdue University helped defray the expenses of archival research.

Parts of two chapters of this book have been published previously in different form. I thank those publishers for permission to reprint. An earlier version of chapter 1 appeared as "Scientific Racism and the Emergence of the Homosexual Body," in *Journal of the History of Sexuality* 5, no. 2 (1994): 243–55. A part of chapter 3 appeared as "Passing Through the Closet in Pauline E. Hopkins's *Contending Forces*" in "Unnatural Formations," a special issue edited by Michael Moon, in *American Literature* 69, no. 1 (1997): 139–66.

Ken Wissoker is a remarkable editor and has provided crucial support for this project from an early stage. I thank him for his enthusiasm and for guiding the book into publication. I also appreciate the dedicated work of the rest of the Duke University Press staff, especially Katie Courtland, Rebecca Danes, Paula Dragosh, and Becky Filene Broun. For his careful copyediting, I thank Bill Henry.

Big thanks go to my sister Una Somerville and to Scott Olsson for offering steady encouragement and necessary breaks from writing. I also thank Kevin and Kate Olsson for lovingly reminding me how to play and read for fun.

I am also grateful to friends whose kindness and imagination have kept me going, especially Charles Clifton, Madelyn Detloff, Ron Gregg, Oscar Groves, Bruce Hainley, Vanessa Haney, Julee Raiskin, John Vincent, Angela Williams, Mary Wood, Martha Wright, and Margaret Wrinkle. Individually, John D'Amico and Jane Levey made life happier: I miss them both. For conversations that sharpened my thinking, and for much more, I thank Beth Povinelli.

Lisa Cohen is a true friend; her advice and exacting criticism have been crucial to the writing of this book. I am grateful for the care and insight with which she has read so much of it. Regina Kunzel understood this project long before it was a book and, at every step, helped shape it in vital ways. Her comments on countless drafts, along with her steady encouragement, have been invaluable. For her generosity, judgment, and example, I am grateful. I had the good luck to meet Kristin Bergen during the final stages of writing this book; her affection, wit, and encouragement helped me finish it. For that, and for so much else, I owe her enormous thanks.

I dedicate this book to my parents, Bridget and Brendan Somerville, whose creativity and generosity have always guided my efforts. I am profoundly grateful for all the ways they have supported my writing and especially for their steadfast love and encouragement.

Introduction

In 1892 Homer Plessy defied a Louisiana law that required railroad companies carrying passengers within the state to "provide equal but separate accommodations for the white, and colored, races."[1] Fully aware of the law and intending to challenge it, Plessy took a seat in a train car designated for white passengers, announced that he was a "Negro" to the conductor, and refused to move. As he expected, Plessy was promptly arrested. In a series of trials and appeals, Plessy and his lawyers eventually took the case to the United States Supreme Court, which, despite a vigorous dissent by Justice Harlan, upheld the segregationist Louisiana law through its infamous "separate but equal" pronouncement in 1896. In the aftermath of the failures of Reconstruction, the Supreme Court ruling marked a moment when the racialization of American culture had been dramatically articulated and reconfigured. Although racial segregation had long been entrenched as a de facto practice in many regions of the United States, the 1896 ruling formally and explicitly hardened racialized boundaries in new ways. This legalized system of segregation recalled slavery's racialized distinctions between "slave" and "free" but reconfigured this binary by articulating it in exclusively racial terms, the imagined division between "black" and "white" bodies. In effect, *Plessy v. Ferguson* ushered in a nationwide and brutal era of "Jim Crow" segregation, an institutionalized apartheid that lasted well into the twentieth century.[2]

The *Plessy* decision was only one of many sites at which antiblack violence, symbolic and embodied, was enacted during this period. The ruling legitimated the white-supremacist logic that also accounted for the unprecedented numbers of lynchings that took place between 1889 and 1930.[3] Foreign policy mirrored the racialized violence taking place internally. During this same period, the United States pursued expansionism in Cuba, Puerto Rico, Hawaii, Panama, and the Philippines, justifying such domination through the discourse of a "civilizing mission" to enlighten the "darker" races. Social anxieties about racial identity during this period led to a deluge of Jim Crow and antimiscegenation laws, laws that can be understood as an aggressive attempt to classify, separate, and racialize bodies as either "black" or "white."[4]

Meanwhile, as racialized social boundaries were increasingly policed, so too were emerging categories of sexual identity. In 1892, exploited by a sensationalist press, the highly publicized trial of Alice Mitchell, who had murdered her female lover Freda Ward, focused public attention on the meanings of sexual attachments between women.[5] Although Mitchell's case hinged on whether or not she was insane, its effect was to increase public consciousness of and to criminalize a new type of woman, the female "invert." This public consciousness of homosexuality was piqued further three years later during the trial of Oscar Wilde, which was covered widely in the popular press in the United States and Europe. Wilde was charged with "gross indecency" between men, which had been outlawed in England by the Criminal Law Amendment Act of 1885, known as the Labouchère Amendment.[6] After a series of trials, Wilde was found guilty and sentenced to the maximum punishment, two years' imprisonment with hard labor.[7] Although Wilde's trial and imprisonment took place in England, he became a transatlantic icon of homosexuality and decadence. According to one report, between 1895 and 1900, more than nine hundred sermons were preached against him in churches in the United States.[8]

The larger context for the cases of Wilde and Mitchell was the shift in understandings of sexual identity that occurred during the late nineteenth century. One of the most important and, by now, familiar insights developed in the fields of lesbian and gay studies and the history of sexuality is the notion that homosexuality and, by extension, heterosexuality are relatively recent inventions in Western culture, rather than transhistorical or "natural" categories of human beings. As Michel Foucault and other historians of sexuality have argued, although sexual acts between two people of the same sex had been punishable during earlier periods through legal and religious sanctions, these sexual practices did not necessarily define individuals as homosexual per se.[9] Only in the late nineteenth century did a new understanding of sexuality emerge, in which sexual acts and desires became constitutive of identity. Homosexuality as the condition, and therefore the identity, of particular bodies was thus a historically specific production. In Foucault's much quoted words, "Homosexuality appeared as one of the forms of sexuality when it was transposed from the practice of sodomy onto a kind of interior androgyny, a hermaphrodism of the soul. The sodomite had been a temporary aberration, the homosexual was now a species."[10] This shift brought about changes in the organization of not only bodies but knowledge itself. As Eve Sedgwick has claimed, "many of the major nodes of thought and knowledge in twentieth-century Western culture as a whole are structured—indeed, fractured—by a chronic, now endemic crisis of homo/heterosexual definition."[11]

In this book, I ask what this "crisis of homo/heterosexual definition," which emerged in the United States in the late nineteenth century, had to do with concurrent conflicts over racial definition and the presumed boundary between "black" and "white." Although some scholarship has drawn parallels between discourses of racial difference and sexuality, their particular relationship and potentially mutual effects remain largely unexplored. I am interested in interrogating how negotiations of the color line, which W. E. B. Du Bois pronounced to be the "problem of the Twentieth Century,"[12] shaped and were shaped by the emergence of notions of sexual identity and the corresponding epistemological uncertainties surrounding them. I show that it was not merely a historical coincidence that the classification of bodies as either "homosexual" or "heterosexual" emerged at the same time that the United States was aggressively constructing and policing the boundary between "black" and "white" bodies. In doing so, this study responds to and challenges a persistent critical tendency to treat late-nineteenth-century shifts in the cultural understanding and deployment of race and sexuality as separate and unrelated. Through the study of a range of literary, scientific, and cinematic texts that foreground the problems of delineating and interpreting racial and sexual identity, I argue instead that the simultaneous efforts to shore up and bifurcate categories of race and sexuality in the late nineteenth and early twentieth centuries were deeply intertwined.

By historicizing and denaturalizing the interconnections between late-nineteenth-century discourses of race and sexuality, I hope to rethink what have been seen as separate strands of American culture. This separation is often unintentionally reproduced through analogies between race and sexuality and between racialized and sexualized bodies. I show that these analogies have a specific history and became mobilized at the turn of the century: the formation of notions of heterosexuality and homosexuality emerged in the United States through (and not merely parallel to) a discourse saturated with assumptions about the racialization of bodies. These assumptions and the heightened surveillance of bodies in a racially segregated culture demanded a specific kind of logic, which, as I will argue, gave coherence to the new concepts of homo- and heterosexuality.

This project is directed also more broadly at a number of theoretical and disciplinary questions, including the ways in which scholarship on questions of race and sexuality has been organized institutionally. To date, the field that has sustained and produced some of the most vital work on ideologies of race and racial segregation in the United States is African American studies. Likewise, the field of lesbian and gay studies has more recently developed a rich body of scholarship on the discourses of homo- and heterosexuality. Both of these interdisciplinary areas have grown as a response to the absence of inquiry into race and sexuality in traditionally bounded disciplines. African American studies and lesbian and gay studies have been constituted out of a similar logic of identity-based scholarship and are, for me and others, the location of some of the most exciting and productive inquiry of the last two decades. Yet at this theoretical and historical juncture, the analogy often drawn between lesbian/gay and African American studies has produced unfortunate effects, including the illusion that they are parallel, rather than intersecting, bodies of scholarship. In lesbian/gay studies, questions of race and racialization tend to be subordinate to analyses of sexuality. In scholarship on race, with a few notable exceptions, there has been a general critical tendency to minimize the role of sexuality, and particularly homosexuality. The relative absence of questions of race until recently in existing work in lesbian and gay studies is partly a function of its historical position. In establishing the field, scholars have been preoccupied with distinguishing and separating categories of gender, race, and sexuality from one another. But it is now necessary to account for the ways in which these formulations have often depended on fixing other categories of difference. Biddy Martin, for example, in critiquing work that has attempted to explore the epistemological specificities of the homo/hetero divide, has registered her concern that "these kinds of formulations project fixity onto race and gender."[13] The challenge is to recognize the instability of multiple categories of difference simultaneously rather than to assume the fixity of one to establish the complexity of another.

My work builds on the analytical insights articulated most fully and consistently by critics who have challenged the tendency within dominant critical discourses to treat race and gender separately.[14] Their insistence on the importance of understanding the *intersectionality* of race and gender has opened up space in turn to ask how sexuality might also intersect with multiple categories of identification and difference. Kobena Mercer and Isaac Julien, for instance, have offered suggestive comments about the historical and theoretical links between race and sexuality:

> The prevailing Western concept of sexuality . . . *already contains racism.* Historically, the European construction of sexuality coincides with the epoch of imperialism and the two inter-connect. . . . The personage of the savage was developed as the Other of civilisation and one of the first "proofs" of this otherness was the nakedness of the savage, the visibility of its sex.[15]

Building on these preliminary insights, my study attempts to show that questions of race—in particular the formation of notions of "whiteness" and "blackness"—must be understood as a crucial part of the history and representation of sexual formations, including lesbian and gay identity and compulsory heterosexuality in the United States. I use methodologies from both African American studies and lesbian/gay studies in my readings of texts and engage them critically in perhaps unexpected ways. For instance, I focus a critical lens on constructions of race in my readings of texts that have been discussed primarily as sites for the analysis of gender and sexuality. Correspondingly, I foreground questions of (homo)sexuality in texts that have been understood previously within the framework of a critical emphasis on race. My aim is not to abandon either focus but to understand the ways in which critical questions of race and sexuality are refracted through each other in literary, scientific, and visual representation.

My methodology draws on and reformulates recent developments loosely gathered under the approach of queer studies. "Queer" may be understood as pointedly critiquing notions of stable lesbian and gay (or "straight") identification. Building on and simultaneously challenging earlier work that called itself lesbian and gay studies, queer theory has emerged as a site at which the very assumption of the utility of stable sexual orientations, such as "gay" or "lesbian," has undergone critique. "Queer" approaches also bring into question received notions of evidence, proof, and argumentation. Rather than asserting its own authenticity as a discrete field of study, at its best, queer studies has implicitly and explicitly challenged the seemingly "natural" status of epistemological assumptions of established disciplines.[16] However, as I will show, queer approaches have not yet been fully responsive to the ways in which these methodologies might be useful in addressing questions of race. This responsiveness is part of the goal of this study and is enabled by my training in literary and cultural studies, fields whose notions of evidence have historically been receptive to some degree of ambiguity and connotation. My method perhaps demands an even wider berth for doubt and skepticism because I ask readers to see what may be counterintuitive, given the ways in which we have grown accustomed to dividing texts—like bodies—according to a mistaken logic of transparent racial or sexual identity. My readings, therefore, listen for "the inexplicable presence of the thing not named"[17] and are attuned to the queer and racial presences and implications in texts that do not otherwise name them. I employ the techniques of queer reading but modulate my analysis from a singular focus on sexuality to one equally alert to the resonances of racialization.

Before I describe the organization of the chapters that follow, it is necessary to define two key terms that are used throughout my analysis. "Sexuality" is used throughout this study to refer to a historically and culturally contingent category of identity. As such, "sexuality" means much more than sexual practice per se. One's sexual identity, while at times linked directly to one's sexual activities, more often describes a complex ideological position, into which one is interpellated based partly on the culture's mapping of bodies and desires and partly on one's response to that interpellation.[18] Thus there is no strict relationship between one's sexual desire or behavior and one's sexual identity, although the two are closely intertwined.

The term "race" in this study refers to a historical, ideological process rather than to fixed transhistorical or biological characteristics: one's racial identity is contingent on one's cultural and historical location. Concepts of race in Brazil, South Africa, and the United States, for example, are all embedded within histories of imperialism and slavery, but each nation uses a different (and contradictory) logic of racial classification to determine who is "white," "black," or "colored."[19] Similarly, even within national cultures, racial meanings change over time: Irish immigrants in the early-nineteenth-century United States were not considered part of the "white" population, but were seen as a distinct and savagelike racial other.[20] Although popular notions of race often assume that it refers to self-evident and visible characteristics, there exist no discrete markers of racial difference, in scientific discourse or otherwise, uniformly distinguishing one "race" from another. To avoid fixing race as a transhistorical or natural category of identity, I foreground instead processes of "racialization," which Michael Omi and Howard Winant explain as "the extension of racial meaning to a previously racially unclassified relationship, social practice or group. Racialization is an ideological process, an historically specific one."[21] This crucial notion of racialization enables me to connect the ideological work of race to the historical emergence of models of homo- and heterosexuality at the turn of the century.

Although I trace the intersections of these two discourses of race and sexuality, I also resist erasing the important distinctions between them and the often starkly irreconcilable aspects of their cultural deployment. It is important to emphasize that I do not posit simple analogies between racial and sexual identities but rather attempt to historicize and therefore denaturalize their relationship. All too often, it is assumed that being a person of color is "like" being gay and that sexual orientation is "like" racial identity. Yet these analogies have a history and perform specific kinds of cultural work, often with contradictory political effects. In the ongoing debates about the right to same-sex marriage in the United States, for instance, activists often invoke legal precedents granting the right to interracial marriage.[22] Proponents argue that the legal system eventually recognized that it was unconstitutional to prohibit interracial marriage and that, by the same logic, the courts should recognize the unconstitutionality of prohibiting same-sex marriage. On the other hand, the analogy may be used to demonize "minority" populations, as became all too evident in the tendency to link and pathologize gay and black populations as "high-risk" groups in governmental responses to AIDS in the 1980s. In either case, whatever its other effects, the analogy obscures those who inhabit both identifications. As bell hooks has noted, "to make synonymous experience of homophobic aggression with racial oppression deflects attention away from the particular dual dilemma that non-white gay people face, as individuals who confront both racism and homophobia."[23] Further, such analogies implicitly posit whiteness and heterosexuality as the norm. To say that gay people are "like" black people is to suggest that those same gay people are not black. The underlying assumption is that white homosexuality is like heterosexual blackness. Rather than suggesting that race, gender, and sexual orientation are somehow "natural" analogies, then, this study offers an analysis of the historical construction of intersections among these categories of identity at a particular cultural moment.

To return to that moment and the juridical landscape of the 1890s, the juxtaposition of the Plessy, Mitchell, and Wilde trials points undeniably to the institutional efforts undertaken during this period to bifurcate identity into "black" or "white," "heterosexual" or "homosexual," and thus to simplify socially constructed boundaries of race and sexual orientation. Importantly, these shifts were embedded in anxieties over the control of language and representation. Albion Tourgée, who oversaw Plessy's challenge, argued that the primary question in the case was "not as to the *equality* of the privileges enjoyed, but *the right of the State to label one citizen as white and another as colored.*"[24] Unwilling to allow individuals to determine the racial status of their own bodies, the Supreme Court reinforced a cultural fiction of racial opposites and authorized the individual states to define and separate any bodies in question. Contests over language similarly vexed the court proceedings of the Wilde trial, a trial that revolved around the central problem of the "Love that dared not speak its name."[25] As Neil Bartlett has written:

What Wilde and the court were contesting was not the evidence, but who had the right to *interpret* that evidence. It is no accident that the line *the Love that dare not speak its name* haunted the trial, and has stayed with us ever since. It is not the love itself which was on trial. . . .

What was on trial was the right to speak (invent and articulate) the name of that love.[26]

These trials, then, reveal the existence of a cultural desperation regarding rights in language and the control of language over the social construction of identity. As Wilde himself wrote after the trial, "I saw then at once that what is said of a man is nothing. The point is, who says it."[27]

While racial and sexual identities were being contested discursively, their construction, of course, dramatically shaped and depended on the ways in which those identities were embodied. Plessy's lawyers understood the problem of their case as a struggle over the control of both language and property rights. As Tourgée noted, "in any mixed community, the reputation of belonging to the dominant race, in this instance the white race, is *property*, in the same sense that a right of action, or of inheritance, is property."[28] Although unsuccessful as a legal argument, Tourgée's emphasis on the connection between racial identity and property refigured the assumptions about ownership and bodies embedded in slavery. His evocation of property rights underscores the ways in which profound material effects were and continue to be at stake in the social construction of identities. Those whose bodies were culturally marked as nonnormative lost their claim to the same rights as those whose racial or sexual reputation invested them with cultural legitimacy, or the property of a "good name."

The following chapters foreground my concerns with understanding how a range of discourses constructed the divisions between "blackness" and "whiteness" and homo- and heterosexuality. These discourses had varying degrees of power to shape cultural understandings of bodies in the late nineteenth and early twentieth centuries. In the first part, I consider questions of race and sexuality in two nascent cultural institutions, sexology and cinema. That the physical body offers transparent evidence of its history, identity, and behavior is a deeply held cultural fiction in the United States, one that seems a necessary starting point for this study. During the nineteenth century, human anatomy was treated as a legible text, over which various fields of science, including the nascent field of sexology, competed for authority as literate readers and interpreters of its meaning. As an emerging (and self-consciously) "expert" discourse, sexology became a privileged, though not exclusive, site for the explicit articulation of newly emerging models of homo- and heterosexuality. Although most of the population may not have had direct knowledge of the texts produced by sexologists and the earlier "experts" of scientific racism (comparative anatomists), their theories and conclusions increasingly assumed enormous cultural power to organize and pathologize those marked as sexually deviant or racially "other." In chapter 1, I analyze works by late-nineteenth- and early-twentieth-century sexologists in order to consider the relationship between the emergent scientific discourse on homosexuality and existing scientific discourses on racial difference. My discussion centers on the rhetorical strategies and structures of important sexological works such as Havelock Ellis's *Sexual Inversion,* volume 2 of his *Studies in the Psychology of Sex* (1897). This early work in sexology, poised at the crossroads of anthropometry and psychoanalysis, illustrates the ways in which the development of new sexual categories was mediated by methodologies and conclusions borrowed from previous studies of racial difference.

The emphasis on the surveillance of bodies that was embedded in expert discourses such as sexology was part of the profound reorganization of vision and knowledge in American culture between the 1890s and the 1920s. This period saw the emergence of a number of new visual technologies, particularly the development of cinema as a popular medium. Because race and sexuality pose representational problems centered on the possibilities and impossibilities of the physical legibility of identity, chapter 2 explores the ways in which the emergent film industry in the United States articulated and simultaneously evaded links between racial difference and homosexuality. Although recent work in feminist and early film criticism and history has begun to address questions of race and sexual orientation, there exists surprisingly little work that draws together these analytical categories in order to understand their intersections. I consider these questions through a comparison of the film comedy *A Florida Enchantment* (Vitagraph, 1914) with its literary and stage sources, asking how and why the film masks its underlying racial narrative within its overt fascination with sexual transformation and boundaries of gender and sexuality. I situate these questions in the context of the shifts that occurred in the construction of categories of black/white, female/male, and homosexual/heterosexual during the period, and within a discussion of the vexed cultural status of the emergent film industry of the 1910s.

Stuart Hall points out that "the ideologies of racism remain contradictory structures, which can function both as the vehicles for the imposition of dominant ideologies, and as the elementary forms for the cultures of resistance." [29] The second half of this book turns from the culturally dominant discourses of scientific racism and cinema to literary texts, a crucial site of African American self-representation in the late nineteenth and early twentieth centuries, particularly as the "New Negro" movement gained momentum through the 1920s. Virtually absent as subjects in dominant discourses such as sexology and the emerging film industry, African Americans found in fiction an important medium for instantiating political agency and for contesting dominant cultural stereotypes. These texts demonstrate the stakes of the emerging discourse of homosexuality/heterosexuality for African Americans in both stark and subtle ways. Because existing cultural stereotypes of African Americans were largely sexualized, the new discourse of sexual pathology was intertwined with these racialized images. To varying degrees, these authors were able to resist, contest, and appropriate these dominant cultural discourses. At the same time, they often reinscribed them. It is important to emphasize that I do not see the authors (or readers) of these texts necessarily offering heroic resistance to the pathologizing discourses of race or sexuality. Instead, what interests me is the extent to which the discourse of homosexuality began to shape their texts, and the often contradictory ways in which these writers registered its effects.

Chapter 3 shows how the discourses of homosexuality circulated in significant ways in Pauline E. Hopkins's attempts to revise cultural constructions of black womanhood in her novels *Contending Forces* and *Winona*. As recent scholarship has demonstrated, Hopkins played an important part in the development of African American literature and an African American reading audience in the early twentieth century.[30] I place her work within the historical contexts not only of racial segregation but also of emerging categories of sexual identity during this period in the United States. My discussion considers how the often unstable division between homosexuality and heterosexuality circulates as part of Hopkins's exploration of the barriers to desire imposed by the color line.

Antiblack discrimination and violence reached alarming heights in the two decades before World War I, and in response, many African Americans chose to migrate in unprecedented numbers toward northern urban centers. The anonymity resulting from this mobility made it possible for many light-complexioned African Americans to "cross the color line" into the white population at rates unparalleled during any other period, making this era "the great age of passing."[31] In chapter 4, I discuss one of the most important novels of passing written during this period, James Weldon Johnson's *Autobiography of an Ex-Coloured Man,* a text that enacted even as it narrated the phenomenon of passing. First published anonymously in 1912, the novel raised crucial questions about the epistemology of identity: just as the text's status as truth or fiction could not be detected by its readers, so the "ex-coloured man's" movement across the color line demonstrated that race had no ontological certainty. I show that Johnson's innovative revisions of the genre of the novel of racial passing had to do as much with the circulation of a discourse of forbidden sexuality as with the protagonist's liminal racial status.

In chapter 5, I focus on writing by and about Jean Toomer, whose refusal to be identified as "black" or "white" after the publication of *Cane* (1923) has tended to set the terms for the critical discussion of his life and writing. This critical focus on race has created a blind spot around the possibility that questions of sexuality circulated simultaneously with race within Toomer's writing and life. Drawing on published and unpublished biographies, autobiographies, and short stories, I discuss first the ways in which queer theoretical approaches open up new directions for understanding Toomer's representational strategies with regard to racial questions, and in turn how Toomer and his work demonstrate the need to resituate questions of racialization at the center of queer approaches.

It is crucial to the integrity of the arguments put forward in this study that I acknowledge their limitations, which I have either chosen in an effort to manage the scope of this project or have as yet been unable to overcome. First, I emphasize that my conclusions hold only for a specific historical period in the United States. Thus whereas some of my discussions may resonate with or even accurately describe the intersections of race and sexuality during other historical moments, the work of characterizing the particular formations of those periods remains to be completed. Although some of the more disturbing current invocations of links between racial and sexual discourses have propelled me in this project, I would resist applying my arguments uncritically to our own historical moment (or others).

Next, the range of texts analyzed here is highly selective and is not necessarily representative of the entire historical period or the entire United States. What I have sacrificed in terms of "coverage" I hope to have compensated for in depth. My goal is to provide productive new readings of a variety of texts rather than to assert a single story that each text discretely supports. I have put a number of texts into conversation, but it is important to remember that they commanded varying degrees of cultural authority during the period under study. In limiting my study to these particular texts and to sexology, fiction, and cinema, I have attempted to be vigilant about their differing means of production and cultural authority, a vigilance that has frequently prevented me from generalizing more broadly about related medical, literary, or cinematic movements.

Further, my analysis of "race" in this study is limited to constructions of "blackness" and "whiteness," primarily because prevailing discourses of race and racial segregation in late-nineteenth- and early-twentieth-century American culture deployed this bifurcation more pervasively than other models of racial diversity. This framework is an obvious limitation, resulting in the omission of racial distinctions erased by the black/white divide. Significant and urgent questions remain about how those who identified as neither "white" nor "black" were situated in relation to the emergence of a discourse of homo- and heterosexuality. I do not specifically interrogate the cultural constructions of Asian, Jewish, or Native American bodies, for instance, but recent work by scholars such as Lisa Lowe, Sander Gilman, and others suggests that this line of inquiry deserves further research.[32] My hope is that my focus on the black/white bifurcation, while admittedly circumscribed, will usefully inform future studies that complicate the intersecting representational histories of sexuality and race in—and perhaps even beyond—American culture.

Despite the increasingly pervasive cultural authority of the socially constructed dichotomies "black" versus "white" and "homosexual" versus "heterosexual" during the period of this study, ideological bound-aries of race, sexuality, and gender were and continue to be sites of on-going contestation. The marked proliferation of medical and scientific texts that investigated homosexuality during this period, for example, suggests that categories of sexual identity were far from self-evident. It is important to see that the particular meanings of socially constructed identities gain currency through repetition, resistance, and appropria-tion. The emergence of "new" sexual identities and the reconfiguration of racialized identities in the late nineteenth and early twentieth cen-turies were not singular "events" through which those meanings were simply established once and for all but rather ongoing processes of con-testation and accumulation.

I

Scientific Racism and the Invention of

the Homosexual Body

"I regard sex as the central problem of life," wrote Havelock Ellis in the general preface to the first volume of *Studies in the Psychology of Sex,* one of the most important texts of the late-nineteenth-century medical and scientific discourse on homosexuality in the United States and Europe. Justifying such unprecedented boldness toward the study of sex, Ellis explained:

> And now that the problem of religion has practically been settled, and that the problem of labour has at least been placed on a practical foundation, the question of sex—*with the racial questions that rest on it*—stands before the coming generations as the chief problem for solution.[1]

In spite of Ellis's oddly breezy dismissal of the problems of labor and religion, which were far from settled at the time, this passage points suggestively to a link between sexual and racial anxieties. Yet what exactly did Ellis mean by "racial questions"? More significantly, what was his sense of the relationship between racial questions and the "question of sex"? Although Ellis himself left these issues unresolved, his elliptical declaration nevertheless suggested that a discourse of race—however elusive—somehow hovered around or within the study of sexuality.

This chapter begins with Ellis's provocative linkage between "racial questions" and "the question of sex" and explores the various ways in which they were intertwined in late-nineteenth- and early-twentieth-century medical literature on sexuality. I focus on "expert" literature about sexuality, broadly defined to include the writings of physicians, sexologists, and psychiatrists, because it has been integral to the project of situating the "invention" of homo- and heterosexuality historically.[2] Although medical discourse was by no means the only—or necessarily the most powerful—site of the emergence of new sexual identities, it does nevertheless offer rich sources for understanding the complex development of these sexual categories in the late nineteenth and early twentieth centuries. Medical and sexological literature not only became one of the few sites of explicit engagement with questions of sexuality but also held substantial definitional power within a culture that sanctioned science to discover and tell the truth about bodies.

Previous literary, historical, and theoretical work on the emergence of notions of homosexuality in the late nineteenth century has drawn primarily on theories and histories of gender. George Chauncey, for instance, has provided an invaluable discussion of the ways in which medical paradigms of sexuality shifted according to changing ideologies of gender between 1880 and 1930.[3] He notes a gradual change in medical models of sexual deviance, from a notion of sexual inversion, understood as a reversal of one's sex role, to a model of homosexuality, defined as deviant sexual object choice. These categories and their transformations, argues Chauncey, reflected concurrent shifts in the cultural organization of sex and gender roles and participated in prescribing acceptable behavior, especially within a context of white middle-class gender ideologies.

Although gender insubordination offers a powerful explanatory model for the "invention" of homosexuality, ideologies of gender also, of course, shaped and were shaped by dominant constructions of race. Indeed, although rarely acknowledged, it is striking that the emergence of a discourse on homosexuality in the United States occurred at roughly the same time that boundaries between "black" and "white" were being policed and enforced in unprecedented ways, particularly through institutionalized racial segregation.

Although some historians of the scientific discourse on sexuality have included brief acknowledgment of nineteenth-century discourses of racial difference in their work, the particular relationship and potentially mutual effects of discourses of homosexuality and race remain unexplored.[4] This silence may be due in part to the relative lack of explicit attention to race in medical and sexological literature of the late nineteenth and early twentieth centuries. These writers did not self-consciously interrogate race, nor were those whose gender insubordination and sexual transgression brought them under the medical gaze generally identified by race in these accounts.[5] Yet the lack of explicit attention to race in these texts does not mean that it was irrelevant to sexologists' endeavors. On the contrary, given the upheavals surrounding racial definition during this period, it is reasonable to claim that these texts were as embedded within contemporary racial ideologies as they were within ideologies of gender. My aim is not to replace a focus on gender with that of race but rather to understand how discourses of race and gender buttressed one another, often competing, often overlapping, in shaping emerging models of homosexuality. I suggest that the structures and methodologies that drove dominant ideologies of race also fueled the pursuit of knowledge about the homosexual body: both sympathetic and hostile accounts of homosexuality were steeped in assumptions that had driven previous scientific studies of race.

My approach is both literary and historical in method, relying on a combination of close reading and contextual analysis. I am particularly interested in the discursive strategies of those who sought to explain and naturalize the categories of "black" and "white," "heterosexual" and "homosexual." My goal, however, is not to garner and display unequivocal evidence of the direct influence of racial science on those who were developing scientific models of homosexuality. Further, although the texts that I study here reproduce the culturally dominant racist ideologies of the nineteenth century, identifying the racism of these writers as individuals is not the goal of this chapter. Rather, my focus here is on how these writers and thinkers conceptualized sexuality through a reliance on, and deployment of, racial ideologies, that is, the cultural assumptions and systems of representation about race through which individuals understood their relationships within the world.[6]

I begin with an overview of the history of sexology and scientific racism in the United States. I then suggest three broadly defined ways in which discourses of sexuality seem to have been particularly engaged—sometimes overtly, but largely implicitly—with the discourse of scientific racism. All these models constructed both the nonwhite body and the nonheterosexual body as pathological to greater or lesser extents. Although I discuss these models in separate sections here, they often coexisted despite their contradictions. These models are speculative and are intended as a first step toward understanding the myriad and historically specific ways in which racial and sexual discourses shaped each other at the moment in which medical and scientific discourse articulated a notion of homosexuality.

The Emergence of Sexology in the United States

The field of sexology in the United States developed in conversation with slightly earlier developments in Europe, particularly in Germany in the late nineteenth century. What characterized the growth of sexology as a field was its attempt to wrest authority for diagnosing and defining sexual "abnormalities" away from juridical discourse and to place it firmly within the purview of medical science.[7] Thus what was once considered criminal behavior gradually came to be described in terms of disease, as the title of the German sexologist and psychologist Richard von Krafft-Ebing's *Psychopathia Sexualis* (1886) made clear. Same-sex attraction was one of many such sexual "pathologies," which also included pedophilia, necrophilia, fetishism, sadism, and masochism, among others. Part of Krafft-Ebing's work first appeared in the United States in 1888, when a selection from his *Psychopathia Sexualis* entitled "Perversion of the Sexual Instinct" was translated into English and published as an article in an American medical journal.[8] During the 1880s and 1890s, American medical journals also began to devote attention to "Urnings" and "Uranism," terms that had first been used by Karl Heinrich Ulrichs in 1864, to describe the model of a female soul in a male body.[9] Another term, "contrary sexual feeling," adapted from the German *Konträre Sexualempfindung,* first used by Carl von Westphal in 1869, also began to appear in medical journals of the 1880s and 1890s. Although these texts used differing terms, they shared the assertion that medicine, not law or religion, should be the primary site for determining society's response to those who practiced such behaviors.[10]

   In the 1890s, the work of the British sexologist Havelock Ellis became perhaps the most widely influential and authoritative source in American discourses on sexuality. Prominent in the medical community, he was an honorary member of the Chicago Academy of Medicine, a member of the Medico-Legal Society of New York, and vice president of the International Medical and Legal Congress of New York in 1895.[11]

His work first appeared in the United States in 1895, when his article "Sexual Inversion in Women" was published in an American medical journal.[12] Apparently the first study of such depth to be published in the United States, this article was included in Ellis's subsequent book, *Sexual Inversion,* published in the United States in 1900. Initially appearing as the first volume of *Studies in the Psychology of Sex, Sexual Inversion* became a definitive text in late-nineteenth-century investigations of homosexuality.[13] Despite the series's titular focus on the psychology of sex, *Sexual Inversion* was a hybrid text, poised in methodology between the earlier field of comparative anatomy, with its procedures of bodily measurement, and the nascent techniques of psychology, with its focus on mental development.[14] Like Ulrichs, Krafft-Ebing, and Westphal, Ellis hoped to provide scientific authority for the position that homosexuality should be considered not a crime but rather a congenital (and thus involuntary) physiological abnormality. Writing *Sexual Inversion* in the wake of England's 1885 Labouchère Amendment, which prohibited "any act of gross indecency" between men, Ellis intended in large part to defend homosexuality from "law and public opinion," which, in his view, combined "to place a heavy penal burden and a severe social stigma on the manifestations of an instinct which to those persons who possess it frequently appears natural and normal."[15] In doing so, Ellis attempted to drape himself in the cultural authority of a naturalist, eager to exert his powers of observation in an attempt to classify and codify understandings of homosexuality.[16]

Ellis's *Sexual Inversion* gained attention in the United States partly because of the censorship scandal that surrounded it. On publication in England in 1897, *Sexual Inversion* was judged to be not a scientific work but "a certain lewd, wicked, bawdy, scandalous libel"; effectively banned in England, subsequent copies were published only in the United States.[17] Yet the importance of Ellis's *Sexual Inversion* to American understandings of homosexuality lay not only in its reception but also in Ellis's reliance on American sources for his case studies, many of which were provided by Dr. James G. Kiernan, then secretary of the Chicago Academy of Medicine.[18] Although medical and legal practitioners were the primary audience of *Sexual Inversion,* there is abundant evidence that the book also became an important source for nonexpert readers attempting to find representations of themselves. Letters written by the American lit-

erary critic F. O. Matthiessen to his companion Russell Cheney in the
1920s, for instance, mention having read Ellis's works, which apparently
had profound effects on Matthiessen's understanding of his own sexuality: "For the first time it was completely brought home to me that I
was what I was by *nature*."[19]

Matthiessen's letter also mentioned that he had "marked and checked
some passages that struck me particularly" in the works of another
writer, Edward Carpenter.[20] Not medically trained, but widely influential among sexologists in the United States and Europe, Carpenter, a
British socialist, proposed understanding those who had same-sex desires through a model of intermediate types. Like Ellis's work, though
with a slightly different approach, Carpenter's influential essay "The
Intermediate Sex" was first published in the United States in 1911. Carpenter, who had long-term sexual relationships with men, offered an
idealized model of inverts as "intermediate types" on a continuum of
male and female characteristics, reversing the pervasive pathologization
of homosexuality in medical discourses. Responding to negative characterizations such as Krafft-Ebing's, Carpenter wrote, "Nor does it appear
that persons of this class are usually of a gross or specially low type,
but if anything rather the opposite—being most of refined, sensitive
nature."[21] This characterization struck a chord among readers such as
Matthiessen, who remarked on the "beautiful pictures [Carpenter] gives
of love between men."[22]

The early sexological model of inversion prevailed in the United
States until the 1920s, when a notion of homosexuality as "abnormal"
sexual object choice began to emerge.[23] By that time, Sigmund Freud's
views on sexuality, which had been widely circulated since the 1910s,
began to be popularized. Psychoanalytic discourse defined itself in
part through its differences from sexology, which had relied largely on
physiological models. Freud viewed the debates about whether homosexuality was congenital or acquired as specious and instead argued that
homosexuality played a part, to differing degrees, in everyone's sexuality. Thus, in contrast to the earlier sexologists, he refuted models that
set "homosexuals" apart as a discrete group.[24] Yet the older model of
inverts as a special type did not disappear altogether, from either expert or popular discourse. As Eve Sedgwick has noted, "universalizing"
models (such as Freud's) and "minoritizing" models (articulated by Ellis,

Krafft-Ebing, and others), while contradictory, have both continued to coexist simultaneously as explanatory frameworks for homosexuality in American culture.[25]

Part of the reason that Freud's views did not fully supersede the models of the early sexologists, as my discussion will suggest, may be that minoritizing accounts resonated with and reinforced prevailing American models of racialized bodies. Psychoanalysis did not incorporate an explicit discourse of race, perhaps intentionally as a response to growing anti-Semitism in Europe. As Sander Gilman has suggested, "As virtually all of Freud's early disciples were Jews, the lure of psychoanalysis for them may well have been its claims for a universalization of human experience and an active exclusion of the importance of race from its theoretical framework."[26] In contrast, with their emphasis on physiological models, sexologists appealed to those invested in somatic theories, reinforced in the United States by concurrent discourses about racial difference.

It is worth noting here that although my discussion focuses on medical and sexological texts, the delineation of that genre of writing as separate from other spheres is, of course, highly unstable. Despite their claims to scientific objectivity and truth, these writers' investigations were inevitably shaped by contemporary political and cultural ideologies. Further, as Lisa Duggan has demonstrated, some of these writers, particularly Ellis, drew on newspapers and popular accounts both for the "data" of their work (i.e., case studies) and for the subsequent interpretation of those "data."[27] There was considerable overlap between the sensationalistic accounts of "lady lovers" that appeared in newspapers and the supposedly "scientific" studies of writers like Ellis. Popular and scientific representations should be considered with equal skepticism; each was inextricable from the ideological biases of the day.

Nineteenth-Century Scientific Racism

Before turning to my readings of particular sexological studies, it is useful to discuss briefly the history of scientific studies of race in the nineteenth century. In the United States, the term "race" has always been contested. In nineteenth-century scientific usage, it might refer to groupings based variously on geography, religion, class, or color.[28]

Scientific studies of race before Darwin tended to fall into two general schools of thought, monogeny and polygeny, both of which foregrounded the question of racial origins.[29]

Monogeny, which had been the prevailing theory in eighteenth-century studies of racial difference, held that all of the so-called races were members of the same species and that they had descended from common ancestry. Racial differences were thought to be caused primarily by environmental conditions. Conveniently, monogenist theories meshed with the standard Christian origin narrative, in which, at the moment of the Fall in the Garden of Eden, humankind had begun to disperse and degenerate into multiple races from a single original source represented by Adam and Eve. Some proponents of this theory of degeneration believed that these differences were fixed and irreversible; others held that degeneration might be reversed in appropriate climates. Although monogenists emphasized environmental factors as the key explanation for racial differences, it is important to emphasize that monogenists did not generally advocate racial equality. Samuel Stanhope Smith, a major authority among monogenists, held that whites were the pure and original race from which others had degenerated. His ideas, developed primarily in his *Essay on the Causes of the Variety of Complexion and Figure in the Human Species,* first published in 1787, held sway until the 1830s.

The other major theory of racial origins, polygeny, held that different races were actually different species with distinct biological and geographic origins. Although theories of polygenesis had begun to be developed in the early nineteenth century, it was not until the 1840s and 1850s that this view came to be accepted widely among scientists. Polygeny was a predominantly American theoretical development and was widely referred to as the "American school" of anthropology. As George Fredrickson has pointed out, the emergence and greater acceptance of polygenesis rather than monogenesis among scientists during these decades cannot be divorced from political and cultural debates about slavery in the United States: "The full scientific assault on environmentalism came at a time . . . when it was bound to have some influence on the discussion of slavery and Negro prospects."[30] Polygenists such as Samuel George Morton, Josiah Nott, and Louis Agassiz held that blacks were permanently inferior to whites and that racial mixture would have dangerous social and biological consequences. According to polygenist models, the mulatto was a hybrid that would eventually die out of existence.

However they differed, adherents to both polygeny and monogeny nevertheless shared many epistemological assumptions and relied on the same empiricist methodologies, comparative anatomy and anthropometry.[31] Behind these anatomical measurements lay the assumption that the body was a legible text, with various keys or languages available for reading its symbolic codes. In the logic of biological determinism, the surface and interior of the individual body rather than its social characteristics, such as language, behavior, or clothing, became the primary sites of its meaning. "Every peculiarity of the body has probably some corresponding significance in the mind, and the causes of the former are the remoter causes of the latter," wrote Edward Drinker Cope, a well-known American paleontologist, summarizing the assumptions that fueled the science of comparative anatomy.[32] Although scientists debated which particular anatomical features carried racial meanings (skin, facial angle, pelvis, skull, brain mass, genitalia), the theory that anatomy predicted intelligence and behavior remained remarkably constant. As Nancy Stepan and Sander Gilman have noted, "The concepts within racial science were so congruent with social and political life (with power relations, that is) as to be virtually uncontested from inside the mainstream of science."[33]

Supported by the cultural authority of an ostensibly objective scientific method, these readings of the body became a powerful instrument for those seeking to justify the economic and political disenfranchisement of various racial groups within systems of slavery and colonialism. As Barbara Fields has noted, however, "Try as they would, the scientific racists of the past failed to discover any objective criterion upon which to classify people; to their chagrin, every criterion they tried varied more within so-called races than between them."[34] Although the methods of science were considered to be outside the political and economic realm, in fact, as we know, these anatomical investigations, however professedly innocent their intentions, were driven by racial ideologies already firmly in place.[35]

With the publication of Darwin's *Origin of the Species* in 1859, prevailing theories of polygeny had to be reformulated in light of the theory of evolution. Darwin's controversial innovation was an emphasis on the continuity between animals and human beings. Evolutionary theory held out the possibility that the physical, mental, and moral characteristics of human beings had evolved gradually over time from apelike ancestors.[36] Although the idea of continuity depended logically on the blurring of boundaries within hierarchies, it did not necessarily invalidate the methods of comparative anatomy or polygenist theories. The Darwinian model might seem to contradict the belief that different races originated separately, but believers in polygeny modified their theories to make them compatible with evolutionary models. Thus they argued that blacks were an "incipient species," holding that there had been no racial progress or intellectual development of blacks in recorded history, and that, by the tenets of natural selection, blacks remained biologically inferior.

Evolutionary theory also tended to reinforce the notion of racial hierarchies through the method of ranking and ordering bodies according to stages of evolutionary "progress." The theory of recapitulation, often summed up by the phrase "ontogeny recapitulates phylogeny," emerged as a crucial concept, holding that in its individual maturation, each organism proceeds through stages that are equivalent to adult forms of organisms that have preceded it in evolutionary development.[37] Thus the children of "superior" groups embodied phases equivalent to the mature adult phases of "inferior" groups. Importantly, analogies between gender and race structured the logic of hierarchal rankings of bodies. According to the logic of recapitulation, adult African Americans and white women were at the same stage as white male children and therefore represented an ancestral stage in the evolution of adult white males.[38] These types of analogies had already been mobilized earlier in the nineteenth century by comparative anatomists such as Carl Vogt, who in his study of brains argued that "the grown-up Negro partakes, as regards his intellectual faculties, of the nature of the child, the female, and the senile white."[39] As Robyn Wiegman comments, "Such an analogy simultaneously differentiated and linked two of the nineteenth century's primary forms of social difference, instantiating and perpetuating the visible economies of race and gender by locating their signification on bodies that could not claim the disembodied abstraction accorded those both white and male."[40] The powerful analogies that structured the theory of recapitulation, as I will show, became crucial for later characterizations of homosexuality.

Visible Differences: Sexology and Comparative Anatomy

Comparative anatomy, which had been the chief methodology of nineteenth-century racial science, gave sexologists a ready-made set of procedures and assumptions with which to scan the body visually for discrete markers of difference. Race, in fact, became an explicit, though ambiguous, structural element in Ellis's *Sexual Inversion*. In chapter 5, titled "The Nature of Sexual Inversion," Ellis attempted to collate the evidence contained in his collection of case studies, dividing his general conclusions into various analytic categories. Significantly, "Race" was the first category he listed, under which he wrote, "All my cases, 80 in number, are British and American, 20 living in the United States and the rest being British. Ancestry, from the point of view of race, was not made a matter of special investigation" (264). He then listed the ancestries of the individuals whose case studies he included, which he identified as "English . . . Scotch . . . Irish . . . German . . . French . . . Portuguese . . . [and] more or less Jewish" (264). He concluded that "except in the apparently frequent presence of the German element, there is nothing remarkable in this ancestry" (264). Ellis used the term "race" in this passage interchangeably with national origin, with the possible exception of Jewish identity. These national identities were perceived to be at least partially biological and certainly hereditary in Ellis's account, though subordinate to the categories "British" and "American." Although he dismissed "ancestry, from the point of view of race," as a significant category, its place as the first topic within the chapter suggested its importance to the structure of Ellis's analysis.[41]

As scholars such as Nancy Stepan, Londa Schiebinger, and Sander Gilman have pointed out, scientific assertions about racial difference were often articulated through gender.[42] Gilman has commented that "any attempt to establish that the races were inherently different rested to no little extent on the sexual difference of the black."[43] This association was made not only in scientific discourses but also in popular racist mythology as well. However, although nineteenth-century American popular cultural forms such as blackface minstrelsy focused on the supposed differences in size between African American and white men's genitalia, the male body was not necessarily the primary site of medical inquiry into racial difference.[44] Instead, as a number of medical journals from the 1870s demonstrate, comparative anatomists repeatedly located racial difference through the sexual characteristics of the female body.[45]

In exploring the influence of scientific studies of race on the emerging discourse of sexuality, it is useful to look closely at a study from the genre of comparative anatomy. In 1867 W. H. Flower and James Murie published an "Account of the Dissection of a Bushwoman," which carefully cataloged the "more perishable soft structures of the body" of a young Bushwoman.[46] They placed their study in a line of inquiry concerning the African woman's body that had begun at least a half century earlier with French naturalist Georges Cuvier's description of the woman popularly known as the "Hottentot Venus," or Saartje Baartman, who was displayed to European audiences fascinated by her "steatopygia" (protruding buttocks).[47] Significantly, starting with Cuvier, this tradition of comparative anatomy located the boundaries of race through the sexual and reproductive anatomy of the African female body, ignoring altogether the problematic absence of male bodies from these studies.

Flower and Murie's account lingered on two specific sites of difference: the "protuberance of the buttocks, so peculiar to the Bushman race," and "the remarkable development of the labia minora," which were "sufficiently well marked to distinguish these parts from those of any ordinary varieties of the human species" (208). The racial difference of the African body, implied Flower and Murie, was located in its literal excess, a specifically sexual excess that placed her body outside the boundaries of the "normal" female. To support their conclusion, Flower and Murie included corroborating "evidence" in the final part of their account. They quoted a secondhand report, "received from a scientific friend residing at the Cape of Good Hope," describing the anatomy of "two pure bred Hottentots, mother and daughter" (208). This account also focused on the women's genitalia, which they referred to as "appendages" (208). Although their account ostensibly foregrounded boundaries of race, their portrayal of the sexual characteristics of the Bushwoman betrayed Flower and Murie's anxieties about gender boundaries. The characteristics singled out as "peculiar" to this race—

the (double) "appendages"—fluttered between genders, at one moment masculine, at the next moment exaggeratedly feminine. Flower and Murie constructed the site of *racial* difference by marking the sexual and reproductive anatomy of the African woman as "peculiar"; in their characterization, sexual ambiguity delineated the boundaries of race.

Sexologists writing in the late nineteenth and early twentieth centuries inherited this tendency to racialize perceived sexual ambiguity, but they used a new framework to interpret its meaning. Producing "data" about their newly created object of study, the invert, they also routinely included physical examinations in their accounts, reproducing the methodologies employed by comparative anatomists such as Flower and Murie. Many of the case histories in Krafft-Ebing's *Psychopathia Sexualis,* for instance, included a paragraph detailing any anatomical peculiarities of the body in question.[48] Krafft-Ebing could not draw any conclusions about somatic indicators of "abnormal" sexuality, but physical examinations nevertheless remained a staple of the genre. In Ellis's *Sexual Inversion,* as I will show, case studies often focused more intently on the bodies of female "inverts" than on those of their male counterparts.[49] Although the specific sites of anatomical inspection (hymen, clitoris, labia, vagina) differed in various sexological texts, the underlying theory remained constant: women's genitalia and reproductive anatomy held a valuable and presumably visual key to ranking bodies according to norms of sexuality.

Sexologists reproduced not only the methodologies of the comparative anatomy of races but also its iconography. One of the most consistent medical characterizations of the anatomy of both African American women and lesbians was the myth of an unusually large clitoris.[50] As late as 1921, medical journals contained articles declaring that "a physical examination of [female homosexuals] will in practically every instance disclose an abnormally prominent clitoris." Significantly, this author added, "This is particularly so in colored women."[51] In an earlier account of racial differences between white and African American women, one gynecologist had also focused on the size and visibility of the clitoris; in his examinations, he had perceived a distinction between the "free" clitoris of "negresses" and the "imprisonment" of the clitoris of the "Aryan American woman."[52] In constructing these oppositions, such characterizations literalized the sexual and racial ideologies of the nineteenth-century "Cult of True Womanhood," which explicitly privileged white women's sexual "purity" while implicitly suggesting African American women's sexual accessibility.[53]

Like the studies of comparative anatomists, the case histories in Ellis's *Sexual Inversion* differed markedly according to gender in the amount and degree of attention given to the examination of anatomical details. "As regards the sexual organs it seems possible," Ellis wrote, "so far as my observations go, to speak more definitely of inverted women than of inverted men" (256). Ellis justified his more zealous inspection of women's bodies in part by invoking the ambiguity surrounding women's sexuality in general: "We are accustomed to a much greater familiarity and intimacy between women than between men, and we are less apt to suspect the existence of any abnormal passion" (204). To Ellis, the seemingly imperceptible differences between "normal" and "abnormal" intimacies between women called for greater scrutiny into the subtleties of their anatomy. He included the following detailed account as potential evidence for understanding the fine line between the female invert and the "normal" woman:

> *Sexual Organs.* — (a) Internal: Uterus and ovaries appear normal. (b) External: Small clitoris, with this irregularity, that the lower folds of the labia minora, instead of uniting one with the other and forming the frenum, are extended upward along the sides of the clitoris, while the upper folds are poorly developed, furnishing the clitoris with a scant hood. The labia majora depart from normal conformation in being fuller in their posterior half than in their anterior part, so that when the subject is in the supine position they sag, as it were, presenting a slight resemblance to fleshy sacs, but in substance and structure they feel normal. (136)

This extraordinary taxonomy, performed for Ellis by an unnamed "obstetric physician of high standing," echoed earlier anatomical catalogs of African women. The exacting eye (and hand) of the investigating physician highlighted every possible detail as meaningful evidence. Through the triple repetition of "normal" and the use of evaluative language such as "irregularity" and "poorly developed," the physician reinforced his position of judgment. Without providing criteria for what constituted "normal" anatomy, the physician simply proclaimed irregularity based on his own powers of sight and touch. Moreover, his characterization of what he perceived as abnormal echoed the anxious account by Flower and Murie. Although the description of the clitoris in this account is a notable exception to the tendency to exaggerate its size, the account nevertheless scrutinized another site of genital excess. The "fleshy sacs" of this woman, like the "appendages" fetishized in the earlier account, invoked the anatomy of a phantom male body inhabiting the lesbian's anatomical features.

The attention given to the apparent gender ambiguity in these accounts took on specific significance in the context of evolutionary theory. One of the basic assumptions within the Darwinian model was the belief that, as organisms evolved through a process of natural selection, they also showed greater signs of sexual differentiation. Following this logic, various writers used sexual characteristics as indicators of evolutionary progress toward civilization. In *Man and Woman,* for instance, Ellis himself cautiously suggested that since the "beginnings of industrialism, . . . more marked sexual differences in physical development seem (we cannot speak definitely) to have developed than are usually to be found in savage societies."[54] In articulating this idea, Ellis drew from theories developed by biologists such as Patrick Geddes and J. Arthur Thomson, who stated in their important work *The Evolution of Sex* that "hermaphroditism is primitive; the unisexual state is a subsequent differentiation. The present cases of normal hermaphroditism imply either persistence or reversion."[55] In characterizing either lesbians' or African American women's bodies as less sexually differentiated than the norm (always posited as white heterosexual women's bodies), anatomists and sexologists drew on notions of natural selection to dismiss these bodies as anomalous "throwbacks" within a scheme of cultural and anatomical progress.

Eugenics, Sexology, and the Mixed Body

Evolutionary assumptions played a significant role in the development of eugenics, a form of racial science explicitly entwined with questions of sexuality and reproduction. Francis Galton (a cousin of Charles Darwin) introduced and defined the term "eugenics" in his *Inquiries into Human Faculty and Its Development* (1883) as "the cultivation of the race" and "the science of improving stock, which . . . takes cognisance of all influences that tend in however remote a degree to give to the more suitable races or strains of blood a better chance of prevailing speedily over the less suitable than they otherwise would have had."[56] In the United States, eugenics advocated selective reproduction and "race hygiene," a political and scientific response to the growth of a population beginning to challenge the dominance of white political interests. The widespread scientific and social interest in eugenics was fueled by anxieties expressed through the popularized notion of (white) "race suicide." This phrase, invoked most famously by Theodore Roosevelt, summed up nativist fears about a perceived decline in reproduction among white Americans. The new field of eugenics worked hand in hand with growing antimiscegenation sentiment and policy, provoked not only by attempts for political representation among African Americans but also by the influx of large populations of immigrants.[57] As Mark Haller has pointed out, "Racists and [immigration] restrictionists . . . found in eugenics the scientific reassurances they needed that heredity shaped man's personality and that their assumptions rested on biological facts."[58]

As American culture became increasingly racially segregated at the turn of the century, the figure of the mulatto carried contradictory meanings in relation to the discourse of eugenics and the larger field of racial science. Edward Byron Reuter's *The Mulatto in the United States,* for instance, pursued an exhaustive quantitative and comparative study of the "mulatto" population and its achievements in relation to those of "pure" white or African ancestry. Reuter traced the presence of a distinct group of mixed-race people back to early American history: "Their physical appearance, though markedly different from that of the pure blooded race, was sufficiently marked to set them off as a peculiar people."[59] Reuter, of course, was willing to admit the viability of "mulattoes" only within a framework that emphasized the separation of races. Far from using the notion of the biracial body to refute the belief in discrete markers of racial difference, Reuter perpetuated the notion by focusing on the distinctiveness of this "peculiar people." In contrast, others denied any positive (or neutral) effects of race mixture. Arguing that any intermixture was a threat to "white" purity, Charles Davenport, who dominated the early eugenic movement in the United States, claimed that "miscegenation commonly spells disharmony—dis-

harmony of physical, mental and temperamental qualities. . . . A hybrid-
ized people are a badly put together people and a dissatisfied, restless,
ineffective people."[60] The mulatto, as an embodiment of the object of
eugenist efforts, also became an important, if contradictory, figure in
sexologists' attempts to characterize the sexual invert.

In its emphasis on sexual reproduction, eugenics was tied to the
concerns of sexology, even though most eugenicists did not generally
emphasize questions of homosexuality. Sexologists, however, invoked
the concerns of eugenicists in pathologizing homosexuality. William
Robinson, a doctor who was a prominent sexologist and editor of two
medical journals concerning sex research, used the unmistakable rhetoric of eugenics to describe homosexuality. In 1914, in an article entitled
"My Views on Homosexuality," he wrote that he considered homosexuality "a sign of degeneracy" and that it was "a sad, deplorable, pathological phenomenon. Every sexual deviation or disorder which has for
its result an inability to perpetuate the race is *ipso facto* pathologic, *ipso
facto* an abnormality, and this is pre-eminently true of homosexuality."[61]
Some sexologists who developed models of homosexuality also participated directly in the eugenics movement.[62] Ellis's sense of the "racial
questions" inherent in sex, for instance, was surely informed by his own
involvement with eugenics. On behalf of the British National Coun-
cil for Public Morals, Ellis wrote several essays concerning eugenics,
including *The Problem of Race Regeneration,* a pamphlet advocating "voluntary" sterilization of the unfit as a policy in the best interest of "the
race."[63] He was also active in the Eugenics Education Society in England.[64] Further, in a letter to Francis Galton in 1907, Ellis wrote, "In
the concluding volume of my Sex 'Studies' I shall do what I can to in-
sinuate the eugenic attitude."[65]

The beginnings of sexology, then, circulated within and perhaps
depended on a pervasive climate of eugenicist and antimiscegenation
sentiment and legislation. Even at the level of nomenclature, anxieties
about miscegenation shaped sexologists' attempts to find an appropriate and scientific name for the newly visible object of their study.
Introduced into English through the 1892 English translation of Krafft-
Ebing's *Psychopathia Sexualis,* the term "homosexuality" stimulated a
great deal of uneasiness. In the 1915 edition of *Sexual Inversion,* Ellis reported that "most investigators have been much puzzled in coming to a

conclusion as to the best, most exact, and at the same time most color-less names [for same-sex desire]" (2). Giving an account of the various names proposed, such as Ulrichs's "Uranian" and Westphal's "contrary sexual feeling," Ellis admitted that "homosexuality" was the most widely used term. Far from the ideal "colorless" term, however, "homosexuality" evoked Ellis's distaste for its mixed origins; in a regretful aside, he noted that "it has, philologically, the awkward disadvantage of being a bastard term compounded of Greek and Latin elements" (2). In the first edition of *Sexual Inversion,* Ellis stated his alarm more directly: " 'Homosexual' is a barbarously hybrid word."[66]

A similar view was expressed by Edward Carpenter, who, like Ellis, winced at the connotations of illegitimacy in the word: " 'Homosexual,' generally used in scientific works, is of course a bastard word. 'Homogenic' has been suggested, as being from two roots, both Greek, i.e., 'homos,' same, and 'genos,' sex."[67] Carpenter's suggestion, of course, resonated both against and within the vocabularies of eugenics and miscegenation. Performing these etymological gyrations with almost comic literalism, Ellis and Carpenter expressed pervasive cultural anxieties about questions of racial origins and purity. Concerned above all else with legitimacy, they attempted to remove and rewrite the mixed origins of "homosexuality." Ironically, despite their suggestions for alternatives, the "bastard" term took hold among sexologists, thus yoking together, at least rhetorically, two kinds of mixed bodies—the racial "hybrid" and the invert.

Although Ellis exhibited anxieties about biracial bodies, for others who sought to naturalize and recuperate homosexuality, the evolutionary emphasis on continuity and the figure of the mulatto offered potentially useful analogies. Edward Stevenson, who wrote pseudonymously as Xavier Mayne, one of the earliest American advocates of homosexual rights, stated, "Between whitest of men and the blackest negro stretches out a vast line of intermediary races as to their colours: brown, olive, red tawny, yellow."[68] He then invoked this model of race to envision a continuous spectrum of gender and sexuality: "Nature abhors the absolute, delights in the fractional. . . . Intersexes express the half-steps, the between-beings."[69] In this analogy, Mayne reversed dominant cultural hierarchies that privileged purity over mixture. Drawing on irrefutable evidence of the "natural" existence of biracial people, Mayne posited a direct analogy to a similarly mixed body, the intersex, which he positioned as a necessary presence within the natural order.

Despite Carpenter's complaint about "bastard" terminology, he, like Mayne, also occasionally appropriated the scientific language of racial mixing in order to resist the association between homosexuality and degeneration. In *The Intermediate Sex,* Carpenter attempted to theorize homosexuality outside of the discourse of pathology or abnormality; he too suggested a continuum of genders, with "intermediate types" occupying a place between the poles of exclusively heterosexual male and female. In an appendix to *The Intermediate Sex,* Carpenter offered a series of quotations supporting his ideas, some of which drew on racial analogies:

> Anatomically and mentally we find all shades existing from the pure genus man to the pure genus woman. Thus there has been constituted what is well named by an illustrious exponent of the science "The Third Sex." . . . As we are continually meeting in cities women who are one-quarter, or one-eighth, or so on, *male* . . . so there are in the Inner Self similar half-breeds, all adapting themselves to circumstances with perfect ease."[70]

Through notions of "shades" of gender and sexual "half-breeds," Carpenter appropriated dominant scientific models of race to construct and embody what he called the intermediate sex. The analogy between the sexual invert and the mixed racial body was thus mobilized in contradictory ways within sexological discourse: it could exhibit this body as evidence either of degeneration or of a legitimate place within the natural order.

Sexual "Perversion" and Racialized Desire

By the early twentieth century, medical models of sexuality had begun to shift and incorporate a notion of homosexuality based on sexual object choice rather than inversion. It seems significant that this shift took place within a period that also saw a transformation of scientific notions about race. As historians have suggested, in the early twentieth century, scientific claims for exclusively biological models of racial difference were beginning to be undermined by scientists such as Franz

Boas, although, of course, these models have persisted in popular understandings of race.[71]

In what ways were these shifts away from biologized notions of
sexuality and race related in scientific literature? One area in which
they overlapped and perhaps shaped one another was through models
of interracial and homosexual desire. Whereas previously two bodies,
the mulatto and the invert, had been linked together in a visual economy, now two tabooed types of desire—interracial and homosexual—
became linked in sexological and psychological discourse through the
model of "abnormal" sexual object choice.

This convergence of theories of "perverse" racial and sexual desire
is evident in the assumptions of psychologists such as Margaret Otis,
whose analysis of "A Perversion Not Commonly Noted" appeared in a
medical journal in 1913. Otis noted that in all-girl institutions, including reform schools and boarding schools, she had observed widespread
"love-making between the white and colored girls."[72] Otis's explicit discussion of racial difference and homosexuality was relatively rare amid
the burgeoning medical literature on sexuality in the early twentieth
century.[73] Both fascinated and alarmed, Otis remarked that this perversion was "well known in reform schools and institutions for delinquent
girls," but that "this particular form of the homosexual relation has perhaps not been brought to the attention of scientists" (113). Performing
her ostensible duty to science, Otis carefully described these rituals of
interracial romance and the girls' "peculiar moral code." In particular, she noted that the girls incorporated racial difference into courtship rituals self-consciously patterned on traditional gender roles: "One
white girl . . . admitted that the colored girl she loved seemed the man,
and thought it was so in the case of the others" (114). In Otis's account,
the actions of the girls clearly threatened the keepers of the institutions,
who responded to the perceived danger with efforts to racially segre-
gate their charges (who were, of course, already segregated by gender).
Otis, however, left open the motivation for segregation: Did the girls'
intimacy trouble the authorities because it was homosexual or because
it was interracial? Otis avoided exploring this question and offered a
succinct theory instead: "The difference in color, in this case, takes the
place of difference in sex" (113). She used a simple analogy between race

and gender to understand their desire: black was to white as masculine was to feminine.

Racial difference performed an important visual function in Otis's account. In turn-of-the-century American culture, where Jim Crow segregation erected a structure of taboos against any kind of public (non-work-related) interracial relationship, racial difference visually marked the alliances between the schoolgirls as anomalous and therefore the object of scientific scrutiny. In a culture in which Ellis could remark that he was accustomed to women being on intimate terms, race became a marker for the sexual nature of that liaison. As Kathryn Hinojosa Baker has noted, "Had the 'love-making' been intraracial rather than interracial, Otis might not have seen any need to write an article detailing these relationships; race makes the situation notable."[74] In effect, the institution of racial segregation and its cultural fiction of "black" and "white" produced a framework in which the girls' interracial romances became legible as "perverse."

Otis's account also demonstrates the ways in which the color line was fundamentally eroticized in the early twentieth century. We might recall here that the supposed need for racial segregation, as it was formalized by the *Plessy v. Ferguson* case in the 1890s, was articulated through a discourse of panic about sexual mobility. One strategy was to demonize all black men as a sexual threat to white women. As an editorial in a Louisiana newspaper in favor of racially segregated train cars put it, "A man that would be horrified at the idea of his wife or daughter seated by the side of a burly negro in the parlor of a hotel or at a restaurant cannot see her occupying a crowded seat in a car next to a negro without the same feeling of disgust."[75] The assumption driving this reasoning reveals a racial fantasy inextricably tied to the logic of compulsory heterosexuality. Both legalized and de facto racial segregation served not only to demand constant adherence to the fictions of racial identity but also to police sexual mobility. In the context of the all-girls' spaces of reform schools, this eroticization of the color line remained in force, from both Otis's perspective and perhaps those of the girls themselves. Otis's case reveals that the imposition of segregation marked the "white" and "colored" girls as differently gendered, even in the space of a supposedly single-sex institution.

Otis's statement that "the difference in color, in this case, takes the place of difference in sex" resonates with recent critical discussions of lesbian desire and identification, which have invoked similar analogies between the visual function of butch-femme roles and racial difference. For instance, film critic Ruby Rich has suggested that "racial difference operates for lesbians in the same way as, let's say, butch-femme, or s&m roles do, that is, as a form of differentiation between two people of the same gender."[76] Elsewhere, Rich has speculated further that "race occupies the place vacated by gender. The non-sameness of color, language, or culture is a marker of difference in relationships otherwise defined by the sameness of gender."[77] Commenting on Rich's analysis, however, Biddy Martin points out that "race does not operate just like butch-femme . . . it also operates to secure butch-femme roles."[78] Although it is important to emphasize that "butch-femme" as a particular construction of lesbian desire is anachronistic in the context of Otis's article, Martin's comments point usefully to an analysis of the scopic function of racial difference in this account. Martin adds, "Making lesbian desire visible as desire, rather than identification, requires an added measure of difference, figured racially."[79] Thus, within prevailing models that assumed that sexual desire depended on difference, homosexual desire was made legible through the girls' transgression of the color line.

It is also possible that a corollary process was at work in Otis's account: that the figure of the color line itself instantiated desire, regardless of gender. Otis admitted that "the separation seemed to enhance the value of the loved one, and that she was to a degree inaccessible, added to her charms" (113). Regarding a different historical and cultural context, that of nineteenth-century Orientalist painting, art historian Linda Nochlin has asserted that "the conjunction of black and white, or dark and light female bodies, whether naked or in the guise of mistress and maidservant, traditionally signified lesbianism."[80] Although Nochlin does not elaborate further on this assertion, it resonates with Otis's account of the American institution. The proximity of "white" and "colored" girls attracted the pathologizing gaze of Otis's clinical eye and made this "particular form of the homosexual relation" worth noting.

The discourse of sexual pathology, in turn, seems to have informed scientific understandings of race as well. In 1903, for instance, a southern physician drew on the language of sexology to legitimate a particularly racist fear: "A perversion from which most races are exempt, prompts the negro's inclinations towards the white woman, whereas other races incline toward the females of their own."[81] Using the medical language of perversion to naturalize and legitimate the dominant cultural myth of the black rapist, this account characterized interracial desire as a type of congenital abnormal sexual object choice. In the writer's terms, the desire of African American men for white women (though not the desire of white men for African American women) could be understood and pathologized by drawing on emergent models of sexual orientation.[82]

This chapter has focused on the various ways in which late-nineteenth- and early-twentieth-century scientific discourses on race provided a logic through which sexologists and other medical "experts" articulated emerging models of homosexuality in the United States. These interconnections fall into three broad areas. Methodologies and iconographies of comparative anatomy attempted to locate discrete physiological markers of difference by which to classify and separate races. Sexologists drew on these techniques to try to position the "homosexual" body as anatomically distinguishable from the "normal" body. Likewise, medical discourses on sexuality appear to have been steeped in pervasive cultural anxieties about "mixed" bodies, particularly the mulatto, whose symbolic position as a mixture of black and white bodies was literalized in scientific accounts. Sexologists and others writing about homosexuality borrowed the model of the racially mixed body as a way to make sense of the "invert," an individual who appeared to be neither completely masculine nor completely feminine. Finally, racial and sexual discourses converged in psychological models that understood "unnatural" desire as perversion: in these cases, interracial and same-sex sexuality became analogous within later conceptions of sexual object choice. As in Otis's account, the proximity of "white" and "colored" bodies under segregation elicited expert scrutiny and provided a visual marker of transgressive sexual desire.

At about the same time that the first articles on sexual inversion appeared in medical journals in the United States, experiments with a new visual technology—the cinema—were just beginning to change the landscape of American popular culture. In April 1896 the first public exhibitions of Thomas Edison's vitascope, which projected motion pictures "upon a white screen in a darkened hall," took place in New York City.[83] Although expert discourses on sexuality and race asserted enormous cultural authority during this time, as the new medium of cinema emerged in the next three decades, it would also hold increasing power to shape cultural assumptions about the visibility of sexual and racial identities. As the next chapter will explore, racial and sexual discourses became deeply intertwined in the popular imagination as the new medium reinforced and reinterpreted scientific emphases on the visualization and embodiment of racial and sexual identities.

2

The Queer Career of Jim Crow

Racial and Sexual Transformation

in Early Cinema

In the last chapter, I argued that nascent models of sexual inversion and homosexuality in the "expert" discourse of sexology were entwined in various ways with the logic of American scientific racism. Efforts to describe the traits of a discrete body—that of the invert—called on the methodologies of comparative anatomy, as well as the tropes developed to represent its objects of study. The body of the invert was scanned, as African bodies had been, for markers of difference, at the same time that the invert's apparent gender ambiguity could be understood alternatively as a mixed body, akin to scientific constructions of the mulatto. As sexologists eventually developed a new emphasis on sexual object choice rather than the physiology of the "invert" per se, homosexual desire and interracial desire also became linked as "unnatural" sexual desires.

While the "expert" discourse of sexology was a powerful site for the emergence of these models of homosexuality and their imbrication with racial discourses, it was also a relatively exclusive discourse (although, as I have pointed out, it drew from "nonexpert" discourses and appealed to "nonexpert" readers as well). Many critics have warned against attaching too much weight to sexology and have insisted that we need to look beyond this explicit medical discourse to see the meaning of homosexuality in the culture at large. For this reason, this chapter takes up a robust popular text from the same period, *A Florida Enchantment,* and traces its transformation over a twenty-three-year period, from 1891, when it was first published as a novel, through 1896, when it became a stage production, to 1914, when it was adapted as a film. I focus on this text because it widens the scope of my discussion of the imbrication of race and sexuality at this historical moment and because it allows me to trace how this interconnection was negotiated in American popular culture. My argument will suggest the different ways in which dichotomies between "whiteness" and "blackness" structured the emergence of a discourse of homosexuality in popular representations and how cinema, in particular, managed that linkage as it struggled over the visualization of racialized and homosexual bodies.

Assessing the popular novels of Archibald Clavering Gunter, a critic wrote in 1902 that these ubiquitous books "were not made to be kept in the library, but to be read and thrown away."[1] Although Gunter himself remains an obscure figure in literary history, his (perhaps literally "trash") novel *A Florida Enchantment* proved to be a remarkably durable text, appearing in three different popular cultural contexts in the United States over a period of twenty-three years. It was published as a novel in 1891, performed on the stage in 1896, and finally produced as a film by Vitagraph in 1914. Originally cowritten by Gunter with Fergus Redmond, *A Florida Enchantment* concerned the comic transformation of two women into men.[2] In the novel, Lillian Travers, a white heiress, arrives in Florida with her "mulatto maid" Jane to visit Lillian's elderly aunt. Lillian's fiancé, Fred, also happens to live in the same town. During her visit, Lillian purchases a mysterious box that contains magical "sex-change seeds" that originated from a tree in Africa. After a tiff with her fiancé, Lillian swallows one of the magical seeds and begins her transformation into "Lawrence" (fig. 1). Realizing that as a proper gentleman, s/he will need a valet rather than a maid, Lillian/Lawrence forces Jane to swallow a seed also. The rest of the novel concerns the comedy of errors and confusion that result from the women's dual sex changes (figs. 2 and 3).

The Vitagraph film adaptation of *A Florida Enchantment* is today more widely known than Gunter's original novel. Through the development of the fields of early cinema studies and lesbian and gay studies, the film has recently begun to emerge as the starting point for discussing lesbian and gay film history and representation.[3] The program copy for the 1989 San Francisco Lesbian and Gay Film Festival, for instance, buoyantly advertises *A Florida Enchantment* as an example of early gay-positive images in film. Recuperating the film for its play with gender

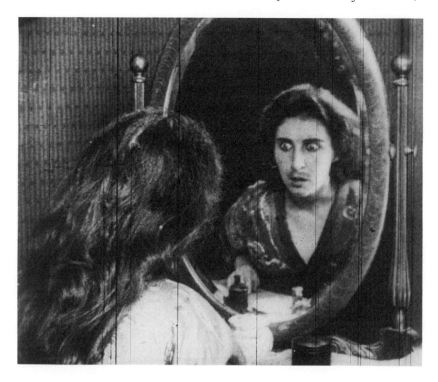

Fig. 1. Lillian Travers (Edith Storey) begins her physical transformation after swallowing a magical sex-change seed in *A Florida Enchantment*. Courtesy of the Library of Congress.

and sexuality, the reviewer exclaims about the "many sexual reversals in the astonishing A FLORIDA ENCHANTMENT from 1914. . . . Its way of toying with gender-specific body gestures remains amazingly witty seventy-five years later."[4] A recent catalog of representations of gay men and lesbians in mainstream cinema lists *A Florida Enchantment* as the first film in its chronology.[5] Vito Russo similarly includes it in his pioneering survey of lesbian and gay images in film, *The Celluloid Closet*. His discussion lingers on the actress Edith Storey, who plays Lillian: "Visually uncanny, especially in her scenes of dapper male attire on a visit to New York, her performance throughout is laced with an insouciance that tempers male arrogance with a secret, barely withheld sensitivity."[6]

It is tempting to valorize the sexually transgressive aspects of *A Florida Enchantment,* which at least temporarily overturns the dominant narra-

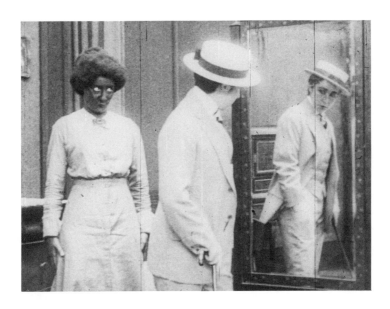

Fig. 2. Lillian (Edith Storey) gazes at herself as "Lawrence Talbot," with the approval of Jane (Ethel Lloyd), in *A Florida Enchantment*. Courtesy of the Library of Congress.

Fig. 3. Jane (Ethel Lloyd) is transformed into "Jack," much to Lillian's amusement, in *A Florida Enchantment*. Courtesy of the Library of Congress.

tive of heterosexual romance. Unlike most gay and lesbian visual pleasure at the movies, which until recently depended on untangling the
coded subtext of images on-screen, *A Florida Enchantment* provides an
unusually sustained and unambiguous display of female homoeroticism.
Indeed, the film playfully foregrounds the subversive possibilities of
"gender trouble."[7] Lillian's name—Travers—itself suggests her association with transvestism and inversion: she literally traverses the boundaries of gender. Edith Storey's depiction of Lawrence, the male version
of Lillian, seems to embody contemporary constructions of the sexual
invert, the male soul trapped in a woman's body.

As it receives more and more attention as a "proto-gay" film, critical
discussions of *A Florida Enchantment* tend to replicate the film's boundless
interest in sexuality and gender and to ignore questions of race. Thomas
Cripps and Daniel Leab have voiced the only exceptions to this tendency: both have briefly noted *A Florida Enchantment* as an example of
early films that portray African Americans through humiliating stereotypes.[8] Their brief comments point to the importance of thinking about
race in *A Florida Enchantment,* yet there is much more to say about the
film's processes of racialization. My approach incorporates the more recent contributions of theorists such as Stuart Hall, Homi Bhabha, and
Eric Lott, among others, who attempt to discuss racial stereotypes, and
particularly blackface, as more than simply derogatory.[9] As Hall has
noted, "the play of identity and difference which constructs racism is
powered not only by the positioning of blacks as the inferior species
but also, and at the same time, by an inexpressible envy and desire."[10]
Once we engage the possibility that the film's representation of race
might have something to do with its figurations of gender, sexuality,
and desire, different questions and readings of *A Florida Enchantment*
emerge. How, for instance, might Jane's presence in the film and her
portrayal in blackface complicate the cross-dressing comedy? And how
is this character related to the narrative's construction of Africa as the
source of the magical sex-change seeds?

The film's seeming indifference toward these issues of race generates
the questions addressed in this chapter. As I will argue, although the
film itself draws little attention to its own systems of racialization, it is
important to interrogate the seeming nonchalance toward racial characterizations in *A Florida Enchantment:* doing so reveals a great deal about

the emerging discourse of homosexuality and its imbrication with racial difference in early-twentieth-century popular culture, particularly the early film industry.

In approaching these questions, this chapter moves between text and context, that is, between intertextual readings of the three versions of *A Florida Enchantment* and discussions of their relationship to popular visual culture and the conflicting meanings of race and sexuality during this period. First, I chart *A Florida Enchantment*'s transformation from novel to motion picture, by way of the stage, in order to illuminate contradictions in the narrative, particularly those that resonated with the changing constructions of sexuality, race, and gender that characterized the period between 1891 (the date of the novel's publication) and 1914 (the date of the film's first exhibition). I then consider the particular difficulties that the narrative presented for the visual medium of film. This translation from novel to film occurred at a crucial moment of transition for the film industry as a whole, as it confronted new questions about its own cultural status. Through the example of *A Florida Enchantment,* it is possible to see how questions of race and sexuality were being negotiated and inscribed not only in film images and narratives but also in the structures of the film industry and in moviegoing practices. Within the historical context of the emergence of lesbian and gay identities and an increasingly racially segregated culture, the vertiginous comedy of Vitagraph's *A Florida Enchantment* reflected deep cultural anxieties about the slippage of bodies out of their conventional systems of visual representation, both on the screen and off.

Novels, Vitagraph, and the Transformation of Early Cinema

Vitagraph created the film adaptation of *A Florida Enchantment* in 1914 when the nascent film industry in the United States had recently undergone a period of transition, in both organization and practice.[11] The period between 1907 and 1915 saw the formation of the Motion Picture Patents Company (MPPC), a trust made up of the most powerful studios at the time, which intended to regulate and control the production, distribution, and exhibition of motion pictures. The MPPC, along with film trade journals, responded to increasing public criticism of the morality of motion pictures and aligned itself with more "respectable" forms of popular entertainment. Film historian Tom Gunning points out that the

> MPPC's drive to improve theatres centred on an issue now almost forgotten—fear of the dark. The darkness of the motion picture theatre blackened film's image for the respectable classes. In that darkness, anything could (and perhaps *did*) happen. Crawling with real or imagined "mashers," the darkened theatre was a place a middle-class patron hesitated to enter (unless, of course, he was a masher).[12]

Although Gunning does not discuss the racial implications of his description of middle-class audiences' "fear of the dark" (a subject that this chapter will address hereafter), he emphasizes the MPPC's attempts to revise the public's associations of the theater with danger. The motion picture industry took deliberate steps during this period to reform the physical appearance of theaters and to associate them with bourgeois standards of respectability through such accoutrements as less darkened theaters, proper ventilation, and comfortable chairs.[13]

Related to this new self-consciousness about the cultural status of the motion picture industry was a transformation in film form and content, moving away from the earlier period's exhibition of short films as part of the variety format of vaudeville to longer "feature" films, which were shown in theaters increasingly devoted to film exhibition alone. The production of feature films based on novels became part of a strategy in the movie industry's attempt to appeal to a larger audience based in the white middle class. Reflecting this shift within the movie industry as a whole, in the years following 1910, Vitagraph began buying and adapting novels by a number of popular authors, including Gunter, as well as Richard Harding Davis, Arthur Train, and Mary Roberts Rinehart.[14] The studio and exhibitors advertised these films as familiar entertainment to middle-class audiences, capitalizing on the previous success of well-known novels or plays. Vitagraph confidently asserted that such films "will not only draw record crowds, but will bring Higher Class Patronage at Higher Prices."[15] In technical terms, the use of novels and stage drama for screenplays demanded a shift to a different format, increasing in length from one reel to three reels or more. It also required a different conception of the actor's importance to the individual film as a commodity. In vaudeville, the development of a middle-class audience had depended in part on attracting "respectable" press attention. One way to receive such attention was for vaudeville shows to recruit leading stars from the legitimate theater (a practice known as the "headliner policy").[16] The film industry followed this successful strategy, recruiting well-known actors from dramatic and vaudeville theaters. In fact, Sidney Drew, who directed and starred in *A Florida Enchantment,* had a respectable acting career on the legitimate stage and in vaudeville. He carried his reputation and presumably at least part of his audience into cinema.[17]

A Florida Enchantment may be considered representative of this larger shift in film production toward literary sources, feature films, and "respectable" entertainment. There are additional reasons why Gunter's *A Florida Enchantment* in particular might have seemed a good candidate for a feature film in 1914. First, its narrative of sex change offered an opportunity to feature cross-dressing, a genre of performance that saw its heyday between 1890 and around 1915.[18] Both female and male cross-dressers appeared frequently onstage and in films from this period, including *Lillian's Dilemma* (1914), *Molly the Drummer Boy* (1914), and Charlie Chaplin's transvestite films, *The Masquerader* (1914) and *The Woman* (1915), to name just a few. These films evoked contemporary excitement and anxiety over changes in gender norms. *A Florida Enchantment* acknowledged its play on "the woman question," for instance, by highlighting the label on the vial of sex-change seeds: it reads "for women who suffer," a punning reference to the women's suffrage movement.

A Florida Enchantment also offered a story ready-made for Florida, which at the time had become the winter home of a number of movie studios, including Kalem, Lubin, Edison, and Selig. Rivaling the nascent film industry in Los Angeles, Florida offered 272 days of "clear cut" sunshine, inexpensive labor, affordable real estate, and relative proximity to studios already established on the east coast.[19] It is estimated that by 1916 more than one thousand actors and thirty companies operated in Jacksonville on a regular or semiregular basis.[20] Florida's association with images of paradise and magical legends such as Ponce de León's search for the Fountain of Youth reinforced the growing industry's cultivation of a public appetite for fantasy. Most of all, the economic vulnerability of laborers in Florida made it attractive to studios. Apparently, because extras could be hired so inexpensively, filming in Florida facilitated the production of so-called mob scenes.[21] One film production manager admitted, "Extras were a whole lot cheaper in Jacksonville than New York because they would work for practically nothing just to get into pictures. In New York you had to pay $8 to $10 tops, but only $3 to $5 tops down here. For a mob scene storming a jail it would really pay to shoot down here."[22]

The practice of filming on location in Florida also points to the growing importance of the film industry to other parts of the economy. An advertisement for *The Octoroon* (Kalem, 1909), subtitled *A Story of the Turpentine Forest* (fig. 4), suggests the symbiotic relationship that was developing between the film industry and the Florida economy: "This is another of the Great Florida Series which has attracted so much attention throughout the country. In addition to giving an intense, dramatic story, it shows the principle [*sic*] features of the turpentine industry."[23] For audiences at a distance, films shot in Florida offered not only entertainment but exposure to the workings of a growing industry in need of investors. Likewise, shooting on location provided indirect advertising for a nascent tourist industry, as a 1914 article implied:

> Many of the pictures feature Florida scenes, thereby extending the fame of the state's beautiful streams and romantic roads, lined with immense moss-covered oaks of stately palmettos. It is the sort of publicity that attracts favorable attention to the state and the vicinity about Jacksonville, so the city proudly includes the studios among its worthy enterprises.[24]

A Florida Enchantment participated in this symbiotic relationship, showcasing Florida's picturesque sights for potential tourists. Its locations included the Ponce de León hotel, an opulent 540-room resort in St. Augustine, and Silver Springs, famous for its remarkably clear water, which eventually grew into a major tourist attraction.[25]

Florida also became the site of the film industry's attempts to develop new race-specific genres during this period. Around this time, various studios began producing comedies with all-black casts that drew on minstrel stereotypes. Unlike the productions of the few studios owned and run by African Americans,[26] these early all-black productions, like Lubin's Sambo and Rastus series, made blackness itself the subject and

Fig. 4. Advertisement
for *The Octoroon*.
Reprinted from
*Moving Picture
World* 4 (23 January
1909): 100.

spectacle of the film. Many of these white-produced all-black comedies
were made in Florida: the Lubin studios, based in Jacksonville, were
best known for these burlesques, including *Rastus in Zululand* (1910),
Rastus among the Zulus (1913), *The Zulu King* (1913), and *Coontown Suffra-
gettes* (1914), which relied on the most hackneyed stereotypes of African
Americans.[27] As Robert Alan Nelson explains:

Most whites and even some blacks laughed at the antics of Rastus and his compatriots, but others were understandably outraged. This criticism didn't seem to bother the Lubin director responsible for these Afro pictures, Arthur Hotaling, nor the Negro performers who participated in them because they offered a (however limited) paid creative outlet for their talents.[28]

Although Nelson underestimates the possible reluctance or resistance of African American performers toward these types of roles, some white viewers did indeed watch these films with remarkable ignorance. A 1909 article about Lubin referred to these films as "startlingly realistic," demonstrating the powerful ideological effects of these images.[29] In an increasingly racially segregated culture, these cartoon images circulated among white audiences much more easily than did the actual bodies of those identified as "black." Such images, in fact, served to justify segregation by depicting and reinforcing images of black bodies as infantile, savagelike, and laughable. Moreover, the very genre of all-black films tended to reinforce and naturalize the spatial segregation of "black" and "white" bodies.

Vitagraph and the Management of Respectability

Vitagraph achieved its greatest success in the second decade of the century, the period in which the studio actively promoted its films as tasteful entertainment.[30] Vitagraph's adaptation of *A Florida Enchantment* was shaped by the studio's efforts to maintain its reputation and to expand the class makeup of its audience during this period of transition in the film industry. A key part of its appeal depended on negotiating its audiences' varied attitudes toward volatile issues such as race and sexuality.

Vitagraph's own promotional materials demonstrate the importance of unspoken but rigidly enforced sexual and racial ideologies to its public image. One of the studio's promotional profiles, "The Home of the Vitagraph," which appeared in a film industry trade journal, provided a detailed account of the physical layout of the Vitagraph studio and its personnel. Although the article focused on architecture and furnishings, it also suggested crucial details about how sexual ideologies shaped the studio's practices. In a description of its dressing rooms, the article mentioned that one building was

> entirely for women, thus separating the sheep from the goats. Each dressing room is equipped with hot and cold water, porcelain basins and all conveniences, and there is a well-fitted bath-room, of goodly size, on each floor. The walls, floors and ceilings are of cement, neatly finished and painted in pleasing designs.[31]

The language used to describe the fixtures emphasizes taste and respectability: the furnishings are "well-fitted," "of goodly size," "neatly finished," and "pleasing." The attention to genteel furnishings suggested that the studio as a whole deferred to respectable ideals of domesticity and femininity. Albert Smith, one of the founders of Vitagraph, stated more explicitly that the reputation of his studio was inseparable from that of the actresses he employed. According to Lary May, Smith "recalled that formality and full names were essential, for 'this was part of a plan to exert every precaution in favor of our young actresses. While it may be regarded as unusual precaution on our part, we nevertheless ordered all couches removed from the dressing rooms and make-up areas.'"[32] In Smith's view, dissociating his "young actresses" from any suggestion of sexual impropriety was essential for securing a good name for his studio.

While the actresses were safely ensconced in decorous (if couchless) dressing rooms, other women working at Vitagraph had important roles in shaping the representation of the studio. The job of adapting Gunter's *A Florida Enchantment* for the screen went to Marguerite Bertsch, one of the most powerful women working at Vitagraph at the time.[33] Bertsch began directing films in 1916 but was perhaps best known for her important role as head of Vitagraph's scenario department, as well as editor and screenwriter at the Famous Players Film Company. As an established scenarist and director, in 1917 Bertsch published a book entitled *How to Write for Moving Pictures: A Manual of Instruction and Information,* a volume that both shaped and reflected the conventions and demands of screenwriting for feature films.[34] In the introduction, Bertsch explained that the aim of her book was to provide readers and potential scriptwriters with the skills "to judge a photoplay so capably that you yourselves could decide fairly on the acceptance or rejection of a manuscript" (13).

In the absence of documents that directly comment on the adaptation of *A Florida Enchantment* for the screen, Bertsch's manual provides some insight into the process of revising the original plot. Bertsch clearly advised, for example, that a central requirement of a screenplay was "a wholesome atmosphere" and the avoidance of "vice," crime, and "the dark, unpleasant side of life" (20). Bertsch's emphasis on a "wholesome atmosphere" may have shaped the most significant changes to the plot of *A Florida Enchantment,* particularly the lesbian overtones of the story. In a chapter on the "power of mental suggestion" Bertsch wrote:

> If we really care for those we serve [the audience], it . . . would be impossible . . . to write anything that might stir up in them vulgar feelings or sexual thought, for such are conveyed by the attitude of the author toward his subject, rather than by the story itself, and a mind that thinks purely, radiates purity by mental suggestion. (267)

Through the rhetoric of moral purity and self-regulation, Bertsch aligned herself and the film industry with agents of social reform, attempting to reverse the public's previous association of cinema with corruption and sexual danger.

While Bertsch's emphasis on moral purity predictably insisted on sexual propriety, she also explicitly engaged the potential effects of cinema in domestic and foreign politics. In a passage that anticipated the self-censoring aims of the industry-wide Hays Production Code, Bertsch clearly stated what was taboo on-screen:

> Sectional difficulties and needs, political, social and religious, calling for, as in the case of the foreign market, the entire elimination of matters pertaining to the church, and demanding in our home markets the avoidance of subjects that give offence to a large class of patrons, or that tend toward industrial or social strife in certain sections. (21)

Such passages attempted to situate cinema outside the realm of the political sphere, through a conscious effort to obscure any engagement in, or advocacy of, overt political or social problems. Despite its attempt to profess an apolitical position, however, this passage also linked the interests of the film industry to the expansionist rhetoric of the day, with its explicit project of appealing to "home markets" and the "foreign market" alike.

Although Bertsch did not mention racial conflict, race played a vital part in the construction of the studio's origins, legacy, and employment practices. Reflecting the pervasiveness of racial segregation in the culture at large, like other motion picture companies, Vitagraph seems to have hired predominantly (if not only) white employees. Its founders, J. Stuart Blackton and Albert E. Smith, seem to have been fascinated with racialized performance, having participated themselves in vaudeville acts. Some of Vitagraph's earliest films were short animated subjects that portrayed racist caricatures, including one entitled *Cohen and Coon,* in which Blackton, one of the studio's founders, "writes Cohen and Coon on a board, then proceeds to change Cohen into a stereotype Jew and Coon into a stereotype Negro."[35] By confounding Jewishness and blackness, this routine enacted the ways in which Vitagraph would later position itself in relation to the rest of the film industry. After the studio's heyday had passed, an article detailing its history explicitly (and in disturbingly glowing terms) characterized Vitagraph's success as a product of imperialist ideals. "Small England grew into the vast British Empire because of the pioneering impulse of the Anglo-Saxon race," wrote William Basil Courtney, "and thus Vitagraph, the only one of the original motion picture companies that was founded entirely by Anglo-Saxons, has ventured first toward every farflung screen frontier."[36] Courtney's pointed references to the "Anglo-Saxon" origins of Vitagraph carry specific anti-Semitic implications: by 1925, when Courtney wrote this article, power in the Hollywood industry had been consolidated within eight major studios, with predominantly Jewish management.[37] Although Courtney's characterization of the studio may have had as much to do with the writer's own racism and anti-Semitism as with the studio's actual practices, Vitagraph does seem to have been a predominantly, if not exclusively, white operation.

Visualizing *A Florida Enchantment*

The process of making a novel into a film, or "picturizing," as it was called, ironically was not necessarily a process of making its meanings and references more visible; as I will show, it was also a process of masking and omission. One of the most obvious differences between the 1891 novel and the 1914 film version of *A Florida Enchantment* is the ending.

The novel invokes the conventional narrative resolution of romantic comedy—marriage—but with a twist: its happy ending is the marriage of Bessie to Lawrence, the post-sex-change version of her friend Lillian. In the last scene of the novel, the newlyweds set sail for their honeymoon and their future: "Lawrence Talbot, who will be a man forever, and his bride, Bessie, who will still remain to him forever a woman, and a joy" (260). With a wink to their readers, Gunter and Redmond presented an ending that on the surface conformed to the conventions of heterosexual romance (a wedding, complete with orange blossoms), at the same time that it mocked and denaturalized those conventions by suggesting that this happy marriage was the fulfillment of love between women. This ending and the novel as a whole received only mild comment from critics. One reviewer of the book wrote, for instance, that "it is alike realistic and improbable" and that "the situations, which might easily have been offensive, are treated with tact and discretion."[38] The potentially offensive "situations" he referred to were apparently understood as sexual, not racial, for he focused on Gunter's treatment of women.

The question of taste and offensiveness, however, did come up when *A Florida Enchantment* was performed onstage in New York City in 1896.[39] Because no script survives for this production, it is impossible to know whether Gunter changed the ending in his adaptation of the novel for the stage. The reviews of the stage production were unanimously negative, all on grounds that it violated codes of taste and decency. It was pronounced "the lowest depth to which the theatrical stage can be sunk by tasteless speculators," "the worst play ever produced in this city," and was charged with presenting "a few of the most indecent ideas . . . that mortal man has ever tried to communicate to his fellow-beings."[40] The play, in one critic's view, seemed intentionally calculated to shock its audience: "Instead of avoiding causes of offense, it almost might be imagined that [Gunter] had sought for them, so grossly and persistently did his characters disregard the ordinary proprieties of life."[41] Given Gunter's success as an entrepreneur in publishing, of course, this ploy might indeed have been intended to attract audiences hungry for scandalous entertainment, despite their professed outrage. Gunter himself refuted this charge, insisting, "It all depends on your view point. Nothing immoral or indecent is intended in *A Florida Enchantment*," adding, a strategic invocation of artistic license, that people simply did not understand the play.[42]

In comparison to the relatively mild reviews of Gunter's novel, these outraged responses to the play may have resulted from the shift to a visual medium. Embodying the antics of Lillian in a live actor brought an immediacy to the transformation not present in the book and apparently violated stage conventions of the period, presenting scenes of an actor in women's clothes in sexual pursuit of another female character. In the first phase of her transformation, Lillian continues to dress as a woman but ostensibly is becoming biologically male. Theater historian Laurence Senelick has suggested that this intermediate stage—when Lillian/Lawrence is still wearing women's clothes—was more offensive to the audience's sensibilities "than the subsequent transformation of the black maid (played by a man) into a valet, and an interfering doctor into a comic nursemaid—both acceptable 'dame' roles."[43] Once Lillian has changed into men's clothing, the play once again conformed to dramatic conventions. I agree that it was not necessarily cross-dressing per se that elicited outrage among the mixed-gender middle-class audiences that attended the theater, but rather the visual representation of two women dressed as women expressing same-sex desire. Yet it is likely that the sheer accumulation of sexual as well as racial boundary crossings had much to do with the audience's reaction.

Cross-Dressing, Inversion, and Lesbian Identity

The twenty-three years that intervened between the novel and the film versions of A Florida Enchantment saw an extended and increasingly intensified struggle among competing discourses over the meanings of erotic relationships between women. Negative responses to the stage version of A Florida Enchantment may have reflected the growing tendency to link cross-dressing with transgressive sexual practice. As historian Lisa Duggan has argued in her discussion of the 1892 trial of Alice Mitchell, what marked Mitchell as different from other women of the same period was not so much her romantic attachment to another woman but the combination of the expression of this desire with her plan to pass permanently as a man.[44] As the figure of the invert gained a more prominent place in public consciousness, gender ambiguity became increasingly interpreted as and conflated with "abnormal" sexual practices.

This conflation of gender ambiguity and nonnormative sexual practices makes it difficult to assert whether the film version of *A Florida Enchantment* is significant for understanding the emergence of lesbian identity. Most scholars have identified the film as an early characterization of lesbians, but others have insisted on separating the issue of gender from sexuality. In a recent history of lesbians and cinema, for instance, Andrea Weiss invokes *A Florida Enchantment* as an example of an early cinematic representation of lesbians only to dismiss it because "female-to-male gender transformation serves as ironic commentary on male privilege but does not imply lesbian identity."[45] Yet Weiss ignores contemporary constructions of inversion in popular consciousness. Historian Sharon Ullman has pointed out that performances of cross-dressing became increasingly associated with homosexuality during this period. Countering the view that the stigmatization of cross-dressing occurred later in the 1930s, Ullman's research "indicates that such stigmatization was widespread by 1913," and that it is evident as early as 1906.[46] Although Ullman focuses on female impersonators, she notes that for male impersonators, "questions of sexual deviancy did arise, [and] other issues not present in female impersonation appear as well — most particularly concerns over public politics and the relationship between . . . male impersonation and the highly contentious suffrage movement."[47]

In *A Florida Enchantment,* what causes other characters to look on Lillian/Lawrence with suspicion is her masculine behavior while she is dressed as a woman. After she first eats the seeds, she rebuffs her fiancé and instead flirts aggressively with Bessie and a local young widow while her aunt and Fred look on worriedly. Later, Lillian/Lawrence smokes cigars and makes a muscle in front of the befuddled Fred. In contrast to the film's almost indulgent responses to these moments, it turns much more anxious when Fred and Jane undergo their gender transformations. Toward the end of the film, Fred eats a seed and performs a grotesque caricature of a woman. Whereas Lillian/Lawrence is represented as delightful, Fred's transformation elicits panic from other male characters. A crowd chases him to the ocean, and he nearly drowns. Similarly, Jane/Jack's advances toward Malvina become so threatening that the town constable must intervene. Clearly, cultural constructions of gender and race shaped the perceived threat of cross-dressing. A young, wealthy white female character like Lillian had more license for gender fluidity than a white male character like Fred or a (supposedly) African American maidservant like Jane.

Off-screen portrayals of actress Edith Storey in the popular press also tended to indulge her seemingly instinctive talent for male impersonation. A promotional piece for *A Florida Enchantment* asserted that "in male attire, Edith Storey is as great a male impersonator as Vesta Tilly [sic]."[48] Indeed, Storey herself apparently relished these roles. In a 1914 interview, Storey claimed that "when it is necessary for me to play male characters, I am always careful to make them just as masculine as possible. Your audience, really looking through the keyhole, is so often offended by the obvious disguise of many girls who try to play male parts; and it therefore sees the artificiality that pervades the whole portrayal."[49] In the same interview, she also described at length her ability to convince a "big, bluff tourist" that she was a man while she was in costume on the set of *A Florida Enchantment*. When the tourist fell for her disguise, Storey pulled off her hat and revealed that she was a woman, much to the onlooker's surprise and alarm. Storey commented that "of course, he didn't know it, but he had given me a splendid compliment. He had as much as told me that I looked a perfect boy."[50] Storey's success at male impersonation was reinforced by numerous profiles in which she was described as an adventurous, tough tomboy affectionately known as "Billy." She recalled playing cowboys in her early roles: "At that time my muscles were too hard to be easily bruised even from the severest bumps."[51] A few years after *A Florida Enchantment* was made, Storey revealed that she was sympathetic to contemporary feminist challenges to gender norms. When asked if she wanted to get married, she responded:

> Only fools say "yes" or "no" to that question. . . . I'll say this: marriage may be a pastime for men, but for a woman it's always a business if she makes a success of it. . . . I have never wished to marry. I don't wish to marry now. . . . When I'm working I'm thinking situation, studying character, all my hours away from the studio. I might forget to get dinner, and if my husband asked me why, I'd probably bite him.[52]

Storey's response, however tongue in cheek, daringly suggested that her male impersonation was in fact linked to a refusal to adhere to normative constructions of heterosexual femininity. Indeed, the rest of her life bore out this refusal: Storey never married.

To return to Weiss's claim that *A Florida Enchantment* is about gender play rather than lesbian desire, it is important to point out that whether or not one sees Lillian as a lesbian, one must take into account the question of Bessie's desire: how do we make sense of this character's unambiguous delight in being courted by Lillian, who she thinks is still a woman? Weiss's tendency to focus only on the cross-dressed woman echoes dominant cultural constructions of lesbian identity since the late nineteenth century, which have consistently erased the sexual desire of feminine women for other women, whether masculine or feminine. Bessie fully returns the desire that Lillian/Lawrence (while dressed as a woman) expresses toward her: Bessie dances with her at the ball, kisses Lillian on the lips, and tries to convince Lillian that they should sleep in the same bed. Although no character in the film marks Bessie's behavior as abnormal, her desire for Lillian is unmistakable.

Given the growing pathologization of women who visibly transgressed cultural standards of proper white femininity, one would have expected the film version of *A Florida Enchantment* to meet with outrage in 1914. Yet contemporary reviews of Vitagraph's *A Florida Enchantment* were lukewarm in comparison, most registering nothing remarkable about the film, with a few responding with contempt toward the transvestite performances. Typical was a response appearing in the *New York Dramatic Mirror* that called the film "satisfactory Summer entertainment. . . . The direction is capable and photography good."[53] One of the most negative reviews appeared in *Variety,* which described the film as "a weary, dreary, listless collection of foolish things."[54] Some of the *Variety* reviewer's irritation suggested a negative response to the lesbian possibilities of the story. "The 'fantasy' is of a young woman who [swallowed] a seed and [became] a man, and not so much a man in this instance as just mannish," the reviewer explained. "To make it 'funnier,' she gave a seed to her colored maid, and the maid became mannish."[55] The review's contemptuous invocation of "mannish" placed Lillian and Jane well within contemporary medical and popular constructions of women who sexually desired other women.[56]

Within the context of the growing popular and scientific awareness and pathologization of "inverts," and given the studio's attempts to attract "respectable" middle-class audiences, Vitagraph seems to have anticipated a negative reaction to ending *A Florida Enchantment* with Lawrence/Lillian and Bessie living happily ever after. Instead of ending with the marriage of Lawrence and Bessie, as the novel had done, the film tempered this resolution. As the narrative accelerates into a panicky chase scene, it cuts to a shot of Lillian fast asleep in her aunt's drawing room. Lillian wakes up, startled, and looks at the seeds, the note, and the box. When she sees the vial intact with the seeds inside, she sighs, relieved to discover that the whole story of transformation has been only a dream. In the final shot of the film, Fred returns and embraces Lillian, diffusing the previous moments of panic with an affectionate laugh.

The movie's dream device resolves the story as it dissolves the sexual ambiguities: it neutralizes Lillian's sex change by relegating it to the realm of fantasy. Further, the dream device restores the characters to their original identities and seals the story with the final shot of the happily engaged "natural" female and male couple, Lillian and Fred. Thus, although most of the film gets its erotic charge from the representation of same-sex desire, the revised ending contains that eroticism within a dream. Homosexual desire and gender confusion are figured as a nightmare, albeit a giddy one, and white heterosexuality becomes the naturalized and reassuring happy ending of this comedy.

Obscuring Nineteenth-Century Popular Entertainment

While Vitagraph had to negotiate the emerging cultural recognition and pathologization of lesbians, it was also engaged in positioning itself in relation to older forms of popular culture, specifically the dime museum, burlesque, and minstrelsy. In comparison with the earlier novel and the stage production, Vitagraph's film version of *A Florida Enchantment* attempted to distance itself from these other (and at times competing) forms of popular entertainment. Whereas the novel had explicitly drawn on them, particularly the dime museum, the film deleted references to them altogether.[57] For instance, the first scene of the novel takes place at "Vedder's extraordinary museum," where Lillian purchases the black box. Gunter and Redmond describe Vedder's as a kind of Barnum museum with a southern twist, noting that it was "devoted to commerce in the form of disposing of Florida curiosities and horrors, to Northern tourists" (7). More explicit references to Barnum emerge later in the novel, when Jane/Jack reveals that s/he has been moonlighting at a dime museum as "the greatest freak on earth," a job that pays a hefty "thousand dollars a week" (161). Significantly, the wealthy and white Lillian herself does not join the dime museum. In fact, for Lillian, the thought of being a museum exhibit becomes the source of "a fearful nightmare," in which she visualizes an advertisement of herself as a sensationalistic attraction. Gunter and Redmond reproduce this poster in the text (fig. 5). Imitating the style of Barnum's advertisements, the poster announces "The Woman Man! . . . The Freak of All Ages." It also promises glimpses of "The Missing Link" and "The Living Skeleton," two acts regularly featured in Barnum's exhibits, as well as the purchase of the seed by "a female member of the Rothschild family," a reference to a famous incident when the Baroness Rothschild invited Barnum and his most famous act, Tom Thumb, to her home.[58] In fact, the plot of *A Florida Enchantment* displaces onto gender what one P. T. Barnum attraction performed with race. According to Morris Robert Werner, in Barnum's constant search for new attractions for his American Museum, he was reported to have exhibited in 1850 "a negro . . . who claimed to have discovered a weed that would turn negroes white."[59]

Gunter and Redmond's references to the dime museum (and particularly its profit-making role) can be read as an ironic comment on the novel's own sensationalistic plot device. The authors appropriate and translate the popular appeal of racial and sexual "freaks" and inexplicable transformations—the staple attractions of the dime museum—into the pages of a popular novel.[60] The film version of *A Florida Enchantment*, however, actively suppressed any echoes of Barnum's museum attractions. In the film, Lillian buys the box at "The Old Curiosity Shop," with an allusion to Charles Dickens, rather than "Vedder's extraordinary museum," with its suggestion of Barnum. Similarly, Jane's employment as a museum attraction and Lillian's nightmare of such exhibition simply dropped out of the plot altogether.

The novel also drew heavily on the tradition of minstrelsy with its blackface stereotypes, particularly in its portrayal of Jane. After Jane's transformation into "Jack," for example, the novel invokes an unambiguously racist portrait: "[Jane] is now a headstrong, wild and harumscarum darky boy, with that peculiar addition called down South

Fig. 5. In a "fearful nightmare," Lillian imagines herself advertised as an exhibit in a dime museum. Reprinted from Archibald Clavering Gunter and Fergus Redmond, *A Florida Enchantment* (New York: Hurst and Company, 1891), 163.

'nigger-brains,' at this time peculiarly dangerous to [Lillian] from its idiotic logic and extraordinary syllogisms" (151). To complete this tableau from blackface minstrelsy, the scene also included the cook Dinah, described as "a darky woman of wondrous potency" and "the nucleus of all domestic bliss" (151). Here again Gunter and Redmond borrowed the stock figures of "Jim Crow" and "Mammy" straight from the minstrel stage, perhaps to capitalize on racist stereotypes that had already been a commercial success. As I will discuss further, the film version of *A Florida Enchantment* had a much more vexed and complicated relationship to the minstrel stage.

Through its casting choices, the stage version of 1896 made explicit the ways in which the character Jane embodied the conventions of the minstrel stage. The stage role of Jane was played by Dan Collyer, a veteran blackface actor from vaudeville.[61] This decision directly linked the play to blackface minstrelsy, in which the combination of blackface and drag was a familiar practice for white male performers, beginning in the 1840s with the low-comedy "wench" role.[62] White women rarely appeared in early blackface minstrel shows, and when all-female minstrel shows later developed, they apparently did not wear blackface.[63]

Whereas the stage version of *A Florida Enchantment* drew on minstrel traditions in casting the white actor Dan Collyer to play Jane, Vitagraph took a significantly different approach in casting Ethel Lloyd, a white actress, to play this part in blackface. In fact, although white actresses did perform occasionally in either blackface or drag, the combination of blackface *and* drag was anomalous for white actresses during this period, according to existing conventions not only of film but also of the minstrel, burlesque, and vaudeville stages. Although this casting choice did not receive much notice at the time, as I will show, it can be seen as part of Vitagraph's attempt to disassociate itself from these other popular-culture traditions.

White women did not appear regularly in the combination of blackface and drag in minstrelsy, but there were numerous other precedents for women either cross-dressing or appearing in blackface onstage. Burlesque, first performed in the United States in 1869, featured all-female performing troupes. Although the burlesque show borrowed the three-part format of the minstrel show, the white women performers did not appear in blackface. According to Robert C. Allen, "as far as can be determined, 'female' minstrels always appeared as white characters, sometimes adorned with blonde wigs."[64] They also frequently played male roles, in such productions as *Ixion, Sinbad,* and *The Forty Thieves.*[65] Allen states that in contrast to blackface minstrelsy, "burlesque had little . . . ethnic or racial basis to its humor."[66] Although Allen provides a valuable history of burlesque, the potentially racialized meanings of burlesque deserve more attention. This question is beyond the scope of my study, but it is clear that understanding whiteness as a racialized category would considerably alter our understanding of the racialized meanings of the burlesque tradition. For instance, Allen notes in passing that critics remarked vociferously on the burlesque performers' (often artificial) blondness.[67] If one recognizes the cultural status of that blondness as an unambiguous marker of whiteness, then its pervasiveness in burlesque—and, perhaps more interestingly, its very artificiality—suggests that it carried, consciously or unconsciously, important racial meanings to its audience.[68]

In vaudeville, which developed rapidly in the 1890s and had reached its height of popularity by 1910, female performers regularly performed in transvestite or blackface acts but rarely, if ever, combined the two. White actresses Vesta Tilley and Kathleen Clifford appeared in top hat and tails and were well-known and popular male impersonators on the vaudeville stage.[69] Likewise, white performers such as the Duncan Sisters, Sophie Tucker, and Eva Tanguay appeared in blackface on the vaudeville stage, but only in female parts. Vivian and Rosetta Duncan were famous for their depiction of "Topsy and Eva," based on the characters in Harriet Beecher Stowe's *Uncle Tom's Cabin*.[70] Tucker sang in blackface and was occasionally billed as "World-Renowned Coon Shouter," and Tanguay was billed as "The Sambo Girl."[71]

Thus, according to prevailing conventions, it would have been more likely for Vitagraph to have cast a white man in the part of Jane (as the stage version of 1896 had done) than to have cast a white woman. Why then did the studio choose Ethel Lloyd? Although it apparently broke with convention, the film, in fact, did not draw much attention to Jane's supposed blackness (or to Lillian's whiteness, for that matter), in comparison with its self-conscious interest in both characters' sexual transformations. Nor did reviewers apparently take much notice of Ethel Lloyd's performance in blackface and drag. To understand why Lloyd's performance did not draw attention to itself despite its break with conventions, it is useful to place it within a larger context of the uses of blackface in film. The lack of attention both by the film and by the audience to Jane, as I will show, is evidence of a transformation not only in technical uses and conventions of blackface but also in the cultural possibilities for racialized performance.

Blackface and Early Cinema

Some early blackface roles in film directly continued traditions developed in the nineteenth-century minstrel show. Thomas Edison, for instance, used blackface minstrel acts in *The Edison Minstrels, Minstrels Battling in a Room,* and *Sambo and Jemima* (c. 1897–1900), early test films in his experiments with synchronizing sound-on-cylinders with film.[72] These blackface performances made a spectacle of racial difference: audiences and performers alike (who for the most part were white and male, though there were occasional exceptions) played out sexual, racial, and class anxieties through theatrical exaggeration. In this way, they participated in what Tom Gunning has called "the cinema of attractions," the tendency of the earliest films to privilege theatrical display over narrative absorption.[73]

Yet slightly later blackface began to function in an entirely different way in cinema as a result of changes both within the film industry and within American culture at large. As discussed, one effect of the film industry's transition between 1907 and 1913 was the shift toward the feature film as the dominant genre. In contrast to the earlier "cinema of attractions," as Gunning has noted, this period saw the "narrativization of the cinema, culminating in the appearance of feature films which radically revised the variety format" and realigned the cinema with the legitimate theater.[74] This shift, I suggest, coincided with a revision of the conventions of blackface: blackface characters now became part of a narrative plot rather than spectacularized attractions. Expanding on the comic and sentimentalized stereotypes developed in minstrelsy and vaudeville, the film industry now incorporated blackface characters into dramatic film roles based on literary sources.

As racial segregation became increasingly institutionalized, the use of black makeup became a way to maintain all-white acting companies while still portraying African Americans on film. D. W. Griffith, the director of *The Birth of a Nation,* for instance, is reported to have forbidden "any 'black blood' among the players who might have to touch white actresses. Those actors were always whites in blackface."[75] According to Cripps, "as late as the mid-1920s major Negro roles went to white men in blackface. Not until after 1925 would a small cadre of Los

Angeles Negroes replace the old white actors."[76] Although blackface minstrel performances and their counterparts in vaudeville continued to be represented directly in films such as *The Jazz Singer* with Al Jolson, ironically many dramatic films transformed "blacking up" into a standard method of portraying racial difference on film while maintaining actual practices of racial segregation.

Blackface was transformed from theatrical spectacle, then, to supposedly naturalistic makeup. The actor and the film did everything possible to make audiences forget that they were watching a racial impersonation. Maintaining and disrupting the fiction of blackness became the subject of white actress Norma Talmadge's reminiscence about making *The Octoroon*. As a form of protest against a director's decision:

> We [white actresses] got together in a corner and deliberately decided to do everything in our power to be thrown out of the picture. . . . So the three of us blackened only our faces and the front parts of our necks, and as the auction block revolved the camera registered the backs of our necks snow-white. Needless to say, we were immediately dragged off the set, bawled out in very inelegant language, and sent home that day with no pay checks.[77]

Talmadge's prank reveals how important a naturalistic use of blackface was to the film and how ineffective it supposedly became when the audience could recognize the white body beneath it. In effect, where minstrel performers had used blackface to produce exaggerated and comic stereotypes of African Americans, the goal of many white movie actors in blackface was to "pass," to act "black" in a mode believable to white audiences. The seeming authenticity of blackface performances on film depended on white audiences' and actors' assumption that race was a transparent visual sign. The naturalization of blackface on film was significantly related to the increasingly naturalized structures of racial segregation within American culture at large.

Ethel Lloyd's portrayal of Jane in *A Florida Enchantment* attempted to achieve precisely this naturalistic effect in blackface. Based on its faith that the audience would accept Lloyd's performance as an African American character, the film constructed a division between "black" and "white" through the seemingly parallel narratives of Lillian and Jane. Lillian's manly swagger and sexual interest in Bessie is mirrored by

Jane's aggressiveness and desire for Malvina, another household servant (also played in blackface by a white actress). During the scenes at the farewell ball, the film also posits a comparison between Lillian and Jane through parallel editing, in which scenes of Lillian stealing Bessie away from her date for a dance are intercut with scenes of Jane fighting over Malvina with Gus Duncan.

The parallelism between Lillian and Jane, however, ultimately breaks down. Although both women swallow the seeds and become men, Lillian does so voluntarily, but Jane does so under duress, both physical and economic. Lillian declares that as a gentleman, she will need a valet instead of a maid, and in one of the most disturbing moments in the film, she traps Jane and forces her to eat one of the seeds. Once the transformation is complete, the constructions of each character's masculinity are anything but parallel. Lawrence swaggers, but he nevertheless remains within genteel codes of behavior. Jack, however, immediately becomes uncontrollable on transformation; to the white characters, his behavior is so threatening that Lillian/Lawrence eventually knocks Jane/Jack unconscious with chloroform. The film thus calls on asymmetrical contemporary cultural constructions of black and white masculinity, reinforcing stereotypes of the aggressive black male and seeming to justify drastic measures to control his violence.[78] Racialized gender stereotypes circumscribe their subsequent pursuits of women: Lillian is successful at courtship with Bessie, whereas Jane repeatedly subjects Malvina to unwanted sexual advances.

While the film constructs an illusion of parallel stories for Lillian and Jane, it insists, too, that these narratives remain separate. Even though we see many scenes of Lillian and Jane changing clothes together and laughing over their secret, the film denies the possibility that Lillian and Jane might be sexually interested in each other. They are portrayed as buddies who share a wink but never gaze sexually at each other. Nor does the film admit the possibility that Lawrence might pursue Malvina or that Jack might desire Bessie. There is no interracial desire, heterosexual or homosexual, anywhere in the film. In this way, the film seems to disavow the eroticization of the proximity of white and "black" women that psychiatrist Margaret Otis found so compelling in her discussion of girls' boarding schools in the same year, as discussed in the previous chapter. While the film seems to embrace, at least temporarily, ambiguities of gender and sexuality, it rigorously contains them within supposedly stable racial boundaries. If the film hints at homosexuality, it does so by denying the possibility of interracial desire.

In addition to shaping the narrative possibilities for the main characters, racialized constructions of gender similarly mark differences between the minor characters Malvina and Bessie. *A Florida Enchantment* can imagine (albeit unconsciously) the desire of a "feminine" white woman (Bessie) for a "masculinized" white woman (Lillian) but cannot admit a similar possibility between the supposedly African American characters. Bessie responds favorably to Lillian/Lawrence's romantic attention, whereas Malvina flatly rebuffs Jane. In the film's frame of vision, a "feminine" black woman is nonexistent. Malvina herself is constructed as somewhat "masculine" in relation to dominant ideologies of womanhood, in which femininity is figured in part through images of passivity and vulnerability. Her repeated rebuffing of Jane contributes to the film's general construction of black male sexuality as aggressive; Jane's advances toward Malvina repeatedly enact and reinforce these stereotypes. Malvina's active refusal to yield to Jane, then, secures rather than upsets contemporary racialized constructions of masculinity and femininity.

It is possible, however, to see that the segregationist tactics of Vitagraph's *A Florida Enchantment* had the potential to backfire and subvert its attempt to fix and naturalize racial difference. By including the practice of blackface in a narrative that self-consciously displayed cross-dressing and gender transformation, the film perhaps inadvertently suggested, even as it repressed, an analogy between race and gender. Although the film attempted to construct a stable division between black and white, the very use of blackface and its proximity to drag threatened to break that division down.

Importantly, the film's farcical treatment of gender play depended on the audience's awareness of the difference between bodies on- and off-screen: the audience knew that it was watching cross-dressed female actors but admitted that they were men within the logic of the movie. Yet the film could not afford this kind of epistemological and representational play around its depiction of race and racial difference. While it pointed up and played on the discrepancies between what audiences knew about the actors' gender and their contradictory appearance on-screen, the film did not engage in the same kind of play around race.

Ethel Lloyd's "real" racial identity, her whiteness, was paradoxically *visible* enough, perhaps unconsciously, to assuage the racial anxieties of a segregated white audience; at the same time, the discrepancy between her "black" appearance on-screen and her "white" identity off-screen had to remain *invisible* to support the film's own insistence on racial separation.

Gender, Consumer Culture, and Racial Segregation

During the year in which *A Florida Enchantment* was released as a motion picture, Alice Guy-Blaché, one of the most successful women film directors during the early period, published an article entitled "Woman's Place in Photoplay Production." In this article, Guy-Blaché discussed the importance of (white) women as audience members: "That women make the [motion picture] theatre possible from the box-office standpoint is an acknowledged fact. Theatre managers know that their appeal must be to the woman if they would succeed, and all of their efforts are naturally in that direction."[79] Guy-Blaché's observation that (white) women made up a valuable part of the moviegoing audience seems to have been acknowledged by the early film industry. Miriam Hansen and Kathy Peiss, among others, have discussed the particular role that cinema played in reconfiguring white women's relationships to leisure and public space and the ways in which exhibitors and producers catered specifically to them. As Hansen notes, "Throughout the 1910s these attempts to respond to and expand an existing market betray an experimental quality and thus register both the upheaval of public and private in terms of gender and sexuality and the generation gap resulting from it."[80] As an example of movies that catered to a younger group of white women, Hansen discusses Kalem's serial *The Hazards of Helen* (1914): "Drawing on successful columns in women's magazines, fashion journals, and newspapers, the serials located pleasure in images of female competence, courage, and physical movement (often involving triumphant transactions between women and technology, especially trains) that marked a striking distance from Victorian ideals of femininity."[81] Certainly, *A Florida Enchantment* bears similarities to this type of character: Lillian and Jane become physically bolder after their transformations, both taking and giving pleasure in their swaggering presences. At the same time, while the bulk of the film presents images of female swashbuckling, the ending tames and neutralizes these images, thus reframing them for an older audience grounded in more Victorian norms of gender.

Importantly, the attendance of white women at the movies was part of the larger cultural shift to a consumer economy in the late nineteenth and early twentieth centuries. This transition from a production-centered to a consumption-centered economy profoundly altered previous notions of separate spheres for white men and women. According to William Leach, by 1915, "women were doing between 80 and 85 percent of the consumer purchasing in the United States."[82] *A Florida Enchantment* thematized this change, for Lillian enacts consumerism in both a literal and economic sense. In her exasperation over her fiancé's neglect, Lillian turns to two forms of consumption for solace: shopping and eating. Lillian has access to money (she is independently wealthy) and explicitly appears as a shopper in two pivotal scenes in the movie: first, when she and Bessie buy the mysterious box at the curio shop, and second, when she and Jane purchase their men's clothes in New York. Significantly, both scenes enact consumption not only as a pleasurable moment but also as a particularly homosocial activity between women. The film also reinforces white women's position within a culture of consumption, at its most literal level, as actual paying audience members in the theater. While this consumption is pleasurable, it is also the source of unintended consequences; Lillian's literal consumption of the seeds is responsible for all of the subsequent upheavals in the film.

The new circulation of white women in movie audiences (and other spheres) may also be seen as an effect of shifting ideologies of race. Jim Crow segregation policed not only racial boundaries but also those of sexuality and gender and therefore shaped the changing demographics of movie audiences. The new visibility of white women in movie audiences, I suggest, was connected to the suppression of visibly black bodies both on the screen and in the audience. Audiences' "fear of the dark" at movie theaters was both literal and figurative. Racial segregation acted as an imagined defense against the powerful myth of black men's sexual threat to white women. According to the logic of Jim Crow, white women could circulate more securely in racially homogeneous social spaces. The increasing control over the mobility of African American men and women coincided with white women being encouraged to circulate as consumers within commodity culture.

By downplaying race and racial narratives, *A Florida Enchantment* helped white middle-class audiences to both forget and feel secure in their own positions within segregated social structures. These relations were not abstractions, of course, but were in fact played out and continually renegotiated in the very space in which a movie such as *A Florida Enchantment* would be viewed. Segregated movie theaters encouraged white viewers to forget about racial difference and reminded African American audiences with a vengeance that they had only limited access to dominant positions of spectatorship. For instance, in his 1932 study of advertising and the African American consumer in the urban South, Paul K. Edwards concluded that the motion picture was not an effective means of reaching an African American market. Southern African Americans were more likely to gather in churches, lodges, and clubs in their own communities rather than in movie theaters, according to Edwards, for several reasons: very few movie theaters catered specifically to African American audiences in southern cities, despite their relatively large African American populations; theaters that did cater to African-American audiences were small and provided inferior entertainment; and finally, theaters were often racially segregated. As Edwards explained:

> A much smaller percentage of Negroes of all classes attend the theatre than is true of whites . . . because of the embarrassment to which the race is often subjected in having to enter and leave the large theatre by segregated side entrances usually opening out on adjoining alleys, and to sit, all classes together, in a restricted part of the gallery.[83]

According to Edwards, this systematic shaming effectively alienated southern African Americans not only from the culture of moviegoing but also from the role of a consumer group, inaccessible to businesses that might use theater attendance in their marketing strategies.

The practices of, and barriers to, African American attendance at the movies that Edwards described in 1932 seem to have held for the earlier period as well. According to Gregory Waller, in 1909 there were approximately 112 "colored" theaters in the United States, but "a good number" of these theaters were probably owned by white investors, "since the [*Indianapolis*] *Freeman* in 1910 put the total number of theaters 'owned and operated by Negroes' at fifty-three."[84] In her study of motion picture exhibition in Chicago from 1905 to 1928, Mary Carbine discusses how movie theaters flourished within the predominantly African American business and entertainment district known as "the Stroll" on Chicago's South Side. Within this area, there were at least two black-owned theaters, and as many as fourteen white-owned theaters that catered specifically to the African American community. In their own communities in northern cities, such black-owned movie theaters provided potential sites for reinforcing positive race consciousness and African American cultural autonomy.[85] African Americans who attempted to see movies outside their own neighborhoods, however, faced conditions similar to those in the South: segregated seating or outright refusals of admission. Carbine notes that African Americans were sometimes employed by theaters catering to white audiences in other parts of the city but were often relegated to the most servile and least visible jobs. The visibility and invisibility of African Americans on-screen and in movie audiences structured the perceptions of white audiences. In practice, of course, many African Americans who could pass for white, temporarily or permanently, were indeed present in segregated theaters—as audience members, as workers, and as actors. Their actual presence, however, depended on their invisibility within racially segregated social spaces.

Africa and the Origins of "Gender Trouble"

The repression of actual African American bodies on-screen through blackface and in the audience through segregated social structures accomplished a process akin to what Michael Rogin has recently called "political amnesia," "a cultural structure of motivated disavowal."[86] As Rogin explains, "since amnesia means motivated forgetting, it implies a cultural impulse both to have the experience and not to retain it in memory. . . . Amnesia signals forbidden pleasure or memory joined with pain."[87] This metaphor of amnesia is useful for seeing how the film version of *A Florida Enchantment* attempted to disavow not only actual African American bodies but, even more so, the histories of those bodies within a context of slavery, imperialism, and gendered hierarchies, a history the film industry and its audiences also sought to evade. To accomplish this disavowal, *A Florida Enchantment* needed to rewrite and refuse to visualize the novel's narrative of the origin of the mysterious sex-change seeds.

In the film version of *A Florida Enchantment*, the origins of the seeds are explained in the note that Lillian discovers inside the antique box:

> *I, Hauser Oglethorpe, in the year of our Lord 1813, was shipwrecked off the coast of Africa. I learned that the tribe of natives which rescued me, recruited their ranks by capturing the women of neighboring tribes. These women soon became men. Quasi, their chief, confessed that he owned a tree, the seeds of which, changed men to women and vice versa.*
>
> *Quasi presented me with the four seeds enclosed herein as a token of the high esteem in which he held me.*[88]

An innocent enough explanation, perhaps. The significance of Oglethorpe's note and this narrative of the seeds' origins, however, becomes more striking when compared with the very different version of the story in the 1891 novel.

In the novel, Oglethorpe's letter is not nearly as brief, spanning instead an entire chapter, "The Marvellous Record of Hauser Oglethorpe," which details a much more complicated relationship to Africa. Whereas the film simply explains that Oglethorpe had been shipwrecked, in the novel Oglethorpe admits that he had gone to Africa "on an excursion after both white and black ivory," the latter being slang for a cargo of slaves (51). Here the Florida setting of the story is crucial to understanding the significance of Oglethorpe's journey: although the importation of slaves had been outlawed in the United States in 1808, it continued legally in the territory of Florida until 1821, when it became a state, and therefore subject to federal laws. Thus Florida became the point of entry for many of the thousands of new slaves brought from Africa into the American South during this period.[89] The letter, dated 1813, is thus an artifact of a period when Florida played a key role in extending importation of new slaves into the nation. Where the film portrays a rather unproblematic relationship between Oglethorpe and Africa, the novel imbeds and implicates him in an international economy of slavery. Oglethorpe's very presence in Africa is no accident or shipwreck in the novel: he is a businessman trading commodities—"beads, muskets and ammunition" for "a cargo of slaves" (51).

The film erases not only the history of slavery behind Oglethorpe's presence in Africa but also the system of violence that accompanied it. In the film, Quassi simply offers Oglethorpe information about the seeds and their magical powers: the letter reports that Oglethorpe merely "learns" and Quassi simply "confesses," exchanges of knowledge that Oglethorpe characterizes as lacking hierarchy or coercion. The seeds are a mere "token of [Quassi's] high esteem." In the novel, however, Oglethorpe and Quassi do not have such an egalitarian relationship: in fact, Oglethorpe threatens to torture Quassi "with the cat-o'-nine-tails, and a brine dip afterward" if he doesn't tell the secret location of the tree (53). At gunpoint, Quassi reveals the tree's location, and ultimately an explosive armed combat erupts over the valuable tree. Here the novel explicitly grounds this violence within a context of capitalist expansion. Oglethorpe and his men eventually burn the tree to the ground to control the supply of seeds in the face of a limitless demand: he wants to establish "a monopoly of the wondrous seeds so that women would beg me for them, and queens and princesses cringe to me the gruff old sailor and the treasures of the earth be poured upon me by beauties who longed to be beauties no more—only simple men" (59). Oglethorpe escapes with four seeds, with which he intends to make a fortune. "For rich women," he explains, "as well as poor ones suffer the pangs of their weak, down-trodden sex, and I can sell them to the princesses and queens of the world" (63).

There are a number of reasons why Vitagraph might have omitted this story of slavery, imperialism, and violence from the film. Vitagraph might have distanced itself from the novel's story of the seeds' origins because it presented an allegory potentially critical of the very history of racial domination and appropriation that the film industry itself depended on and perpetuated. In Gunter's novel, just as the seeds were stolen property, precious and exotic sources of capital, so were the bodies of Africans captured as commodities to be sold on the slave market. To present this allegory, the film would have risked implicating itself in this exploitation of African labor, especially within the context of Florida. For Florida had not only played a key role in the slave trade but, as noted, by 1914 held increasing importance to the film industry as well.

Vitagraph's *A Florida Enchantment* carefully distanced itself from a history of slavery and cultural appropriation. By erasing the involvement of Oglethorpe and Florida in the slave trade from the landscape of the film, it posited a new allegory that rewrote and removed historical guilt or responsibility: the seed was a gift freely given from an African to a white American. This new allegory reasserted the film's, and by extension the film industry's, desired position of innocence in relation to African Americans. In fact, the industry was highly segregated by race, even as it eagerly appropriated African American labor and cultural forms. Eric Lott's analysis of the relationship between minstrelsy and slavery is useful here:

> Whites would like to have imagined the expropriations of minstrelsy to be nonanalogous to those of slavery, to have forgotten or displaced the latter in accounts of the minstrel show. . . . While occasionally the minstrel show becomes a narrative substitute for slavery, a comfortable alternative to the idea of free black labor, generally the intention of this second paradigm is a denial or forgetting of the unremunerated labor of slavery, a denial often difficult to sustain as repressed economic facts return.[90]

The film version of *A Florida Enchantment* induced a similar historical forgetfulness through its strategic omissions and revisions. The novel's detailed accounts of the literal theft of the seeds and the pillaging of the African landscape were elided in the movie. Similarly, the film suppressed the "economic facts" that might threaten to expose the film's relationship to a history of racial exploitation. After Jane has been transformed into a man, for instance, "he" challenges "Lawrence" on the matter of wages: "By de way, Massa Lawrence, I'se been making queries about heah, and twenty dollars a month may be good wages for a maid but fifty's 'bout de figure for a gen'man's body-servant. I rather cal'late my wages has riz by act of Pro'dence, Massa Lawrence" (206). By having "Jack" voice this ironic commentary on the gendered and racialized structure of wages, the novel to some extent critiqued where the movie participated in (and thus attempted to conceal its similarities to) the slave economy that was the very origin of its narrative.

By omitting the narrative of slavery, the film adaptation simultaneously jettisoned a story about gender and sexuality. Although the film's version of Oglethorpe's note included his discovery that the seeds "changed men to women and vice versa," it omitted another more telling incident included in the novel. In the novel's version, as Oglethorpe and his crew get closer to the sex-change tree, they begin to feel the tree's power on their own bodies and desires: "Even the perfume of its flowers had a wondrous effect. As we breathed we seemed to become effeminate and our natures milder, and even our cruel Spanish boatswain became softer in his language and less savage in his blasphemy" (55). The African landscape temporarily inverts the exaggerated masculinity of the "sturdy Yankee tars" (51), whose simultaneous dependence on, and domination of, Africans are bound up with their own intraracial and homoerotic desire. Eventually, each member of the crew, except the Spanish boatswain, tests the seeds: "And soon we all became women, and thought ourselves beautiful and had wench's airs, graces, feelings—and walked down to see our reflections in the limpid water and ask ourselves if we were not lovely" (57). In a moment that reveals the importance of race to this scene, Gunter explicitly rules out interracial desire in this suddenly mixed-gender group: "And after that we five did look lovingly upon the boatswain, for he was the only white man among us" (57).

The novel's narrative of the origins of the seeds links the fantasy of sex change and homoeroticism to a racialized landscape, one negotiated not only through violence and exploitation but also through desire. As Oglethorpe's note tellingly explains before setting out to find the tree, "it was a three days' journey to the object of my desires" (53). The object of Oglethorpe's desires is, it turns out, a "magic" way to make sense of narcissistic and homoerotic desires. The sex change makes legible an underlying miscegenous (and homoerotic) fantasy. The white trader both fears and desires being ravished by a "savage," an ambivalence that is directed toward the Spanish boatswain, "with whom," Oglethorpe admits, "I had fallen deeply in love and of whom I was very much afraid" (58). Even though Oglethorpe calls him the "only white man among us" (57), the boatswain is at the same time identified with the African men:

the Spaniard, Quassi, and the African tribe are all referred to as "savage" (53, 58, 60, 61, 62). The boatswain functions as a pivot in this scene, protecting Oglethorpe and his crew against the sexual threat of Quassi and simultaneously posing his own sexual threat. He exclaims, " 'This is a rare harem for the boatswain of the *Firefly*—I have as many wenches as an Arab sheik!' " (57). The boatswain's ambiguous racial position, however, demands that his masculinity be stabilized; otherwise homoerotic desire would explicitly cross racial lines. For according to Oglethorpe, "upon this scene Quassi looked with grins of pleasure, hoping as I afterwards knew, in his cunning African mind, that the boatswain would eat a seed, so [Quassi] could conquer all of us" (57).

As his letter assures its reader, Oglethorpe's sex change lasts only an hour. When he eats another seed, Oglethorpe restores the previously gendered and racialized hierarchies: "[I] found myself once more a man, and as such the Spaniard's captain" (58). It is possible to speculate why the narrative of Oglethorpe's "one short hour as a woman and very beautiful and very vain" was allowed expression in the literary version of 1891 but excised from the visual text of 1914. In contrast to the novel's exposure of the underlying (homo)sexual narrative of racial domination, the film could not afford to visualize this eroticization of upturned racial and gender hierarchies. Whereas the 1891 narrative of Oglethorpe negotiates the encounter with Africa and African men through a combination of violence and desire, the Vitagraph film of 1914 neutralizes it by depicting it as an unavoidable consequence of natural forces, an accidental shipwreck. It removes the original story of racialized power that explains Oglethorpe's presence in Africa. Further, the resistance of Quassi and the African tribe to Oglethorpe's capitalist aggression is rewritten as voluntary servitude. In the film's note, African defiance is nonexistent; instead the "tribe of natives" rescues Oglethorpe and holds him in "high esteem," naturalizing hierarchies between colonizer and colonized. In 1914 Vitagraph could not afford to make explicit the underlying cultural anxiety—that is, the possibility that white male encounters with black male bodies might lead not to masculine empowerment (as the popular cultural narrative would have it) but to sexual disempowerment nostalgically associated with nineteenth-century ideologies of white womanhood, which had begun to be challenged and resisted by women themselves.

The three versions of *A Florida Enchantment* reveal a number of pressure points in the shifting cultural understandings of race and sexuality between 1891 and 1914 in the United States. Although Gunter and Redmond's novel of 1891 offered a narrative that spoke comically to cultural anxieties about women's increasing independence and visibility in public, *A Florida Enchantment*'s explicit link between sex change and a racial narrative presented problems for Vitagraph in 1914. To salvage the comic plot of gender transformation, the studio used a number of strategies to neutralize the story's sexual and racial meanings. Attempting to consolidate the status of Vitagraph and the film industry at large as a respectable provider of entertainment, the studio distanced *A Florida Enchantment* from other popular cultural forms like the dime museum and blackface minstrelsy, which had appealed to audiences by playing directly on their fascination with racial and sexual transformation. Similarly, by subordinating the racial impersonation of Ethel Lloyd to the device of sex change, the film naturalized blackface performance: it thus reaffirmed the invisibility of actual African American bodies both on the screen and off, replicating and simultaneously masking the cultural architecture of racial segregation. By rewriting the origins of the sex-change seeds, the 1914 film also rewrote its own origins. Vitagraph actively disconnected its comic disruptions of gender and sexuality from a history of racialized desire, fear, and domination. The film reassured white audiences that these cultural anxieties would remain invisible even as it invoked their unspoken presence. For moviegoers in 1914, the enchantment of this film lay in its ability to help audiences forget that the visible upheavals in cultural meanings of gender and sexuality coincided with a racial narrative, whether it was the history of slavery or its reprise in imperialism, racial violence, and segregation.

3

Inverting the Tragic Mulatta Tradition

Race and Homosexuality in Pauline E. Hopkins's Fiction

Acutely aware of the ways in which the supposed boundary between "black" and "white" bodies was built on discourses of sexual pathology, African American women writers of the late nineteenth century embarked on efforts to reconfigure cultural constructions of black womanhood. Excluded from expert discourses such as law and medicine and erased as agents in popular-culture industries such as the emerging cinema, they looked instead to fiction and journalism to carve out some space, however marginalized, to begin to reshape cultural constructions of race, gender, and sexuality.

This chapter focuses on the presence of discourses of homo- and heterosexuality in two novels by one of the most significant African American women writers at the turn of the twentieth century, Pauline E. Hopkins. Between 1900 and 1904, Hopkins wrote four novels, numerous short stories, and biographical articles for the Boston-based *Colored American Magazine,* where she also exerted considerable editorial influence.[1] Hopkins's contributions to the landscape of twentieth-century American fiction have been revalued recently, with one critic remarking that she is "one of the United States's important great experimental novelists."[2] Hopkins is perhaps best known for her efforts to use fiction to intervene in contemporary racial and sexual politics. In the preface to her first novel, *Contending Forces,* she explained her understanding that

> Fiction is of great value to any people as a preserver of manners and customs—religious, political, and social. It is a record of growth and development from generation to generation. *No one will do this for us: we must ourselves develop the men and women who will faithfully portray the*

inmost thoughts and feelings of the Negro with all the fire and romance which lie dormant in our history, and as yet, unrecognized by writers of the Anglo-Saxon race.[3]

Refusing to see literature as a realm of entertainment or leisure activity separate from politics, Hopkins instead insisted on the key role that fiction played in the history and politics of African Americans and, further, the crucial need for African American self-representation.[4]

Hopkins's seemingly straightforward goals of using fiction "to raise the stigma of degradation from my race" (*Contending Forces,* 13), however, proved controversial to both African American and white readers, though for different reasons. In 1904 she was pressured to leave *Colored American Magazine* when it was bought by African American businessman Fred R. Moore, a supporter of Booker T. Washington, who had little interest in Hopkins's outspoken politics and the literary efforts of the magazine. Although the magazine reported that her departure was due to "ill-health," later remarks by William Stanley Braithwaite and W. E. B. Du Bois indicated that her political views clashed with those of the new management.[5]

Hopkins was also criticized by white readers offended by her fictional representations of sexuality. In 1903 Cornelia Condict, a white subscriber to *Colored American Magazine,* wrote to complain that "without exception [the serial stories] have been of love between colored and whites. Does that mean that your novelists can imagine no love beautiful and sublime within the range of the colored race, for each other?"[6] Condict's criticism was directed specifically toward Hopkins, who was the primary writer of fiction for the magazine at that time. Condict complained that "the stories of these tragic mixed loves will not commend themselves to your white readers and will not elevate the colored readers."[7] In a response published with Condict's letter, Hopkins boldly countered these criticisms:

My stories are definitely planned to show the obstacles persistently placed in our paths by a dominant race to subjugate us spiritually. Marriage is made illegal between the races and yet the mulattoes increase. Thus the shadow of corruption falls on the blacks and on the whites, without whose aid the mulattoes would not exist. And then the hue and cry goes abroad of the immorality of the Negro and the disgrace that the mulattoes are to this nation. Amalgamation is an institution designed by God for some wise purpose, and mixed bloods have always exercised a great influence on the progress of human affairs.[8]

Defending her stories, Hopkins used Condict's letter to her own advantage: "I am glad to receive this criticism for it shows more clearly than ever that white people don't understand *what pleases Negroes.*"[9] Refusing to accommodate the racist preferences of her white reader, Hopkins located a powerful political project within her fiction—the right of African Americans to claim and represent their own desires.

Hopkins's insistence on portraying a range of romance narratives, which included stories of interracial desire, was part of her larger attempt to refuse the racialized boundaries that Jim Crow and anti-miscegenation legislation increasingly imposed and naturalized. Nor did Hopkins's fiction focus exclusively on interracial romance, as Condict asserted: in *Contending Forces* and *Of One Blood,* for instance, Hopkins foregrounded desire among African American characters. Ironically, however, Hopkins's response to Condict did resonate within dominant cultural understandings of race that, while not necessarily segregationist, were nevertheless invested in racial hierarchies.[10] In her association of "amalgamation" and "mixed bloods" with "progress," one might argue that Hopkins participated in evolutionary narratives that posited lighter complexions as indicators of progress toward civilization. Hopkins's response to Condict might be interpreted as a suggestion that what did "please Negroes" was not "love beautiful and sublime within the range of the colored race" but precisely interracial (hetero)sexuality, reinforcing cultural myths that African Americans universally desired interracial sex, a myth that was used to justify not only segregation but also systematic racial violence through lynching.

More recently, criticisms of Hopkins's fiction have focused on the frequency of mulatta heroines in her work, interpreted as a reflection of her conservatism and class bias.[11] Yet as Hazel Carby has suggested, it is useful to look at this recurring figure as a literary device within Hopkins's own historical context. Noting the increased prevalence of mulatto figures in American literature of the late nineteenth century,

Carby has suggested that "the figure of the mulatto should be understood and analyzed as a narrative device of mediation."[12]

> After the failure of Reconstruction, social conventions dictated an increasing and more absolute distance between black and white as institutionalized in the Jim Crow laws. In response, the mulatto figure in literature became a more frequently used literary convention for an exploration and expression of what was increasingly socially proscribed. . . . the mulatta figure allowed for movement between two worlds, white and black, and acted as a literary displacement of the actual increasing separation of the races.[13]

Rather than advocating interracial sexuality or racialized hierarchies, as some have interpreted these representations, Hopkins's narratives functioned as literary vehicles for exploring historically specific structures of racialization, sexuality, and power.

The mulatta figure takes on additional significance, as I will show, when Hopkins's texts are placed within concurrent shifts in models of sexual identity during this period in the United States, for the mulatta's movement between black and white worlds represents sexual mobility as well. As discussed in chapter 1, in sexological texts of this period, the figure of the mulatto was often seen, explicitly or implicitly, as analogous to the invert: the mixed-race body evoked the mixed-gender body. This linkage surfaces in Hopkins's texts, particularly in *Contending Forces* and *Winona,* in which two figures associated with emerging models of female homosexuality, the ancient poet Sappho and the cross-dressed woman, converge with the representation of the mulatta heroines. These figures hold an ambiguous position in these novels: they emerge as both useful and dangerous to Hopkins's fictional explorations of African American women's desire.

To clarify my goals, I am not attempting to claim that Hopkins herself was a lesbian or that she wrote "lesbian" novels. Instead, this chapter demonstrates the need to ask how questions of sexuality shaped the work of writers for whom we lack biographical information or who, for other reasons, are not easily classifiable within the terms "homosexual," "heterosexual," "gay," "lesbian," or "queer." As Deborah McDowell has implicitly demonstrated in her insightful discussion of Nella Larsen's *Passing*,[14] one need not rely on biographical evidence to show that questions about gender, homoeroticism, and homosexuality are relevant and often necessary for understanding cultural representations of race and racial difference. In focusing on the presence of a discourse of homosexuality in Hopkins's fiction, my purpose is not to use it as an instrument for disciplining the author (or her text) into recognizable categories of "straight" or "gay." My discussion instead attempts to understand how Hopkins's novels register the ways in which cultural processes of racialization were inextricably bound to questions of sexual identity at the turn of the twentieth century.

The Contending Forces of "Sappho"

Hopkins's first and only nonserialized novel, *Contending Forces,* contains two parts: a brief antebellum story and a narrative about life within an urban middle-class African American community in the 1890s. The first section of the novel, set in the 1790s, introduces the Montforts, a slaveholding family in Bermuda. Responding to pressure from British abolitionists to outlaw slavery in its colonies, including Bermuda, the Montforts move to a plantation in North Carolina to continue agricultural production within a legal slave economy in the United States. The opening four chapters outline the history of the Montforts and end with the family's apparent destruction. White vigilantes bring ruin on the family by suggesting that Grace Montfort, who upholds ideals traditionally associated with nineteenth-century notions of true womanhood, has African American ancestry and has been passing as white. The Montfort history ends with the white vigilantes' violent murder of Charles, the beating and suicide of Grace, and the separation of their two orphaned sons, Charles and Jesse. Hopkins never reveals whether the rumor about Grace's racial identity is true; instead, she shows the destructive power of racialized constructions.

The second part of the novel is set approximately one hundred years later, in Boston in 1896. The story centers on a boardinghouse run by "Ma" Smith and her two adult children, Dora and Will, and follows a melodramatic tale within this middle-class African American community at the turn of the century. The central action of the novel begins with the entrance of a newcomer, Sappho Clark, a stenographer who takes a room in the Smith boardinghouse.

Hopkins's *Contending Forces* can be situated in the tradition of the domestic novel, a genre historically associated with women writers and readers, which became an important site for late-nineteenth-century African American women writers' resistance to cultural stereotypes. Recent feminist analyses have significantly reoriented understandings of the political and cultural work accomplished by African American women's domestic novels at the turn of the century. Whereas some scholars have characterized these novels as texts that reinforced accommodationist views, others, such as Hazel Carby, Ann duCille, and Claudia Tate, have demonstrated the complex ways in which the novels attempted to shape and advance a range of emancipatory political goals.[15] As Tate has stated, "Black women's post-Reconstruction domestic novels aspired to intervene in the racial and sexual schemes of the public world of the turn-of-the-century United States by plotting new stories about the personal lives of black women and men."[16] The marriage plot, traditionally the backbone of domestic fiction, carried different political valences in African American fiction. As duCille has demonstrated, marriage rested within a history of entitlements based on race or one's status as "slave" or "free." Denaturalizing the narrative, cultural, and political meanings of marriage, duCille asks, "What happens to the marriage tradition . . . when it is considered in the context of a literature by and about American men and women who for generations were denied the hegemonic, 'universal truth' of legal marriage?"[17] Rather than simply reinforcing traditional gendered hierarchies, the marriage plot in African American fiction must be seen as a more complex narrative, at times symbolizing the attainment of free citizenship and subjectivity for both African American men and women.

Such scholarship raises important and unanswered questions about other axes of difference through which entitlements to marriage have been denied, particularly those of sexual identity.[18] DuCille's question about "American men and women who for generations were denied the hegemonic, 'universal truth' of legal marriage" also applies, after all, to same-sex attachments. DuCille uses the term "coupling convention," as she explains, "both to destabilize the customary dyadic relation between love and marriage and to displace the heterosexual presumption underpinning the Anglo-American romantic tradition."[19] Yet there remain many questions about how the specific history of the emergence of "heterosexual" and "homosexual" identities in the late nineteenth and early twentieth centuries might inform and be informed by analyses of African American women's cultural production during this period. Although the existence of African American lesbian and gay subcultures in urban centers by the 1920s has been documented, the meanings of same-sex erotic attachments within African American culture before that period remain generally unexplored.[20] Precisely because legal recognition of heterosexual marriage itself was a relatively new civil right for African Americans in the second half of the nineteenth century,[21] it seems particularly important to ask how the meanings attached to same-sex relationships may have been transformed during this period as well.

In her depiction of Sappho, Hopkins also borrows from and revises the conventions of the nineteenth-century novel of passing, in which the light-complexioned protagonist attempts to gain economic and social advancement by fleeing an African American family and community and passing for white in a landscape of anonymity.[22] As a literary genre, the passing narrative offered a space in which to explore contradictory and coexisting beliefs about race. The mobility of the passing figure "proved" that the supposed boundary between "black" and "white" bodies was not universally visible; passing became possible precisely because of the dominant cultural denial that African Americans may look "white." Conversely, although the passing novel offered to challenge the stability of racial categories, it did so within a framework of individualism and often reinforced the cultural biases that posited hierarchies of white over black.

As constructed in the late nineteenth and early twentieth centuries (and perhaps more recently), passing involved immense losses (of family, community, indeed one's own history), great risks (the potential for blackmail, physical violence, and even death), and often betrayal in exchange for the privileges attached to white identity in a culture segregated by law. These licenses and threats structure novels of racial passing. As the passing figure seeks to author his or her own narrative, he or she risks the possibility of any number of people from the past stepping forward to announce their version of his or her "true" identity. In most passing narratives, then, the protagonist's exposure is threatened not by her or his body alone but rather by proximity to another body.

The central character in the late-nineteenth-century novel of passing is often a woman, the tragic mulatta. In her study of the mulatto figure in American fiction, Judith Berzon notes how generic conventions were tied to the gender of the protagonist:

> In most novels with mulatto characters, the male mixed-blood characters are brave, honest, intelligent, and rebellious. . . . Few male mixed-blood characters are tragic mulattoes in the traditional sense. . . . There are almost no male suicides, whereas there are quite a few suicides by female mulatto characters. While there are some female characters who are race leaders . . . there are not many such women in mulatto fiction.[23]

Berzon's useful observation about the narrative conventions attached to the gender of the mulatto/a figure has been echoed by other critics. In her study of gender and ethnicity in the American novel, Mary Dearborn adds that "the tragic mulatto, *usually a woman* . . . is divided between her white and black blood. The tragic mulatto trajectory demands that the mulatto woman desire a white lover and either die (often in white-authored versions) or return to the black community."[24] It is not surprising, then, that a certain amount of erotic tension and narrative curiosity surrounds this figure, as Werner Sollors has pointed out: "In nineteenth-century American culture the figure of the Quadroon and the Octoroon was such a taboo: puzzling, strangely attractive, forbidden (and, perhaps, attractive *because* forbidden)."[25] The figure of the mulatto characteristically symbolizes both psychic and social dilemmas. Positioned as a vehicle for narrative conflict and tension, the mulatta figure's movement between worlds also eroticizes her.

In *Contending Forces,* Hopkins uses the figure of Sappho to both recall and revise the novel of passing and its conventional protagonist. Sappho enters the story as a mysterious stranger, offering little information about her past or family. Physically she resembles the classically beautiful but tragic mulatta who passes for white: "Tall and fair, with hair of a golden cast, aquiline nose, rosebud mouth, soft brown eyes veiled by long, dark lashes" (107). Significantly, although she is "a combination of 'queen rose and lily in one'" (107), Sappho refuses to pass as white. Late in the novel, however, it is revealed that Sappho does "pass" in a different way: she adopts the name "Sappho Clark" to escape her past as Mabelle

Beaubean. Her secret is that she was raped by her white uncle and gave birth to a child as a result. Hopkins builds the narrative around Sappho's silence and the gradual discovery of her past. The novel thus positions the reader to expect, even to desire, the eventual exposure of her secrets.

A number of critics have remarked on the significance of the choice of the name "Sappho," suggesting that Hopkins's invocation of the ancient Greek poet resonated both with the feminist symbolism of this figure and with the fragmentary nature of knowledge about her life and writing.[26] In a discussion of *Contending Forces* that generally criticizes Hopkins's focus on middle-class femininity, Houston Baker suggests that Hopkins's choice of the name is ironic: it "does not refer textually to anomalous sexual proclivities, but only, one assumes, to a classical mastery of the word. Ironically, such mastery for a mulatto woman in nineteenth-century Boston does not yield an island poet, but a clerk typist."[27] In his reading of the allusion and his focus on poetic "mastery," Baker too quickly dismisses the significance of Hopkins's choice for the central figure of her text. What Baker refers to as "anomalous sexual proclivities," that is, the ancient Sappho's sexual attachments to other women, may indeed be relevant to Hopkins's portrayal of her heroine. In fact, it is remarkable that critical discussions of Hopkins have tended to avoid the name's obvious cultural associations with lesbian desire.[28]

During the nineteenth century, two competing narratives circulated around the figure of Sappho of Lesbos. On the one hand, she was considered a courtesan and a dangerous model of female licentiousness; on the other, she was seen as a desexualized figure, a bodiless model of "Greek Love."[29] In 1871, in an article published in the *Atlantic Monthly,* for instance, Thomas Wentworth Higginson was moved to defend Sappho— "the most eminent poetess of the world"—from scholars who had called her "a corrupt woman, and her school at Lesbos a nursery of sins."[30] He instead drew parallels between the ancient Sappho's "maiden lovers" and Boston's literary women of the mid–nineteenth century. Higginson compared Sappho specifically to Margaret Fuller and her "ardent attachments" to other women, which he characterized as passionate but nonsexual.[31]

Toward the end of the nineteenth century, a different sexualized narrative increasingly circulated around the figure of Sappho, who became

enmeshed in emerging understandings of female inversion and homosexuality. Sappho, in fact, came to symbolize the manifestation of this
"new" sexuality in women, as evidenced by the terms used to label it
by literary and medical men alike: "sapphism" and "lesbianism."[32] This
association was so strong that sexologist Havelock Ellis could proclaim,
"above all, Sappho, the greatest of women poets . . . has left a name
which is permanently associated with homosexuality."[33]

A flurry of scholarly activity surrounded Sappho after new papyrus
manuscripts of some of her poems were discovered in 1879 and 1898.[34]
These texts, surviving on remnants of mummy wrappings, were exca-
vated from ancient remains in Egypt.[35] Hopkins was undoubtedly aware
of this renewed interest and perhaps read new studies by Henry Thornton Wharton or John Addington Symonds. Like the earlier account by
Higginson, these studies compared Sappho and her circle of women on
Lesbos to contemporary movements to advance the status of women:
"While mixing freely with male society, they were highly educated, and
accustomed to express their sentiments to an extent unknown elsewhere
in history—until, indeed, the present time."[36] Viewing Sappho and her
circle through the genteel women of his own day, Symonds noted that
they "formed clubs for the cultivation of poetry and music."[37]

For Hopkins, the figure of Sappho may have suggested not only codes
of gentility and a model of an intellectual and artistic woman but also
a potential link to a specifically African past.[38] In the December 1905
issue of the *Voice of the Negro,* a journal to which Hopkins contributed
a number of articles in 1904 and 1905, the African American journal-
ist John E. Bruce published an essay entitled "Some Famous Negroes."
The first to be listed was "Sappho the colored poetess of Mitylene, isle
of Lesbos."[39] Bruce's evidence for Sappho's racial identity was both historical and mythological, and, at best, twice removed, since he cited
Alexander Pope's English translation of Ovid's Latin poem, in which
Sappho is indeed described as "brown," even "glossy jet" like the "Ethiopian dame."[40] Bruce's claim was, of course, speculative, but it was also an
attempt to reclaim a history of African culture denied through colonialism and slavery. If Sappho's identity presented an epistemological gap,
Bruce's attempt to claim her as African was no more problematic than
assuming, as critics had, that she was "white." Although Bruce's article
appeared after the publication of *Contending Forces,* it is possible that

Hopkins, like Bruce, may have discussed or read about the speculation that Sappho had African origins. Whatever Hopkins's actual knowledge of this speculation may have been, however, the emergence of this question demonstrates the increasing prevalence of links between racialized bodies (in this case, African Americans) and homosexuality at the turn of the century.

The figure of Sappho, like her poetry, represented fragmentation and contradiction. She symbolized seemingly irreconcilable notions of womanhood, associated as she was with prostitution, lesbianism, or chastity. Her cultural location—at times Egyptian, at others Greek—remained ambiguous. For Hopkins, this ambiguity reinforced the mystery that structured *Contending Forces:* Who is Sappho Clark? What is her past? Why is she alone? Before Hopkins describes Sappho Clark, she prepares her reader to expect that these questions have something to do with her sexual history. Hopkins introduces Sappho through Dora's fascinated description of her, to which Dora's brother Will responds, "I'll bet you a new pair of Easter gloves that she's a rank old maid with false teeth, bald head, hair on her upper lip" (96). Expressing his sexual anxiety about this unknown woman and his sister's fascination with her, Will invokes specifically masculine characteristics ("bald head, hair on her upper lip") to evoke a stereotype of grotesque female sexuality, a "rank old maid." Much to Will's surprise, when Sappho finally arrives, she appears beautiful beyond belief. Will is not the only character attracted to Sappho. Hopkins describes a deep physical and emotional desire between Dora and Sappho:

> After that evening the two girls were much together. Sappho's beauty appealed strongly to Dora's artistic nature; but hidden beneath the classic outlines of the face, the graceful symmetry of the form, and the dainty coloring of the skin, Dora's shrewd common sense and womanly intuition discovered a character of sterling worth—bold, strong and ennobling; while into Sappho's lonely self-suppressed life the energetic little Yankee girl swept like a healthful, strengthening breeze. Care was forgotten; there was new joy in living. (114)

Hopkins portrays Dora and Sappho's attachment as one of mutual and transforming desire.

Yet Hopkins's attitude toward the possibility of women's mutual desire is contradictory, as might be expected given the uneven historical emergence of lesbian identity at the turn of the century. She seems to oscillate between a certain unself-consciousness about representations of female attachments and an acknowledgment of their potential for transgression. The status of erotic relationships between women in the nineteenth-century United States has been the subject of vigorous debate among feminist literary critics and historians. Much of this scholarship has accepted Carroll Smith-Rosenberg's notion of "romantic friendship," in which passionate attachments between women were seen as acceptable and not incompatible with heterosexual marriage.[41] In a discussion of turn-of-the-century literary representations of lesbians, for instance, Lillian Faderman has suggested that passionate relationships between women were not pathologized. According to Faderman, "popular magazine fiction, well into the twentieth century, could depict female-female love relationships with an openness that later became . . . impossible."[42] Recently this model has been challenged by scholars who have argued for a more complex understanding of erotic relationships between women before the twentieth century. In an insightful article on the representation of same-sex desire between women in popular fiction in the mid–nineteenth century, Marylynne Diggs has identified "the emergence throughout the nineteenth century of a specific sexual identification built upon the pathologizing of erotic and exclusive relationships between women."[43]

Hopkins's depiction of the relationship between Dora and Sappho illustrates this struggle over the definition and representation of women's erotic attachments as she oscillates between models of romantic friendship and lesbian pathology. Although Hopkins does not explicitly name lesbian desire, she does acknowledge that intimacy between two women is potentially dangerous, if not tragic. Dora herself treads cautiously at first in her friendship with Sappho: "She did not, as a rule, care much for girl friendships, holding that a close intimacy between two of the same sex was more than likely to end disastrously for one or the other" (97–98). This remarkably direct indictment of same-sex desire suggests that Hopkins clearly acknowledged the existence of sexual relationships between women and the growing tendency to pathologize them. She nevertheless appears to raise the specter of lesbian desire only to deny it as a characterization of Dora and Sappho's relationship. In spite of her professed reluctance to engage in "girl friendships," Dora cannot resist her attraction to the new lodger: "Sappho Clark seemed to fill a long-felt want in her life, and she had from the first a perfect trust in the beautiful girl" (98). Further, as a means of short-circuiting the inevitable "disastrous ending" of the narrative of desire between Sappho and Dora, Hopkins temporarily allows its expression, albeit only in a carefully controlled space set apart from the main narrative, a space of both containment and transgression, not coincidentally resembling "the closet."

Sappho and the Closet

When an overnight snowstorm makes it impossible for Sappho to leave the Smith boardinghouse for work, she "beg[s] Dora to pass the day with her and play 'company,' like the children" (117). Dora and Sappho take advantage of their enforced isolation to construct an idyllic domestic island:

> By eleven o'clock they had locked the door of Sappho's room to keep out all intruders, had mended the fire until the little stove gave out a delicious warmth, and had drawn the window curtains close to keep out stray currents of air. Sappho's couch was drawn close beside the stove, while Dora's small person was most cosily bestowed in her favorite rocking chair. (117)

Hopkins's description of the scene suggests miniaturization and contraction. The women play "like the children" in a room where the "little stove" suits Dora's "small person." Moreover, phrases such as "delicious warmth," "mended," and "cosily bestowed" suggest specifically domestic comfort, and the repetition of "drawn close" evokes the increasing intimacy between the two women. "Locked" in, Dora and Sappho are ironically now "free" to explore their mutual desire in privacy.

Hopkins may not express any physical desire between Sappho and Dora (nor does she describe explicitly any physical sexual contact, heterosexual or homosexual, anywhere in the novel), but the scene is loaded with sensuality, albeit of a specifically middle-class "flavor": "A service for two was set out in dainty china dishes, cream and sugar looking doubly tempting as it gleamed and glistened in the delicate ware. One plate was piled with thinly cut slices of bread and butter, another held slices of pink ham" (118). Hopkins's description suggests doubleness, not only through the literal "service for two" and "doubly tempting" cream and sugar, but also through syntax, balancing the alliterative adjectives "gleamed and glistened," and the parallel clauses, "One plate . . . , another . . ." (118). Sappho herself is described in the same terms as the food. The sweets that "gleamed and glistened" mirror Sappho's body, described later as "all rosy and sparkling."

The scene is overwhelmingly erotic, in a specifically oral way. As the women complete their feast with cream pie and chocolate bonbons, Sappho teases Dora, "And your teeth, your beautiful white teeth, where will they be shortly if you persist in eating a pound of bonbons every day?" (120). Dora teases back, "I'll eat all the bonbons I want in spite of you, Sappho, and if you don't hurry I'll eat your slice of cream pie, too" (120). Hopkins giddily narrates, "At this dire threat there ensued a scramble for the pie, mingled with peals of merry laughter, until all rosy and sparkling, Sappho emerged from the fray with the dish containing her share of the dainty held high in the air" (120). Hopkins's flowery language — "dire," "ensued," "mingled," "peals," "merry," "fray," "dainty" — suggests the lighthearted and inconsequential diction of respectable drawing-room conversation. This language, stilted and feminized, reinforces the specifically bourgeois sensuality of the scene and its fetishization of color, especially pinks and whites: "cream," "sugar," "bread and butter," "pink ham," "cream pie," and "beautiful white teeth."

In this private, safe, and domestic space, the tea party enacts a displacement of Dora's and Sappho's desire, sensual satisfaction, and veiled sexual aggression. The particular homoerotic significance of this episode is reinforced by the subsequent intimate conversation, a development and extension of the women's oral pleasure. The focus shifts from gastronomic desire to a more direct discussion and simultaneous evasion of the delicate subject of sexual desire. Dora, who at this point is engaged to marry her brother's best friend, asks Sappho earnestly, "Do you ever mean to marry, or are you going to pine in single blessedness on my hands and be a bachelor-maid to the end?" (121). Sappho's reply adds to the ambiguity surrounding her sexuality: " 'Well,' replied Sappho, with a comical twist to her face, 'in the words of Unc' Gulliver, "I mote, an' then agin I moten't"'" (121–22). The rest of their conversation reveals Dora's reason for raising the subject:

> "What troubles me is having a man bothering around. . . . I'm wondering if my love could stand the test."
>
> "That's queer talk for an engaged girl, with a fine, handsome fellow to court her. Why Dora, 'I'm s'prised at yer!'" laughed Sappho gaily.
>
> ". . . I dread to think of being tied to John for good and all; I know I'll be sick of him inside of a week. I do despair of ever being like other girls." (121–22)

This conversation reveals a great deal about Dora and Sappho's understanding of their own sexuality and their relationship. In shaping her novel, Hopkins ostensibly borrowed from nineteenth-century romance conventions, in which the narrative works toward a heterosexual resolution in marriage.[44] This scene, however, presents a potential obstacle to the expected heterosexual coupling; this "queer talk" of "single blessedness" and "bachelor girls" threatens to disrupt the conventional romance narrative. Sappho is not willing to commit herself to any particular desire; her laughing and "comical twist" suggest that a certain anxiety surrounds the subject of heterosexual marriage. Dora's despair stems not from the absence of a potential husband but from her difference from "other girls," for whom heterosexual desire seems effortless and unproblematic. When Sappho recites the traditional maxim of romantic love, "A woman loves one man, and is true to him through all eternity," Dora responds, "That's just what makes me feel so *unsexed*" (122, Hopkins's italics).

Dora's self-diagnosis ripples with anxiety: because her desire does not correspond to the conventional cultural narrative that culminates in heterosexual marriage, Dora can define herself only by the negation of desire. By using the word "unsex," Dora locates herself at the unspecified space between genders and outside traditional romance.[45] Hopkins's use of "unsex" also resonates with the growing discourse of female homosexuality. In his 1915 article on "Inversion and Dreams," for example, the American sexologist James Kiernan included a 1910 report of a young woman who had engaged in both homosexual and heterosexual activity and was troubled by dreams and fantasies in which she appeared as both male and female. Kiernan reported that "this the patient regarded as abnormal, believing herself to be what she called unsexed."⁴⁶ Like Kiernan's patient, Dora both acknowledges and resists her sexual indifference toward men. Yet in a less self-conscious moment, she readily indulges her desire for Sappho: "Dora gazed at her friend with admiration, and wished that she had a kodak, so that she might catch just the expression that lighted her eyes and glowed in a bright color upon her cheeks" (125–26).

Within the novel, this scene of closeted intimacies has great implications for Dora, who here feels "the sincerity of the love that had taken root in her heart for Sappho" (127). Eventually Dora does abandon her engagement to her initial fiancé, John Langley, but she does not completely abandon marriage. She later marries Doctor Arthur Lewis, a promoter of industrial education who resembles Booker T. Washington. Hopkins makes clear, however, that sexual desire has little to do with this marriage. When Doctor Lewis proposes, Dora rationalizes her decision: "No; she could not remain single; she would marry one whose manliness she could respect, if she did not love him. Love was another thing, with which, she told herself, she was done" (360–61). At the end of the novel, after Dora has married Lewis and had a child, her brother Will assesses her emotional state: "If ever a doubt of Dora's happiness had troubled Will's thoughts, it was dispelled now that he saw her a contented young matron, her own individuality swallowed up in love for her husband and child. She had apparently forgotten that any other love had ever disturbed the peaceful current of her life" (389–90). This description suggests the limits of the heterosexual resolution to Dora's narrative: she trades her "individuality" for the role of respectable matron.⁴⁷ Significantly, Dora's voice is also submerged: her thoughts and feelings are now mediated by her brother. Likewise, by leaving Dora's forgotten "other love" unspecified, Hopkins leaves open the possibility that it is Sappho. Despite the heterosexual resolution to each woman's narrative, Hopkins, however mutedly, suggests that marriage does not necessarily represent the complete fulfillment of their sexual or political desires.

Within the context of literary representations of same-sex desire, the scene of Dora and Sappho "locked" pleasurably away has larger implications. The combination of the unspoken acknowledgment and literal marginalization of homoeroticism links *Contending Forces* to the "closet,"

a literary trope that Eve Sedgwick has identified as "the defining structure for gay oppression in this century."[48] A "skeleton in the closet" is
"a private or concealed trouble in one's house or circumstances, ever
present, and ever liable to come into view."[49] To be "in the closet" is to be
palpably invisible in a structure of visibility, proximity, and knowledge.
Although individuals may desire to be "in" or "out" of the closet, one can
never fully control the interpretation of one's status. One must therefore constantly renegotiate the boundary between "in" and "out" in a
culture that simultaneously seeks out and erases lesbian and gay identity.

Panic and Passionlessness

When Hopkins voices Dora's momentary fear that "a close intimacy between two of the same sex was more than likely to end disastrously
for one or the other," she suggests a sense of sexual danger not con-
fined to the relationship between Dora and Sappho. It returns later in a
scene marked by Sappho's intense ambivalence toward a powerful older
woman. In a chapter entitled "The Sewing-Circle," Hopkins presents an
all-female scene of instruction, in which the elder Mrs. Willis, "the bril-
liant widow of a bright Negro politician," guides the younger women of
the community through moral, political, and cultural questions (143).[50]
Significantly, the group's subject for the day is "The place which the
virtuous woman occupies in upbuilding a race" (148). During the discussion, Sappho asks, "how can we eliminate passion from our lives,
and emerge into the purity which marked the life of Christ?" (154).
The question resonates with nineteenth-century racialized constructions of womanhood. As Carby, Tate, and duCille have discussed, the
question of "virtue" was centrally important in constructing African
American womanhood in relation to the "cult of true womanhood"
of the nineteenth century.[51] Because African American women were
associated with sexual accessibility under slavery while white women
were privileged as sexually "pure," it was crucial for African American
women to begin to redefine their own sexuality. Nancy Cott has discussed the potential uses of the ideology that associated passionlessness
with virtuous women: "By replacing sexual with moral motives and de-
terminants, the ideology of passionlessness favored women's power and

self-respect. . . . To women who wanted means of self-preservation and self-control, this view of female nature may well have appealed."[52] For African American women, passionlessness offered a potential model for transforming negative cultural stereotypes.

Cott also notes that the ideology of passionlessness may have been particularly important for securing a sense of solidarity among women who organized collectively on behalf of women's rights. By considering their love for other women to exist on a higher spiritual plane than heterosexual relationships, "that sense of the angelic or spiritual aspect of female love ennobled the experience of sisterhood which was central to the lives of nineteenth-century women and to the early woman's rights movement."[53] This problematic negotiation of desire and sexuality in the construction of a sisterhood is at the heart of Hopkins's sewing-circle scene. Mrs. Willis, "the pivot about which all the social and intellectual life of the colored people of her section revolved" (148), symbolizes ambivalence about the potential for women's solidarity. Willis elicits "the gamut of emotions from strong attraction to repulsion" and seems to have remarkable power over other members of the African American community (144). In responding to Sappho's question about eliminating passion, Willis takes a moderate view: "In some degree passion may be beneficial, but we must guard ourselves against a sinful growth of any appetite" (154). This tentative response does not dismiss the possibility of the *usefulness* of passion, a potentially problematic position for women attempting to revise the cultural stereotype of excessively passionate African American women.

When the two women continue their conversation in a "secluded corner" (155), Sappho is overwhelmed with conflicting emotions toward Willis: "For a moment the flood-gates of suppressed feeling flew open in the girl's heart, and she longed to lean her head on that motherly breast and unburden her sorrows there" (155). Yet this attraction—or "passion"—is immediately tempered by revulsion: "Just as the barriers of Sappho's reserve seemed about to be swept away, there followed, almost instantly, a wave of repulsion toward this woman and her effusiveness, so forced and insincere" (155). Sappho's ambivalence unsettles her: "Sappho was impressed in spite of herself, by the woman's words. . . . There was evidently more in this woman than appeared upon the surface" (157). In this scene, Hopkins raises the potential for intimacy about sexual secrets between Sappho and Willis, only to immediately suppress it. Richard Yarborough suggests that Sappho's ambivalence toward Mrs. Willis reflects Hopkins's own attitude: "Like Sappho, Hopkins never resolves her feelings toward Willis, a powerful figure who captures the author's imagination to a greater extent than her small role in the novel might indicate."[54] Tate has suggested that Hopkins's discomfort may reflect her awareness of the contempt that her contemporaries would probably have felt for the perceived self-promotion of this ambitious and outspoken female figure.[55]

Sappho's passionate ambivalence may also have its source in a powerful identification between these two characters. Just as Sappho elicited Dora's most intimate confessions without "confessing" any details about her own past, so Mrs. Willis extracts facts about other people while withholding information about herself: "Keen in her analysis of human nature, most people realized, after a short acquaintance . . . that she had sifted them thoroughly, while they had gained nothing in return" (144). This scene functions importantly in the narrative, as it piques the reader's appetite for the divulgence of Sappho's secret at the same time that it defers its exposure. In the tea party scene, Dora, ostensibly out of love for Sappho, "subdued her inquisitiveness, and she gladly accepted [Sappho's] friendship without asking troublesome questions" (127). In the sewing-circle scene, Sappho comes dangerously close to divulging her secret: "[Sappho] drew back as from an abyss suddenly beheld stretching before her" (155). Sappho instead veils her own story in terms of an anonymous acquaintance and her hypothetical sin:

> I once knew a woman who had sinned. No one in the community in which she lived knew it but herself. She married a man who would have despised her had he known her story; but as it is, she is looked upon as a pattern of virtue for all women. . . . Ought she not to have told her husband before marriage? (156)

Yet Willis, like Dora, represses as much as she elicits Sappho's disclosure. To Sappho's question about confessing to a future husband, Willis answers simply, "I think not," thus restoring the silence that propels the narrative.

Supporting Characters

Mrs. Willis's potential threat is her power to stop the narrative by eliciting the story about Sappho's secret past. Hopkins eventually dilutes this threat by relegating Willis to a minor role in the rest of the novel. Hopkins sustains a threat of exposure, however, by displacing women's homoerotic desires onto other female subplots, most notably that of Mrs. Ophelia Davis and Mrs. Sarah Ann White, "two occupants of the basement rooms" (104) of the Smith boardinghouse. Just as these "friends of long standing" live in the basement, literally below the main floors of the house, so their narrative occupies a subordinate, yet foundational, position in relation to the marriage plot of the domestic novel. As Hopkins explains,

> They were both born in far-away Louisiana, had been raised on neighboring plantations, and together had sought the blessings of liberty in the North at the close of the war. . . . As their ideas of life and living enlarged, and they saw the possibilities of enjoying some comfort in a home, they began to think of establishing themselves where they could realize this blessing, and finally hit upon the idea of going into partnership in a laundry. (104)

Significantly, Davis and White do not engage in fantasies based on the romance conventions of finding a husband but dream instead of "some comfort in a home" and employment in the North, a fantasy that involves a "partnership" at once affectional and economic, not unlike heterosexual marriage.

Despite their subordinate narrative and class positions, Davis and White represent a risk similar to that of Mrs. Willis toward Sappho and to the narrative itself. When they first meet Sappho, they immediately recognize something extraordinary and uncannily familiar about this beautiful young woman: " 'Lord,' said Ophelia Davis to her friend Sarah Ann, 'I haven't see enything look like thet chile since I lef' home' " (107). Davis's partner confirms her recognition of the familiarity of Sappho: " 'That's the truth, 'Phelia,' replied Sarah Ann; 'that's somethin' God made, honey; thar ain't nothin' like thet growed outside o' Loosyannie' " (107). This scene flirts with the special kind of paranoid knowledge that Sedgwick, in her discussion of the mechanisms of the closet, associates with the phrase, "It takes one to know one." [56] When Sappho confirms her Louisiana upbringing, White exclaims, "I knowed it . . . Ol' New Orleans blood will tell on itself anywhere" (108). The belief that "blood will tell on itself," which depends on the presumed physical legibility of race, provides the suspense that structures novels of passing. In 1913 an anonymous writer summed up the logic of "it takes one to know one" in "Adventures of a Near-White": "I would take a chance with a white man where I would not dare do so with a colored man. Inevitably a colored man knows but usually keeps his mouth shut, aided by a generous tip." [57] Sappho attempts to insulate herself from recognition among northerners who have no access to her past, but she risks exposure by those like Davis and White who are similarly mobile and displaced. Although White's revelation about Sappho is her Louisiana upbringing, the scene nevertheless raises the possibility that Sappho's secret past might betray her at any moment, to or by those who can decode "a story written on her face" (89).

The significance of the characters Davis and White is that they are not only potentially intimate with Sappho's hidden past but also intimate with each other. Hopkins deftly uses class inflections of the two characters to neutralize the potential threat of the laundresses' attachment. Because they are clearly depicted as occupying a social position subordinate to that of the Smiths, they are allowed a wider range of affection (at least until the end of the novel) than Mrs. Willis, who, because of her higher social position, is somehow more threatening in her pursuit of intimacy with Sappho. Hopkins's narrative voice tends to point out and discipline Davis and White's physical and verbal excesses, which run counter to middle-class sensibilities of self-restraint and deference. For instance, Hopkins describes Davis's singing in the parlor in ostensibly comic terms: "With much wheezing and puffing—for the singer was neither slender nor young—and many would-be fascinating jumps and groans, presumed to be trills and runs, she finished, to the relief of the company" (109). Davis and White nevertheless operate as a team throughout the novel, boosting each other with encouragement and taking pride in each other's accomplishments. During Davis's singing in the parlor, "Her friend, Mrs. White, looked at her with great approval" (109). White gives Davis unconditional and enthusiastic praise ("That's out o' sight, 'Phelia!" [109]) and insists on Davis getting recognition *as a woman* for her public accomplishments. When Davis wins a competition at the church fair, Hopkins writes, "And after that the pastor could not forbear saying a few words about how good it was 'to dwell together in brotherly love.' Sister Sarah Ann White said 'the *brothers* had nuthin' to do with it, it was Ophelia Davis an' nobody else'" (218, Hopkins's italics). By using working-class codes to construct a comic role for Davis and White, Hopkins is also able to voice an ironic critique of the public erasure of women while containing it within an ostensibly humorous portrayal of minor characters.

Hopkins sustains the relationship between Davis and White almost to the end of the novel, when she quickly and mechanically introduces Davis's romance with a younger man. Yarborough, in a discussion of problematic aspects of *Contending Forces,* writes that "the neat resolution of the intricate plot may not sit well with modern readers weaned on psychological realism." [58] I would argue further that Hopkins recognized that a resolution that left intact a female couple would be a potentially dangerous break in convention. She thus chose to end the novel by reinforcing the narrative limitations she delineated earlier: "A close intimacy between two of the same sex was more than likely to end disastrously for one or the other" (98). Instead of leaving Davis and White together at the end of the novel, Hopkins disrupts their attachment by producing a fiancé for Davis and replacing women's homosocial bonds with a heterosexual romance.

Dismantling the relationship between White and Davis, however, takes substantial narrative energy, an effort that ironically makes salient the intensity of their attachment. When Davis tells Ma Smith about her plans to marry a younger man, she constructs her new fiancé as a rival to her female companion:

"... Sarah Ann an' me'll have to part after I'm married, she's that jealous." ...

"Now that would be a pity, after you've been together so long," remarked [Ma Smith].

"She's got to drop sayin' ticklish things to me. A 'ooman's got a right to git married, ain't she? ... Mr. Jeemes says he knows the Lord sent me fer to be a helpmeet to him, an' I dassay he's right. Sarah Ann says my money's the 'helpmeet' he's after, an' somebody to cook good vittals to suit his pellet. But I know better; he's a godly man ef he ain't much to look at." (365–66)

In this conversation, Hopkins uses the voice of the absent White to critique the subordinate role of women in marriage, implicitly contrasting it with the relatively equitable arrangement between the two women. The scene ends with Davis's passion focused on White: "Sarah Ann says I'm a mortalized ol' ijit, an' a insane mannyack, an' Jeemes knows what he's a-fishin' fer. She's insultin', mos' insultin'" (368–69). That Hopkins includes a split, however mechanical, between these two characters is evidence that she gave them an important place in the story. That their "breakup" involves jealousy and protectiveness is also evidence that she wanted in some way to express the passion existing between these women, contrasting it with Davis's feelings about her fiancé, who "ain't much to look at." Like Dora, Davis is compelled by cultural custom to agree to marriage, in spite of her indifference for her fiancé and her passionate attachment to her female companion.

Contending Closets

Despite Hopkins's use of the conventional marriage plot in the conclusion of *Contending Forces,* scenes of female homoeroticism structure the narrative in important ways. Hopkins portrays female couples as potential sites for the expression of desire and identification, at the same time that she mitigates their threat to the narrative's overall heterosexual trajectory. Hopkins contains these eruptions of homoeroticism within the literally subordinate spaces—the closets—of the novel: the locked room where Dora and Sappho have their tea party, the all-female "sewing-circle" where Mrs. Willis and Sappho negotiate "passion" and secrecy, and the basement apartment where Sarah Ann White and Ophelia Davis make their home and run their business. Although the sexual secret that threatens to destroy Sappho's claim to respectable womanhood is ostensibly her experience of being raped by a white man, it is also possible to see anxieties about lesbian desire structuring the passing narrative of *Contending Forces.* In fact, if we understand the rape of Mabelle Beaubean as a symbol of the historical negation of African American women's sexual agency, it could be argued that the figure of Sappho,

precisely because of her association with lesbian desire, mediates Hopkins's attempts to imagine a narrative of African American women's
sexual agency. In *Winona,* as I will discuss in the next section, Hopkins
uses another trope associated with homosexuality at the turn of the
century, cross-dressing, to explore the limits and possibilities of African
American women's desire.

"The Prettiest Specimen of Boyhood": Cross-Dressing and Homosexuality in *Winona*

"Many strange tales of romantic happenings in this mixed community
of Anglo-Saxons, Indians and Negroes might be told similar to the one
I am about to relate, and the world stand aghast and try in vain to find
the dividing line supposed to be a natural barrier between the whites
and the dark-skinned race."[59] With this description of a village on the
border between the United States and Canada, Hopkins opens *Winona,*
a novel first serialized in 1902 in *Colored American Magazine.* Hopkins
uses these national and geographic boundaries to symbolize the project
of her novel: to show that the color line is not a "natural barrier," as
segregationists attempted to construct it, but rather an arbitrary and
ultimately unfounded division.

Hopkins demonstrates just how permeable these supposed "natural
barriers" are by foregrounding movement through or over racial, cultural, and national boundaries. Characters repeatedly pass across the
United States–Canada border and between England and North America,
demonstrating the fluidity of racial and cultural identity. For instance,
White Eagle, Winona's father, was formerly a British nobleman, who
fled to Canada to escape a mistaken murder charge. When he provides medical treatment for Seneca Indians suffering from cholera, he
is adopted by the tribe and subsequently disguises himself, assimilating
into Senecan culture. Hopkins notes that White Eagle is one of "many
white men" who "sought to conceal their identity in the safe shelter of
the wigwam" (288). Reversing the familiar conceit of a light-skinned
African American passing for white, Hopkins shows that racial passing is
also practiced by whites: "Nor were all who wore the tribal dress Indians.
Here and there a blue eye gleamed or a glint of gold in the long hair fall-
ing about the shoulders told of other nationalities who had linked their

fortunes with the aborigines" (288). Hopkins emphasizes that notions of racial, cultural, or national purity dissolve in this borderland setting.

As the heroine of the novel, Winona herself embodies these cultural and racial crossings. In appearance, she is described through references to (perhaps stereotypical) signifiers of Indian identity: she rides in a canoe, trails "a slim brown hand through the blue water," and wears "two long plaits of sunny hair" and a dress "of gaily embroidered dark blue broadcloth" (289). Further, this very mixture becomes the source of eroticization. Hopkins notes her "wide brow, about which the hair clustered in rich dark rings, the beautifully chiselled features, [and] the olive complexion with a hint of pink," which is compared with local flowers, the "faint pink stems of the delicate, gauzy Indian-pipes" (291–92). Although contemporary readers might have thought this Indian dress incongruous for the daughter of an African American woman and a white British man, through her description Hopkins naturalizes Winona's position within Indian culture. Like her father, White Eagle, Winona seems fully assimilated into the Senecan community.

Yet Winona later effaces this naturalized identity through a double performance of cross-dressing, disguising herself in men's clothing and darkening her face to appear more stereotypically African American. She dons this disguise in order to enter the prison where Warren Maxwell, the British lawyer, is being held prisoner for assisting John Brown and his fighters. When Maxwell becomes ill, Winona disguises herself as Allen Pinks, a "young mulatto" nurse who volunteers to care for Maxwell and calms the cell with a "soft hush of a tender voice" (386). Whereas Hopkins uses Winona's disguise to develop her theme of dismantling naturalized constructions of gender and race, in doing so, she introduces the specter of homosexuality into her text. As Allen Pinks, Winona becomes both subject and object of erotic fascination, unmistakably evoking the same racialized constructions of the invert that provided the central conceit of A Florida Enchantment.

In fact, the scenes between Pinks and Maxwell are the most overtly erotic in the entire book. At a moment when Maxwell appears to be asleep, Pinks gazes on him with explicit desire: "He stood for some moments gazing down on the Saxon face so pitifully thin and delicate. The brow did not frown nor the lips quiver; no movement of the muscles betrayed the hopeless despair of the sleeper's heart" (387). If this description did not mark out clearly enough Pinks's desire for Maxwell, Hopkins provides unambiguous physical evidence: "There was a light touch on his hair; a tear fell on his cheek; the nurse had kissed the patient!" (387). Hopkins details as she simultaneously tempers the eroticism of this scene. Although Maxwell puzzles over this kiss and questions the identity of his nurse, Pinks deflects both Maxwell's and the reader's curiosity. When Maxwell insists on asking questions about his identity, Hopkins writes, "Allen silenced him firmly and gently" (388). This silencing, however, only kindles Maxwell's own attraction to Pinks:

> Maxwell was fascinated by his nurse; he thought him the prettiest specimen of boyhood he had ever met. The delicate brown features were faultless in outline; the closely cropped black hair was like velvet in its smoothness. He could not shake off the idea that somewhere he had known the lad before in his life. At times this familiarity manifested itself in the tones of the voice soft and low as a woman's, then again it was in the carriage of the head or the flash of the beautiful large dark eyes. (389)

Throughout this scene, Hopkins plays with the reader's knowledge and ignorance. Although the reader may gradually recognize that this "prettiest specimen of boyhood" is Winona in disguise, Maxwell himself ostensibly remains ignorant of the real identity of this "lad," despite his rapt attention to Pinks's body. Thus while the reader may know that their kiss is "really" heterosexual, to Maxwell the kiss is homoerotic, and significantly, self-consciously marked as interracial. The object of Maxwell's desire is "really" a girl, but he ostensibly knows it only as desire for a boy. In the context of turn-of-the-century notions of masculinity and sexuality, as George Chauncey has shown, two men might desire each other, but only the feminized partner would be considered sexually suspect.[60] Thus, especially given Pinks's ostensibly subordinate position within hierarchies of race and age, Maxwell's desire for Pinks could exist well within the range of expected behavior for "normal" men.

Pinks/Winona, however, resembles one of the "intermediate types" that Hopkins's contemporaries, such as Edward Carpenter, Havelock Ellis, and others, attempted to classify in studies of inversion. These different forms of disrupting supposedly stable sexual and racial identities frequently overlap and coexist in individual accounts, as is made apparent in a 1914 report entitled "Invert Marriages." Dr. James Kiernan, whose "Sexology" column appeared regularly in an American medical journal, gave an account of the trial of Cora Anderson, alias "Ralph Kerwineo," who had been accused of "disorderly conduct in wearing male attire." Kiernan quoted from the court records as follows:

> Thirteen years ago [in 1901], two girls, nurses at the Provident Hospital, Chicago, found out how hard it was for a woman (especially a woman with a dark skin) to make an honest living, and decided to double up and form a home. Cora Anderson, looking the Indian she says she is, was the husband and Marie White, plump, pretty and feminine, was the wife.[61]

In response to the cultural and economic limitations attached to her gender, race, and sexual orientation, Anderson had successfully "passed" as "Ralph Kerwineo" for thirteen years until White "outed" her in jealous retaliation for Anderson's affair with another woman.[62] Despite the association of her masquerade with fraud, Anderson professed that she and her "wife" were motivated by a wish "to live honest lives and become respected citizens of the community." In her testimony, Anderson recounted how easily she had adapted to her new identity: "In a short time I thought of myself as a man, and it never entered my mind that I was any different from the men about me with whom I laughed, joked, worked and played my part."[63] Kiernan's account of "Mr. and Mrs. Kerwineo" demonstrated how legal and medical discourses overlapped in their fascination with the boundaries of identity. Anderson's masquerade challenged the stability of the social meanings of those physical differences that science and law held as objective and scientific "facts." Anderson's own words—"[I] played my part"—illustrate her understanding of identity as performance and of gender, race, and sexuality as socially constructed scripts, rather than innate biological differences.

In Hopkins's portrayal of transvestism, she worries the supposedly natural borders between male and female as she pivots between mulatta heroine Winona and the Western sidekick, Allen Pinks. Importantly, Winona's transvestism does not invert but rather blurs her gender. Maxwell sees Pinks as a figure with both conventionally masculine and feminine characteristics: s/he is "the prettiest specimen of boyhood," with a voice "soft and low as a woman's." Like Cora Anderson, Winona internalizes and naturalizes this performance of gender ambiguity.

In stories of impersonation, the exposure of the "true" identity of a character usually signals a return to the established social order of a fictional world. According to these conventions, one would expect the unveiling of Allen Pinks as Winona to resolve the tensions between male/female, black/white. Yet for Winona, exposure inaugurates not a resolution but rather a transformation and a source of new disturbance. After securing Maxwell's escape, Winona herself now experiences a sense of imprisonment outside the walls of the prison. She admits that she had rested more comfortably within her blackface and transvestite *disguise* than in the boundaries of her pre-passing female and biracial body. Although the rescue party exhales a general sigh of relief over Maxwell's escape, Winona feels a distinct sense of discomfort: "Winona was silent and constrained in manner. For the first time since she had adopted her strange dress she felt a wave of self-consciousness that rendered her ashamed" (396). Neither the cross-dressing nor the blackface itself produces Winona's sense of shame (in fact, her disguise gives her license for sexual expression). Rather, her *exposure* deflates her sense of self-worth:

> During her weeks of unselfish devotion when she had played the role of the boy nurse so successfully, she had been purely and proudly glad. Now, little by little, a gulf had opened between [herself and Maxwell] which to her unsophisticated mind could not be bridged. There lay the misery of the present time—she was nothing to him. . . . Fate had fixed impassable chasms of race and caste between them. (404–5)

Paradoxically, the double layering of blackface and cross-dressing had erased the problematic position of Winona's body; without her disguise, she is no longer able to control her own (or Maxwell's) narrative.

One way to understand Winona's response is to situate this scene within the gendered and racialized spaces not only of this particular novel but of American popular fiction more generally. Winona wears men's clothes and blackface not to escape capture but rather to enter an all-male space. This space is not only that of the literal prison but also that of the Western adventure, a literary genre that conventionally has no position for an active female character, much less the figure of the mulatta.[64] Through her disguise, then, Winona is able to escape from the narrative expectations attached to the figure of the mulatta heroine by entering temporarily into the role of Western hero, or at least his male sidekick. Here Hopkins's text reveals that interracial homoeroticism is at the center of male-centered popular fiction and, in fact, seems more desirable and imaginable than interracial heterosexuality. Whereas intimacy between a white man and a younger black man had been sanctioned within the space of the prison, that of a white man and a younger biracial woman remains culturally taboo.

Although Winona's exposure might be read as the reassertion of "black"/"white" boundaries, ironically, Hopkins troublingly implies that Winona, not Maxwell (or larger structures of racist power, for that matter), is herself unable to see that these differences, like the blackface mask, are symbolic rather than natural boundaries: "She tormented herself with fears that were but shadows and railed at barriers which she herself had raised" (405). Winona seems now to internalize all the conventions of the tragic mulatta, at one point even melodramatically lamenting that her only choice now is to become a nun. Thus she seems unable to imagine a position of sexual agency for herself as an African American woman: she can find no place of identification between a desiring boy and a desexualized nun. Hopkins's portrayal of Maxwell, however, suggests that he is unaffected by prohibitions against interracial sexuality. He insists, "In my country we think not of the color of the skin but of the man—the woman—the heart" (405).

It is significant that the object of Winona's sexual desire, Maxwell, is a lawyer. Through this relationship, Hopkins draws an allegorical connection between the romantic hero, Maxwell, and the position of the legal system in its treatment of African American women. The only way that Winona can achieve access to the law, represented by Maxwell, is by disguising herself as a man. This analogy may be Hopkins's ironic commentary on women's actual political disenfranchisement and their struggle for the vote, among other civil rights, during this period. Similarly, Maxwell's literal inability to recognize Winona parallels the construction of law as "blind" to differences of gender and race. The subsequent union of Winona and Maxwell suggests a romantic conception of the law and its possibilities for being a defender and protector of African American women.

Homosexuality and the "Shameful Outrage"

In a brief essay on *Winona* and Bakhtin, Elizabeth Ammons has recently commented on the scenes between "Allen Pinks" and Maxwell:

> The text only permits us to see same-sex attraction, a man tenderly caring for and kissing another man. Complicating the scene even more, the name Hopkins gives Winona in drag, Allen, is the same name she gave herself when she wanted to publish anonymously in the *Colored American Magazine,* Sarah Allen—her mother's name. How do we read this dense network of signs? We know so little about Hopkins's biography that we can say almost nothing about her sexual orientation. At the same time, this scene, so carefully but obviously coded (and therefore inviting decoding), forces us to think broadly rather than narrowly about Hopkins's sexuality.[65]

While I agree that this scene raises a number of questions about sexual orientation, I want to stress that its implications go far beyond biographical speculations about Hopkins's own sexual practices or identity. It seems less urgent to attempt to confirm whether Hopkins herself was a lesbian or that she wrote "lesbian" novels than to ask how she engaged emerging models of homo- and heterosexuality, particularly when these models held very different stakes for African American women and men, whose bodies bore the burden of a history of sexual stereotypes used to demarcate racialized boundaries of normativity in nineteenth-century popular culture.

Although Ammons usefully points to the homoeroticism of this passage, her comments can be developed further by placing the "Allen Pinks" scenes in the context of the entire narrative, particularly because "his" presence is represented by Hopkins as a response to a previous scene of racial and sexual violence between men. In prison, before the arrival of Pinks, Maxwell discovers "a hole for the stove-pipe of the under room to pass through, but the stove had been removed to accommodate a larger number of prisoners. This left a hole in the floor through which one might communicate with those below" (384). This hole positions Maxwell as a kind of voyeur onto the crowded cell below: it "afforded diversion for the invalid who could observe the full operation of the slave system" (384). Just as Maxwell, a British citizen, has observed the U.S. "slave system" as an outsider looking on (or down), so he is literally placed above and outside the "heart-rending scenes . . . enacted before his sight in the lower room" (384). Hopkins inscribes a racialized and asymmetrical structure of looking and power: the white Maxwell is able to gaze on the "free men of color" below, but not vice versa.

This hole in Maxwell's cell is significant not only because it structures a hierarchy of race, vision, and knowledge but also because it becomes the site of a corresponding gap in Hopkins's narration. Hopkins describes a scene in which Maxwell is "aroused to greater indignation than usual" by the sound of "heart-rending cries from the lower room" (385). Yet in the course of this description, Hopkins's narration suddenly meets an obstacle: "Hurrying to the stove-hole [Maxwell] gazed one moment and then fell fainting with terror and nausea upon the floor. He had seen a Negro undergoing the shameful outrage, so denounced in the Scriptures, and which must not be described in the interests of decency and humanity" (385). This crisis in Maxwell's experience of the prison coincides with a crisis in representation: what is "the shameful outrage" that "must not be described" here? In the previous chapter of the novel, Hopkins had been daring enough to include violent and graphic physical details in her description of Maxwell's near lynching. At this moment in the narrative, however, Hopkins, like the repulsed Maxwell, backs away from a direct representation of "the shameful outrage." Abandoning detail, Hopkins resorts instead to a code phrase for sodomy. The content of this "shameful outrage" is left unspecified, a muteness consistent with the history of confusion around the term "sodomy" itself. As Jonathan Goldberg notes:

> Sodomy is, as a sexual act, anything that threatens alliance—any sexual act, that is, that does not promote the aim of married procreative sex (anal intercourse, fellatio, masturbation, bestiality—any of these may fall under the label of sodomy in various early legal codifications and learned discourses).[66]

One cannot be sure what the "outrage" is, but Hopkins's description suggests that a black male prisoner is being raped by a white male guard. Although Hopkins mentions neither homosexuality nor sodomy explicitly, it is important to distinguish between the two. This rape may technically be a homosexual act, but its unambiguous content is violence, not reciprocal desire, and its perpetrator is clearly not a homosexual man. A categorization of sex acts that refuses to acknowledge the context of those acts and the structures of power under which they are performed is the source of this confusion. Thus the same silence surrounds and can collapse two very different acts: consensual sex between two men and the often homophobic, misogynistic, and brutalizing crime of rape by one man against another.[67]

What is curious about Hopkins's depiction is that Maxwell seems to identify with the victim of this rape; his own mental and physical integrity seem threatened by the specter of this penetrative sexual violence between men. Further, racial difference does not circumscribe Maxwell's alliances; in fact, he seems to disidentify with the white guard and to align his own subjectivity and bodily sensation with that of the black prisoner. Maxwell responds to the scene with an embodied sympathy, becoming faint and "delirious." This moment marks a corresponding disorder and disruption in Hopkins's text. As if the very unspeakability of the rape will result in its unbelievability, Hopkins herself steps into the text to address the reader directly: "Unhappily we tell no tale of fiction," she insists (385). On the one hand, Hopkins's appeal to "decency and humanity" as the reason for her elliptical description of the violence establishes the authority of her narrative voice. Clearly asserting her privileged knowledge of "the shameful outrage," she ostensibly "protects" her reader from the explicit facts of what, according to middle-class sexual ideologies of the period, any respectable reader should *not* know. On the other hand, Hopkins follows this crisis with a critique of organized religion: these "unspeakable" horrors would not occur, she writes, "if Christianity, Mohammedanism, or even Buddhism, did exercise the gentle and humanizing influence that is claimed for them" (385). With this gesture, Hopkins abdicates responsibility for the presence of the "shameful outrage" in her text. According to her logic, if organized religion cannot prevent this violence, then Hopkins herself, in an effort to report the truth, cannot be held responsible for its eruption in her text. She invokes the demands of realism to justify her reference to sodomy; at the same time, she removes herself as a cause of its presence, since she is telling "no tale of fiction."[68]

In the final scenes of the novel, Hopkins constructs a utopian revision of the legal system, allowing her to refuse and defy the conventions that construct interracial (hetero)sexuality as inevitably tragic. Back in Canada, Winona and Maxwell are presented with documents left behind by White Eagle. These documents, Winona's parents' marriage license and a birth certificate, prove that she is the legitimate daughter of White Eagle, and thus the heir to the Carlingford estate. This proof of the legal interracial marriage of her parents in Canada provides Winona with a legitimate claim to both black and white identity and to the literal inheritance of her father's property, both of which now entitle her by law to her desire for Maxwell. Yet Hopkins seems to be less than enthusiastic about a heterosexual resolution to the novel. In fact, with decided indifference, she renders Winona's marriage to Maxwell completely predictable and unproblematic:

> They made no plans for the future. What necessity was there of making plans for the future? They knew what the future would be. They loved each other; they would marry sooner or later, after they reached England, with the sanction of her grandfather, old Lord George; that was certain. American caste prejudice could not touch them in their home beyond the sea. (435)

Hopkins's tone here is remarkable for its lack of urgency, its utter nonchalance at the end of a narrative about supposedly taboo sexuality. Claudia Tate has suggested that in Hopkins's serial novels, including *Winona, Of One Blood,* and *Hagar's Daughter,* she subordinated a narrative of romantic love to a project of repudiating racism.[69] It may also be that Hopkins is reluctant to use the marriage plot to resolve the narrative of a character who so fully represented mobility across lines of gender and race.

The two episodes within the prison in *Winona*—first, the "shameful outrage" against a black prisoner by a white guard, and second, the homoerotic fascination between Allen Pinks and Maxwell—present disruptions of narrative conventions of desire, gender, and race. First, the scene of the unspeakable "shameful outrage" insists that interracial sexual violence does not occur only across lines of gender; Hopkins exposes the use of sexual violence as a weapon of racial domination against men, as well as women. Likewise, in a narrative response to this scene of unspeakable violence, Hopkins recuperates the space of the prison for the homoerotic romance of Pinks and Maxwell. As part of her project to revise the mulatta figure and to disrupt the conventions of racialized desire, Hopkins uses Winona's blackface and transvestism to figure Winona's mobility across lines of race and gender, a strategy that cannot avoid associations with homosexuality.

In *Contending Forces* and *Winona,* Hopkins's ambivalent engagement with emerging discourses of homosexuality becomes visible through figures who disrupted conventions associated with the mulatta heroine. Sappho Clark resembles the traditional tragic mulatta but, in her ability to mobilize female homoeroticism, also suggests the emerging figure of the lesbian. Cross-dressed as Allen Pinks, Winona is "the prettiest specimen of boyhood," a subject position that evokes contemporary constructions of the invert and seems more fitting to Winona herself than her supposedly "natural" identity as mulatta heroine. Through these figures, Hopkins demonstrates an awareness of the emergence of new sexual subjectivities and her ambivalence about the emerging cultural tendency to pathologize same-sex desire. In attempting to challenge existing cultural stereotypes of black womanhood, she struggled with both residual and newly emerging pathologizations of desiring female bodies. Without embracing or rejecting the possibility of lesbian desire, she registers its existence as an ambiguous site for renarrating African American women's sexual and political desire.

4

Double Lives on the Color Line

"Perverse" Desire in

The Autobiography of an Ex-Coloured Man

In his autobiography, *Along This Way,* published in 1933, James Weldon Johnson discusses the two literary lives of his fictional autobiography, *The Autobiography of an Ex-Coloured Man,* which was first published anonymously in 1912 and subsequently reissued in 1927 "affixed" (in Johnson's words) with his identity as the author. Addressing the reception of the book's initial publication, Johnson explains:

> I did get a certain pleasure out of anonymity, that no acknowledged book could have given me. The authorship of the book excited the curiosity of literate colored people, and there was speculation among them as to who the writer might be—to every such group some colored man who had married white, and so coincided with the main point on which the story turned, is known.[1]

Johnson emphasizes his pleasure at witnessing his text "passing" as a "human document": like the (unnamed) ex-coloured man himself, the text circulates anonymously without being clearly marked as "truth" or "fiction." Yet this passage also asserts a key—and, as I will argue, strategic—characterization of the narrative of *The Autobiography of an Ex-Coloured Man:* that the "main point" of the text concerns "some colored man who had married white." For, as I will explore in this chapter, the pursuit of interracial (heterosexual) marriage is hardly the main trajectory of desire in this text. In fact, it is both integral to, and subordinated by, another form of desire figured as "perverse" that shapes the ex-coloured man's narrative, that of male homosexuality. In this way, Johnson's text participates in the uneven transitions occurring in early-twentieth-century American cultural understandings of bodies and desires that I have discussed in previous chapters. Specifically, in *The Autobiography of an Ex-Coloured Man*, the representation of the mulatto body is mediated by the iconography of gender inversion, and interracial heterosexual desire functions in the text as both an analogy to homosexual object choice and a screen through which it can be articulated. As he shuttles between racialized subject positions, the ex-coloured man is constructed simultaneously as the subject and object of multiple trajectories of desire. The very proximity of these oscillating racialized and sexualized "perversions" is integral to Johnson's fascination with, and critique of, his unnamed protagonist.

"A Pretty Boy": Gender Inversion and the Mulatto Body

A key turning point in most fictional narratives of the tragic mulatto/a figure is the protagonist's confrontation with an epistemological crisis about her or his racial identity.[2] In American fiction about mulatto/a characters—including, for example, Frances Harper's *Iola Leroy,* Mark Twain's *Pudd'nhead Wilson,* Kate Chopin's "Désirée's Baby," Zora Neale Hurston's *Their Eyes Were Watching God,* and William Faulkner's *Light in August*—the protagonist is unaware of his or her racial identity or assumes herself or himself to be white until some external source of knowledge steps forward to present evidence of her or his African American ancestry. Typically these epistemological and ontological crises are rendered as moments when the subject is interpellated into a racialized position by institutions and their technological apparatuses, such as the school, the law, the hospital, the orphanage, or, in the case of Hurston's Janie, an itinerant photographer.[3] In *The Autobiography of an Ex-Coloured Man,* the scene of recognition occurs in a classroom, when the teacher separates the white students from "the others."[4] When the protagonist, who has never before consciously considered the question of his racial identity, stands with the white children, the teacher excludes him from the group. Given this new "knowledge," the narrator later confronts his own image in a mirror:

I had often heard people say to my mother: "What a pretty boy you have!" I was accustomed to hear remarks about my beauty; but now, for the first time, I became conscious of it and recognized it. I noticed the ivory whiteness of my skin, the beauty of my mouth, the size and liquid darkness of my eyes, and how the long, black lashes that fringed and shaded them produced an effect that was strangely fascinating even to me. I noticed the softness and glossiness of my dark hair that fell in waves over my temples, making my forehead appear whiter than it really was. How long I stood there gazing at my image I do not know. (17)

As this passage so richly demonstrates, although the narrator initially frames his crisis as one of racial identification, this moment in the narrative coincides with a (somewhat pleasurable) renegotiation of his gender. Where one might expect the narrator to respond to his new knowledge about his African American identity by suddenly recognizing features associated with racial stereotypes, the narrator presents a scene in which he enters instead a new consciousness of his own "beauty." His description presents a series of contrasts between light and dark: the "ivory whiteness" of his skin and forehead brings out the "liquid darkness" of his eyes, "long, black lashes," and "dark hair." This play between light and dark is itself erotic and the source of the "strangely fascinating" effect on the narrator. Through descriptions such as "fringed and shaded" and his focus on the "softness and glossiness" and "waves" of his hair, the narrator is also distinctly feminized, recalling descriptions of the highly eroticized mulatta of nineteenth-century fiction.[5]

As discussed in the previous chapter, the narrative trajectories of male and female mulatto characters in nineteenth-century fiction differed considerably, with tragedy as the more likely end for a female character. In Charles Chesnutt's The House Behind the Cedars, for instance, the very light complexioned character John Warwick successfully passes into the white world (and out of the text). His beautiful sister Rena, however, is exposed in her attempt to pass as white and subsequently dies young, fleeing the attentions of rival suitors into a wilderness that ultimately punishes and destroys her.[6] In a recent discussion of black masculinity and passing narratives, Philip Brian Harper has resituated the meanings of this gendered difference, arguing that "the tragic mulatto has been conceived as a specifically feminine character."[7] In his reading of the "mirror scene" in *The Autobiography of an Ex-Coloured Man,* Harper argues that the feminization of the protagonist calls into question his sexual orientation: "This feminized orientation itself potentially constitutes the protagonist's personal tragedy, indicating a gender identity that is anything but properly masculine, and verging dangerously on a sexual identity that is anything but hetero."[8] I fully agree with Harper's point that Johnson figures the disruption of the narrator's sense of a stable racial identification through a corresponding slippage in gender and sexuality. It may be argued more precisely, too, that rather than simply "feminizing" the narrator, Johnson characterizes him through a model of gender inversion. That is, as a "hybrid" racialized subject, symbolically both black and white, the narrator is also gendered "between" male and female, like the bodies of the inverts who were subjected to the taxonomizing gaze of sexologists. In the case of the ex-coloured man, his *own* gaze importantly constructs and internalizes an eroticized version of the mulatto as invert.

Racialized Homoerotics

The gaze through which the narrator so powerfully eroticizes his own biracial body in this early recognition scene also turns on and eroticizes other male bodies throughout the book. Although he does not direct this gaze exclusively at men, as I will show, the narrator's homoerotic attachments hold a much more powerful place in the narrative than do his erotic attachments with women. Johnson's repeated use of these scenes to destabilize the narrator's masculinity is an integral part of the novel's overall project of critiquing racial passing and the narrator's racial naïveté. These homoerotic attachments begin early in the narrative, when the narrator is a child in school, with descriptions of his crushes on two boys, symbolically one white and the other African American. These attachments oscillate between identification and desire. On the one hand, his identifications with the white and black boyhood friends literalize the ex-coloured man's seemingly split identification with white and black culture. On the other hand, these figures are also rendered as objects of the protagonist's nascent homoerotic desire, which will shape his most important adult relationship later in the narrative.

The narrator describes his meeting with his first "staunch friend," a white boy nicknamed "Red Head":

This friend I bound to me with hooks of steel in a very simple way. He was a big awkward boy with a face full of freckles and a head full of very red hair. . . . I had not been at school many hours before I felt that "Red Head"—as I involuntarily called him—and I were to be friends. I do not doubt that this feeling was strengthened by the fact that I had been quick enough to see that a big, strong boy was a friend to be desired at a public school; and, perhaps, in spite of his dullness, "Red Head" had been able to discern that I could be of service to him. At any rate there was a simultaneous mutual attraction. (11)

This description foregrounds a number of issues that recur in the narrator's relationships with white men later in the novel. Importantly, the "simultaneous mutual attraction" depends explicitly on the relationships of power between the narrator and this boy within the world of the schoolroom. Clearly, as the narrator admits, he was partly attracted to the power that "Red Head" represented: the narrator sees this older boy as a reliable ally and protector against the other boys at school, some of whom, the narrator remembers, "seemed to me like savages" (10), an unself-consciously racialized construction of his own superiority. In return for this protection, the narrator is quite willing to "be of service to him" by coaching Red Head in his academic work, often simply giving his friend the correct answers on exams. As the narrator writes, "through all our school-days, 'Red Head' shared my wit and quickness and I benefited by his strength and dogged faithfulness" (13). A similar system of patronage and service characterizes the narrator's subsequent relationship to white men, as the narrator foreshadows: "And when I grew to manhood, I found myself freer with elderly white people than with those near my own age" (23).

If the narrator eroticizes the position of power granted to Red Head by means of his white identity, gender, age, and sheer physical bulk, he also eroticizes black male bodies, but in very different ways. At the same time that the narrator bonds with Red Head, he also meets "Shiny," who, he writes, "strongly attracted my attention from the first day I saw him" (14). The narrator gives great attention to Shiny's physical characteristics:

> His face was as black as night, but shone as though it were polished; he had sparkling eyes, and when he opened his mouth, he displayed glistening white teeth. It struck me at once as appropriate to call him "Shiny Face," or "Shiny Eyes," or "Shiny Teeth," and I spoke of him often by one of these names to the other boys. These terms were finally merged into "Shiny," and that name he answered good-naturedly during the balance of his public school days. (14)

The narrator's description of Shiny unself-consciously draws on popular cultural stereotypes of the black male body, particularly those that had circulated through the conventions of blackface minstrelsy.[9] The narrator constructs Shiny's body as a collection of fetishized parts, fixating on his "polished" face, "sparkling eyes," and "glistening" teeth. Indeed, the narrator expands the imaginative hold of these fetishizations by using them metonymically to name his friend: in the narrator's eyes, his friend's identity becomes synonymous with the "shiny" characteristics on which he fixates. When Shiny makes a speech at grammar school graduation, the narrator again expresses his fascination with his friend's physical presence:

> He made a striking picture, that thin little black boy standing on the platform, dressed in clothes that did not fit him any too well, his eyes burning with excitement, his shrill, musical voice vibrating in tones of appealing defiance, and his black face alight with such great intelligence and earnestness as to be positively handsome. (44)

In this portrait of Shiny, who later in the novel becomes a professor at a "Negro college," Johnson borrows the tropes of the African American hero, dignified spiritually and physically. In contrast to the narrator, who repeatedly demonstrates his lack of spiritual or physical defiance, Shiny represents a race leader, one whose racial and gender identifications are, not coincidentally, never in question. In this scene, however, the narrator's desire for Shiny takes on the form of a powerful identification with this heroic figure: "I felt leap within me pride that I was coloured; and I began to form wild dreams of bringing glory and honour to the Negro race" (46).

The figure of Shiny resurfaces at a crucial moment in the closing pages of the novel, when the narrator is passing for white, and again his

presence has the effect of eliciting the narrator's desire for racial identification. Standing in line at a theater with his white fiancée, who at
that point does not know about the narrator's African American ancestry, the narrator spots Shiny in the crowd. Although the ex-coloured
man perceives Shiny as a threat to his secret and thus to his potential
status as husband to this white woman, Shiny protects him from exposure: "[Shiny] seemed, at a glance, to divine my situation, and let drop
no word that would have aroused suspicion as to the truth" (202). Although Shiny participates in the narrator's passing, this incident has the
ironic effect of making the narrator want to reveal his African ancestry
to his fiancée. As in the earlier scene, however, so the narrator's identification with Shiny is fleeting and ultimately replaced by his desire,
however ashamed, to be an "ordinarily successful white man" (211).

The narrator's early fascinations with Shiny and Red Head prefigure
perhaps the central and most powerful erotic relationship in *The Autobiography of an Ex-Coloured Man,* that of the narrator and his patron, a
wealthy white man whom the narrator meets while performing as a
ragtime pianist in New York. The narrator describes his fascination with
this figure on his first encounter with him:

> Among the other white "slummers" there came into the "Club" one
> night a clean-cut, slender, but athletic-looking man, who would have
> been taken for a youth had it not been for the tinge of grey about his
> temples. He was clean-shaven and had regular features, and all of his
> movements bore the indefinable but unmistakable stamp of culture.
> He spoke to no one, but sat languidly puffing cigarettes and sipping
> a glass of beer. He was the centre of a great deal of attention; all of
> the old-timers were wondering who he was. (116)

This eroticized and lone figure gradually focuses his attentions on the
narrator and begins a slow seduction of him, leaving a five-dollar tip
each time he visits the club. The man, later referred to by the narrator
as "my millionaire friend," symbolizes a somewhat sinister version of
fin de siècle decadence, a figure of wealth and forbidden sexuality. At a
party in the millionaire's home at which the narrator is a hired enter-
tainer, the narrator observes: "The men ranged in appearance from a
girlish-looking youth to a big grizzled man whom everybody addressed
as 'Judge.' None of the women appeared to be under thirty, but each

of them struck me as being handsome. I was not long in finding out that they were all decidedly blasé. Several of the women smoked cigarettes, and with a careless grace which showed they were used to the habit" (118). This scene suggests the existence of a spectrum of gender and sexual identities that exceed the boundaries of bourgeois norms, a certain outlaw sexuality possible within wealthy social circles at the time.[10] The male figures are thus described in language that exaggerates conventions of femininity ("a girlish-looking youth") and masculinity ("a big grizzled man"). Likewise, the female figures do not conform to standards of middle-class femininity: described as "handsome," they are associated with gender transgression through their accomplished cigarette smoking, a taboo for respectable women at the time and a symbol of sexual freedom.

The relationship of the narrator to his "millionaire" recalls that of both son and lover. The millionaire's position as an admirer of the musical abilities of the ex-coloured man echoes the earlier position of the narrator's white father, described as "a tall, handsome, well-dressed gentleman of perhaps thirty-five," evoking a figure much like the suave patron (32). During one of his father's rare visits, the piano similarly mediates the emotional relationship between father and son:

> My father was so enthusiastic in his praise that he touched my vanity
> —which was great—and more than that; he displayed that sincere
> appreciation which always arouses an artist to his best effort, and too,
> in an unexplainable manner, makes him feel like shedding tears. I
> showed my gratitude by playing for him a Chopin waltz with all the
> feeling that was in me. When I had finished, my mother's eyes were
> glistening with tears; my father stepped across the room, seized me
> in his arms, and squeezed me to his breast. I am certain that for that
> moment he was proud to be my father. (34–35)

Both the narrator's father and the millionaire are older male figures who support both emotionally and materially the narrator's efforts to have a musical career. Just as his father rewards his performance with the gift of a new piano, so the millionaire provides him with cash, travel, and a new wardrobe.

At the same time that the relationship between the narrator and his patron is one of son to father, however, it also has associations with a more directly sexual relationship. Robert Stepto has noted that in his portrayal of the narrator's mother as a "kept woman" to a wealthy white man, Johnson borrows and recasts antislavery literature's "haunting image of the snug cottage in the clearing," provided for the slaves who became concubines for their white masters.[11] I suggest that there is also at work here an implicit analogy between the narrator's relationship with the patron and his mother's relationship with his father: both echo the figure of the slave mistress, who is given a minimal amount of financial and material security in exchange for her sexual service to the white master.[12] Through an identification between the narrator and his mother, Johnson foregrounds the ways in which processes of racialization shape and resituate codes of masculinity.

Johnson clearly delineates the racialized hierarchies of ownership and property that define the relationship between the protagonist and the patron, implicitly connecting this instance of patronage with the historical legacy of slavery. The complex interplay of economic power and eroticism between the narrator and his patron becomes increasingly apparent as their "friendship" progresses. Eventually, the millionaire develops an exclusive arrangement with the narrator, and the full dimensions of the patron's economic control are revealed in the narrator's comment that "occasionally he 'loaned' me to some of his friends. And, too, I often played for him alone at his apartments" (120). Although the narrator defends his patron—"Between him and me no suggestion of racial differences had ever come up" (145)—clearly "racial differences" are central to the structure of their relationship.

Johnson implicitly criticizes the protagonist's inability to see the class and racial hierarchies that structure his relationship to his patron, a blindness that implicates the narrator in his own exploitation. After detailing the odd habits of the millionaire, who demands that the narrator play for him alone late at night in his home for hours at a time, the narrator begins to sense that something is askew:

> During such moments this man sitting there so mysteriously silent, almost hid in a cloud of heavy-scented smoke, filled me with a sort of unearthly terror. He seemed to be some grim, mute, but relentless tyrant, possessing over me a supernatural power which he used to drive me on mercilessly to exhaustion. (121)

In this passage, the narrator seems close to articulating and acknowledging the millionaire's underlying sadistic and exploitative powers. Yet he immediately disavows this possibility: "But these feelings came very rarely; besides, he paid me so liberally I could forget much" (121). And indeed the narrator does forget much, dismissing his earlier portrait of the millionaire as a "grim, mute, but relentless tyrant," and instead insisting that the two men had "a familiar and warm relationship," and that "[the patron] had a decided personal liking for me" (121). In fact, the narrator seems to idolize this man and his position of power: "On my part, I looked upon him at that time as about all a man could wish to be" (121). Here the narrator's attempts to convince himself that their relationship is about mutual regard rather than power and money echoes his mother's romantic attachment to his father: "She loved him; more, she worshipped him, and she died firmly believing that he loved her more than any other woman in the world" (43). Although the narrator casts a skeptical eye on his parents' relationship ("Perhaps she was right. Who knows?" [43]), he is unable to doubt his millionaire's motives.

Although Johnson portrays the narrator as a naive participant in his own economic exploitation, he also characterizes the patron as skillful at securing his own power through its very erasure. Nowhere is this process more apparent than in the scenes in Paris, where the millionaire has brought along the narrator as his "valet." Because they have left New York for Europe quite suddenly, the narrator has few clothes when he arrives in Paris, a situation quickly remedied by the patron: "He bought me the same kind of clothes which he himself wore, and that was the best; and he treated me in every way as he dressed me, as an equal, not as a servant. In fact, I don't think anyone could have guessed that such a relation existed" (130). The narrator mistakes the superficial appearance of similarity between the two men as evidence of their equal status. Although the narrator never explicitly suggests that their relationship might have a sexual component, his descriptions have all the characteristics of a sexual liaison: "He kept me supplied with money far beyond what ordinary wages would have amounted to. For the first two weeks we were together almost constantly, seeing the sights, sights old to him, but from which he seemed to get new pleasure in showing them to me" (130). At one point, the narrator seems to go out of his way to deny that their relationship is erotic. During a discussion between the narrator and the millionaire about the ex-coloured man returning to the United States, Johnson writes, "When I had finished [telling him my plans] he put his hand on my shoulder—this was the first physical expression of tender regard he had ever shown me—and look[ed] at me in a big-brotherly way" (144). The narrator's characterization of their relationship as that of siblings is ironic, after his previous descriptions of inequality and exploitation. His description of the patron's look as "big-brotherly" masks the condescension (and perhaps sexual desire) of the white patron; the narrator wants to remember this gesture as one of benevolence rather than subjugation. Further, it is significant that the narrator interrupts this sentence with the explanation that "this was the first physical expression of tender regard he had ever shown me." This assertion marks a self-conscious disavowal of the powerful eroticism, whether physical or not, that has structured their relationship.

While Johnson depicts the relationship between the narrator and his patron as fraught with inequities, he also implicates the narrator's own acquisitive motivations; in addition to the literal money and possessions he receives, the ex-coloured man gains enormous cultural capital through exposure to Europe. The narrator ends his relationship with the patron by temporarily reidentifying with African American culture when he decides to try to pursue a career as a black composer in the United States (one of Johnson's own successful careers). In this way, he also seems to avert the inevitably tragic end that the patron meets by "leaping into eternity" (143). Yet Johnson implicitly criticizes the narrator, who, despite his physical departure, remains nostalgically attached to "this peculiar man" and refuses to recognize the racialized discrepancies in power that shaped their relationship. In fact, the narrator elevates the formative effects of the patron on his life: "And so I separated from the man who was, all in all, the best friend I ever had, except my mother, the man who exerted the greatest influence ever brought into my life, except that exerted by my mother. My affection for him was so strong, my recollections of him are so distinct, he was such a peculiar and striking character, that I could easily fill several chapters with reminiscences of him" (148). Through this effusive and arbitrary resolution to their relationship, Johnson suggests that the narrator's feelings toward the patron exceed the limits of what is representable. With what seems a disingenuous concern for "tiring the reader," the narrator ends his discussion of this "peculiar and striking character."

In his discussion of the text, Harper describes the function of the wealthy patron as ultimately bearing the burden of representing homosexuality and thus relieving the ex-coloured man from such a stigmatizing characterization. He notes that the patron's suicide, his "leap into eternity," removes the threat of homosexuality from the text: "Luckily for the protagonist . . . the relationship that he undertakes that most nearly approximates a homosexual coupling also functions as the means by which the narrative can exorcise this unwholesome element."[13] Yet as I will show in the next section, the narrator's sexuality is not rendered normative through the various heterosexual relationships that he enters. Two forms of taboo desire, incest and interracial sexuality, function as evidence of his perversity and are linked symbolically to the potentially tragic narrative of homosexuality.

Deviant Heterosexuality

Although his relationship with the white patron is arguably the most fully rendered erotic bond in *The Autobiography of an Ex-Coloured Man,* the narrator's attachments are not exclusively homoerotic. The narrator presents brief portraits of girls and women to whom he is attracted: a young musician for whom he is an accompanist, a schoolteacher he meets in Florida, a young girl he believes to be his stepsister, a rich widow he meets in the Club, and his wife. All of his attachments to these women, however eroticized, are aborted in some way beyond the narrator's control, as if they must be expelled from the narrative. For example, despite the narrator's secret rhapsodic infatuation with an older teenage girl, a violinist, the attraction is entirely one-sided, with no possibility that his affection will be returned. Likewise, the narrator's attachment to his first fiancée, "a young school-teacher," with whom he entertains "dreams of matrimonial bliss," is described fleetingly. He introduces her and dismisses her, all in a single sentence, alluding to "another turn in the course of my life [that] brought these dreams to an end" (83). When the factory in which he works closes, the narrator's visions of middle-class heterosexuality ("marrying the young school-teacher" and "raising a family") are replaced by "a desire like a fever" to return to New York (88). Importantly, there are racial as well as sexual implications to the narrator's flight: marrying the schoolteacher would have committed the narrator to a permanent identity within a black middle-class community.

The narrator's adult attractions to women are represented as transgressive, fleeting, inevitably tragic, and culturally taboo. In his representation of these relationships, Johnson depicts as dangerous the narrator's attraction to women who (like the white patron), by law and custom, are prohibited objects of sexual desire for black men. But unlike the rendering of the protagonist's attachment to the patron, these relationships are represented as explicitly sexual, thus providing, according to the cultural logic of segregation, a recognizable pattern of deviant sexual object choice. For example, while attending the opera during his trip to Europe, the narrator becomes enchanted by "a beautiful, tender girl" (134). Recalling this encounter, the narrator describes her as a disembodied presence: "I cannot describe her either as to feature, or colour of her hair, or of her eyes; she was so young, so fair, so ethereal, that I felt to stare at her would be a violation; yet I was distinctly conscious of her beauty" (133–34). When he realizes that the man accompanying this girl is his own father, the narrator is overwhelmed by the tragic implications of his incestuous desire. Staring at her is indeed a "violation": within the historical context of the early twentieth century, his desire for his white stepsister transgresses cultural prohibitions against both incest and interracial heterosexuality.[14]

Similarly, the narrator presents his brief relationship with the "widow," a wealthy white woman, as transgressive and dangerous. He describes her as "an exceedingly beautiful woman of perhaps thirty-five . . . [who] had glistening copper-coloured hair, very white skin, and eyes very much like Du Maurier's conception of Trilby's 'twin grey stars'" (108). The widow is one of a group of white women, "regular habituées" of the Club, who have a specifically racialized erotic orientation: they seek out "coloured men" as their sexual companions (108). The narrator portrays this woman and her exclusive desire for African American men in terms of a femme fatale: when he is warned about her jealous lover, the narrator writes, "the woman was so beautiful that my native gallantry and delicacy would not allow me to repulse her; my finer feelings entirely overcame my judgment" (122). Their relationship and the woman's life come to a tragic and violent end when her lover murders her. The narrator is haunted by the scene of "that beautiful white throat with the ugly wound. The jet of blood pulsing from it had placed an indelible red stain on my memory" (125). This murder serves as a brutal punishment for the widow's sexual and racial transgression. Significantly, it is also the catalyst responsible for the narrator's decision to travel to Europe with his white male patron. According to the logic of the narrative, male interracial homoeroticism becomes an antidote to the potentially horrific consequences of interracial heterosexuality, one not entirely unwelcome for the protagonist.

Likewise, the narrator's heterosexual courtship and marriage receive relatively little attention in contrast to the narrative space and intensity devoted to his relationship with the white patron. The first description of the narrator's future wife does not occur until the final chapter of the book: "She was almost tall and quite slender, with lustrous yellow hair and eyes so blue as to appear almost black. She was as white as a lily, and she was dressed in white. Indeed, she seemed to me the most dazzlingly white thing I had ever seen. But it was not her delicate beauty which attracted me most; it was her voice, a voice which made one wonder how tones of such passionate colour could come from so fragile a body" (198). This description eroticizes a contrast between, on the one hand, the overwhelming whiteness of her image and its distinct lack of physical presence (she is "almost tall and quite slender," with a "delicate beauty," and a "fragile . . . body") and, on the other hand, the "passionate colour" of her overpresent voice. Again, as if the narrative cannot sustain interracial heterosexuality, the narrator's wife dies a tragically young death, a death significantly linked to childbirth, seemingly punishing her for the miscegenous results of her sexual behavior. Although the narrator does not describe her death directly, he states that "it was for [their second child, a son] that she gave all; and that is the second sacred sorrow of my life" (209). Echoing the death of the widow earlier in the novel, the death of the narrator's wife works narratively as retribution for interracial heterosexuality. Although he laments that "her loss to me is irreparable," he also admits that she represented a threat that her death coincidentally removes: "I no longer have the same fear for myself of my secret's being found out" (210). The death of the narrator's wife removes a threat to his performance not only of whiteness but also of masculinity. Despite their "supremely happy" marriage, her very presence had made the narrator wonder "if she was scrutinizing me, to see if she was looking for anything in me which made me differ from the other men she knew. . . . I began even to wonder if I really was like the men I associated with; if there was not, after all, an indefinable something which marked a difference" (199–200). The "indefinable something"—the hidden identity that could be rendered as either his mulatto or invert status—is at once racial and sexual.

"Like Van Vechten, Start Inspectin'"

So far this chapter has enacted a primarily textual account of the ways in which questions of mixed-race identity and interracial desire in Johnson's *Autobiography of an Ex-Coloured Man* became enmeshed with those of emerging (and contradictory) cultural understandings of gender inversion and homosexual object choice.[15] Johnson's "cover story" that the text hinged on the narrative of "some colored man who had married white" belied the ways in which his text participated in constructing homosexuality, along with interracial sexuality, as deviant sexual object choice and the "hybrid" mulatto as a figure of gender inversion. In this section, I turn to issues of reading and reception, shifting my focus away from the intersecting constructions of race and sexuality *within* the text, toward the ways in which these issues circulated *around* the text and its publication. In this context, Johnson's 1933 assertion that the narrative of *The Autobiography of an Ex-Coloured Man* pivoted on interracial marriage can be read as a strategic (if unconscious) intervention into potential reinterpretations of the text after its republication in 1927. In its second life, the text was "affixed" with not only Johnson's name but also that of Carl Van Vechten, the white (gay) patron of modernism and the "Harlem Renaissance" who initially suggested to Knopf the text's republication and whose introduction accompanied the text.[16] If Johnson's name signaled the closing of an epistemological gap concerning the text's authorship and genre, the attachment of Van Vechten's persona to the text through his introduction made more palpable the imbrication of interracial and homosexual desire, both among characters within the book and between the text and its various audiences.

And so, fifteen years after the book's first anonymous publication, the 1927 Knopf edition of the *Autobiography* found a new and wider readership that had become familiar with, and eager for, creative work—writing, music, and visual arts—about African American culture beginning in the early 1920s. Van Vechten's introduction to the text was, of course, in keeping with his friendships and promotion of numerous writers and artists during this period, including Countee Cullen, Ronald Firbank, Langston Hughes, Nella Larsen, Rudolph Fisher, and Gertrude Stein, among others. Johnson and Van Vechten met and became close friends in 1924, when Van Vechten first began participating in Harlem's social and artistic circles.[17] As many critics have noted, Van Vechten's motivations for supporting African American cultural production were ambiguous, mixing admiration and savvy literary judgment with colonizing voyeurism and appropriation.

With his introduction to the *Autobiography,* Van Vechten mediated between Johnson and his new audience, a gesture echoing that of nineteenth-century white editors who authenticated slave narratives, such as Lydia Maria Child, who presented Harriet Jacobs's *Incidents in the Life of a Slave Girl,* and William Lloyd Garrison, who provided a preface to Frederick Douglass's narrative.[18] Unlike those introductions, however, which functioned to verify the slave's identity and story as authentic, Van Vechten's introduction had a more complicated purpose in the context of the text's modernist aesthetic. On the one hand, he affirmed the "inauthenticity" of the text, emphasizing that it had "little enough to do with Mr. Johnson's own life" (xxxiii). On the other hand, he verified the accuracy of the experiences that Johnson chronicled, positioning the text as the raw material out of which other representations of African Americans, including his own novel *Nigger Heaven* (1926), could be produced: "When I was writing Nigger Heaven I discovered the Autobiography to be an invaluable source-book for the study of Negro psychology" (xxxv).

Although Van Vechten supported (and appropriated) a broad range of modernist and African American artistic production, his position as a white gay man arguably played a significant part in the circulation and production of these texts. Van Vechten's sexual identity was complex, since he had sexual relationships with both women and men, but homoeroticism and the growth of a more visible gay subculture in 1920s Manhattan (in which he energetically participated) did seem to shape his selection and construction of particular writers and texts. More specifically, by reprinting and attaching himself to the *Autobiography,* Van Vechten rehearsed prototypically the strategies of queer reading and reassemblage that would become more explicit in his later life. One of the motivations for republishing the *Autobiography* may have stemmed from the way it had begun to articulate an identity and subculture more recognizable as gay to readers in 1927 than in 1912. In attaching his introduction, Van Vechten staged, whether consciously or not, a position of reading and subjectivity that had as much to do with the sexual as racial subcultures associated with the Harlem Renaissance.

Although Van Vechten's introduction never explicitly identifies himself or the text as "gay" or "queer," it is useful to speculate about his attachments to this particular narrative. It is possible, for instance, to imagine Van Vechten's dual identifications with its characters. In the image of the ex-coloured man's white patron, the "clean-cut, slender, but athletic-looking man [with] . . . a tinge of grey about his temples," the fortyish Van Vechten may have seen an eroticized or idealized version of himself. But he may also have identified with the ex-coloured man—a man who shuttled among the nightclubs and drag balls of Harlem, the downtown world of the white literary industry, and the expatriate modernist salons of Paris—a figure resembling himself. The multiple worlds and identities inhabited by the ex-coloured man may have uncannily echoed, or perhaps provided a map for, Van Vechten's own movement among diverse social circles. A particularly compelling set of caricatures by Mexican artist Miguel Covarrubias also makes explicit the ways in which Van Vechten's identity was mediated by his racial identifications. In a caricature entitled *A Prediction,* Covarrubias represented Van Vechten in blackface (fig. 6). A kind of "ex-coloured man" in reverse, the title—*A Prediction*—suggested that Van Vechten was an imminently coloured man. This image makes explicit the logic of using racial discourse to articulate Van Vechten's sexualized "difference" from normative white culture.[19]

These resonances become more obvious when one takes into account

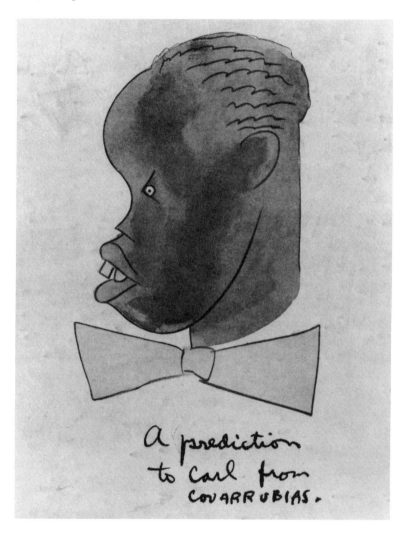

Fig. 6. *A Prediction,* caricature of Carl Van Vechten by Miguel Covarrubias. Courtesy of the Van Vechten Trust. Yale Collection of American Literature, Beinecke Rare Book and Manuscript Library, Yale University.

the more than twenty scrapbooks that Van Vechten put together in the mid-1950s, which contained various collages of photographs, mostly of nude men, juxtaposed with texts clipped from newspapers and magazines. One page, for instance, shows a photograph of a young man in a sailor suit, labeled with two captions, "Boy Crazy," and "My Queer." Art historian Jonathan Weinberg has analyzed these "homemade sex books" in detail.[20] As he points out, what makes the scrapbooks compelling is not so much the actual images but the way they provide evidence of Van Vechten's strategies of reading and "writing" images and text as a gay man: "Van Vechten appears to have been scanning the newspapers looking not only for the public naming of homosexuality, but for the way in which same-sex love can only be deduced by reading between the lines."[21] Weinberg explains that the scrapbooks demonstrate the acts of assertive reappropriation at the heart of Van Vechten's processes of queer reading: "He found homosexuality where homosexuality had been suppressed—the crime reports—and he found homosexuality where it was not supposed to be—the tennis court or the wrestling mat."[22]

Given this evidence of Van Vechten's prolific re-production of "mainstream" culture as decidedly queer in the scrapbooks, we might read a similar, though more veiled, process occurring in Van Vechten's earlier promotion of the *Autobiography*. If, as we know, the meaning of a text is produced in acts of reading, then Van Vechten's public performance of his own reading of the *Autobiography* in the introduction to the 1927 edition produced a different text, one that spoke to the presence of a more explicitly gay culture woven into the artistic and social fabric of both the literal and imagined space of Harlem. As historians such as Eric Garber, George Chauncey, and Kevin Mumford have noted, during the 1920s, two neighborhoods in Manhattan—Greenwich Village and Harlem—developed flourishing enclaves of gay culture.[23] Indeed, many of the writers who were central to the Harlem Renaissance movement actively participated in these lesbian and gay cultures.[24] As Henry Louis Gates Jr. has contended, the Harlem Renaissance "was surely as gay as it was black, not that it was exclusively either of these."[25]

In *Along This Way*, Johnson admitted that he was writing his "real" autobiography in part to make clear once and for all that *The Autobiography of an Ex-Coloured Man* "was not the story of my life."[26] While Johnson's assertion had a great deal to do with distancing himself from the ex-coloured man's tendencies toward assimilationist racial politics, it may also have been compelled by the questions of sexuality that the text and its circulation raised. Just as the ex-coloured man's narrative offered a space in which to explore forbidden desires to "pass" and "marry white" in a racially segregated culture, so it registered the existence of other forbidden desires, most notably homosexuality. Part of the enduring fascination of readers with the *Autobiography* lies in the ways in which the text mapped culturally taboo sexual desires onto the color line, a relationship that was integral to the literary and artistic landscape of the 1920s. In the next chapter, I explore the ways that this landscape and subsequent critical responses to it shaped the career of Johnson's contemporary Jean Toomer.

5

"Queer to Myself As I Am to You"

Jean Toomer, Racial Disidentification, and Queer Reading

On the publication of his best-known work, *Cane* (1923), Jean Toomer was received as a new and promising voice in African American literature by numerous critics and writers, including W. E. B. Du Bois, William Stanley Braithwaite, and Sherwood Anderson. Much of this praise emphasized Toomer's position as a gifted voice for African American culture. Braithwaite, for instance, claimed that "we come upon the very first artist of the race, who . . . can write about the Negro without the surrender or compromise of the artist's vision. . . . Jean Toomer is a bright morning star of a new day of the race in literature."[1] Likewise, Anderson wrote to Toomer that his writing was "the first negro work I have seen that strikes me as being really negro."[2] Although Toomer welcomed such critical attention, as he gradually realized that he was being positioned as an authentic "Negro" writer, he began to resist these constructions of his authorship. In negotiations with his publisher, he reacted strongly against any tendency to commodify African American identity in advertisements for the book, reasoning that "as I was not a Negro, I could not feature myself as one."[3] By 1930, when he was asked by James Weldon Johnson for permission to reprint portions of *Cane* in *The Book of American Negro Poetry,* Toomer declined: "My poems are not Negro poems, nor are they Anglo-Saxon or white or English poems. My prose likewise. They are, first, mine. And, second, in so far as general race or stock is concerned, they spring from the result of racial blending here in America which has produced a new race or stock. We may call this stock the American stock or race."[4]

Despite Toomer's resistance to identifying his writing or authorship as unambiguously African American, *Cane* has been claimed unequivocally as a key modernist text firmly situated in the "Harlem Renaissance" canon, and Toomer himself is often portrayed as naive, at best, or a race traitor, at worst. Whether sympathetic or critical, discussions of Toomer often point out the irony that the author of *Cane,* a book invested so thoroughly in a lyrical evocation of southern African American culture, could divest himself of claims to authenticity as a "Negro" writer. Alice Walker, for instance, has explained the necessity of distinguishing between the author and his text, writing that with *Cane,* Toomer was "saying goodbye to the Negro in himself. *Cane* then is a parting gift, and no less precious because of that. I think Jean Toomer would want us to keep its beauty, but let him go."[5] Underscoring the irony of Toomer's reluctance to claim African American identity, critics often note that Toomer's grandfather was P. B. S. Pinchback, an eminent politician in Louisiana during Reconstruction, who played a part in the team of lawyers led by Albion Tourgée in *Plessy v. Ferguson.* Pinchback's public claims to African American ancestry had everything to do with his political career.[6]

Toomer's resistance to identifying himself as "Negro" is often located in accounts of his career as a moment of arrogance or confusion, one of many instances in a tragic pattern of self-destructiveness. This interpretation has been shaped by the contexts in which interest in Toomer has been greatest: the "New Negro"/Harlem Renaissance movement of the 1920s and the Black Arts movement of the 1960s and 1970s, both of which were consolidated around an affirmative reclamation of African American identity and cultural production. Within these contexts, Toomer's ambivalence could be understood only as a betrayal of solidarity with "the race," a mistaken withdrawal from a collective movement whose existence in fact facilitated publication and developed a readership for African American authors. Arna Bontemps, for instance, who played a significant role in the recovery of *Cane* and the development of Toomer scholarship in the 1960s, understood his career this way: "Despite his promise . . . Jean Toomer rejected his prospects and turned his back on greatness."[7] Bontemps posited a causal relationship between Toomer's racial disidentification and the decline of his writing career after *Cane,* a trajectory that seems to fit neatly into familiar narrative conventions, particularly that of the tragic mulatto and the narrative of racial passing. Poet Robert Hayden also used these tropes in his attempt to give coherence to the perplexing ironies of Toomer's literary career: "Toomer published relatively little after *Cane* and nothing which equalled that work. Eventually he gave up writing altogether, having beforehand turned away from Negro material. In fact, he ceased to identify himself as a Negro and 'crossed the color line.'"[8] More recently, Henry Louis Gates Jr. has elaborated these characterizations of Toomer. In fact, Gates positions James Weldon Johnson's novel *The Autobiography of an Ex-Coloured Man* as a literary precursor for both the life of Jean Toomer and his major published work, *Cane:* "Toomer's *Cane* revises key tropes found in Johnson's novel, just as Toomer's biographical details parallel uncannily those of Johnson's protagonist."[9] Specifically, the "key tropes" and "biographical details" that Gates traces are those that have to do with crossing racial borders. He also uses the figure of Johnson to mark the "death" of Toomer as an African American writer: "It was in 1930 that Toomer officially passed from the literary black race, since in that year he denied James Weldon Johnson reprint rights to publish his works in the *Book of American Negro Poetry;* such a gesture, made to Johnson, a dean of black arts and letters, most certainly constituted a rite of passage from within to without."[10] Gates superimposes an Oedipal relationship between Johnson and Toomer: in a single gesture, Toomer ultimately rejects his racial and literary lineages, both symbolically embodied in the figure of James Weldon Johnson.[11] On the one hand, Gates emphasizes the importance of Toomer for understanding the connection between race and literary traditions: Toomer "forces us to abandon any definition of Afro-American literature that would posit the racial identity of an author as its principal criterion."[12] On the other hand, by invoking Johnson, Gates restates, however tentatively, the pervasive tendency among critics to understand Toomer through the narrative of racial passing, even as he acknowledges this interpretation as a "received, wishful opinion."[13]

Like other narrative conventions, the narrative of passing appeals to critics because it offers one way to make sense of the often perplexing contradictions of Toomer's ideas about race and his racial identifications. Yet the use of the narrative of passing also tends to foreground certain questions as it erases others. Because it emphasizes a disjunction between the racial fictions of "black" and "white," and the corresponding temporal separation of "before" and "after," the narrative of racial passing tends to project a familiar genre onto Toomer's life: like the conventional figure of the tragic mulatto, he appears caught in an unresolvable dilemma, alienated from either white or black identity.[14] Invoking this narrative of passing also has the effect of containing the ambiguity of racial categories within a model that posits "black" and "white" as the only possible authentic identities, a model that Toomer rejected. Recognizing that he had been "accused of passing," he insisted instead that "as for me personally, I see myself an American, simply an American."[15]

This chapter sets out to shift the scope of critical discussions of Toomer from an almost exclusive focus on race to one that also brings into view related questions of gender and sexuality. Thus I avoid the question of whether Toomer did or did not racially pass and am not concerned with the intricacies of his racial identifications and evasions. Specifically, I focus on the ways in which crises of masculinity and sexuality are linked to negotiations of the imaginary color line institutionalized by Jim Crow segregation. Following Gates, I also link Johnson and Toomer, but for different reasons: both authors were acutely concerned with how masculinity and sexuality were inflected through racial structures in the United States. The comparison between Toomer and Johnson is useful, but we need to understand that they are linked not only through the term "race" but through the (often different) ways in which their work is concerned with representing racialized masculinity and corresponding issues of sexual orientation. I consider the ways in which the construction of the racially ambiguous male body as a simultaneously sexually suspect body has been deployed both by and about Toomer. In his fiction and autobiographical writing, as I will show, Toomer was centrally concerned with male homoeroticism and its relationship to race. Not coincidentally, questions of sexual orientation and masculinity have also shaped critical discussions of race in Toomer's life and writing, in important, though not necessarily explicit, ways.

"A False Soprano" Meets Queer Theory

In novels of racial passing, as we have seen in the previous chapter's discussion of *The Autobiography of an Ex-Coloured Man,* movement across "the color line" usually carries with it the symbolic potential for sexual transgression as well. Because Toomer's biography is often (perhaps mistakenly) understood through a narrative of passing, the entanglement of racial and sexual boundary crossing, not surprisingly, has come into play in critical constructions of Toomer. In the study mentioned earlier, Gates enacts one of the most telling, and the most complicated, of these discussions, in which he constructs Toomer's racial disidentification as a simultaneous movement across categories of gender and sexuality. Borrowing and revising the approach of feminist literary critic Barbara Johnson, Gates asks, "What is the 'critical difference' . . . between the black Toomer and the white?"[16] He then marks this "critical difference" through highly sexualized metaphors:

> In a curious and perhaps perverse sense, Toomer's was a gesture of racial castration, which, if not silencing his voice literally, then at least transformed his deep black bass into a false soprano. Toomer did not want so much to be white as most of us . . . would have it; rather, he sought to be racially indeterminate, which [Barbara] Johnson suggests to be the nature of the castrato. Toomer's curiously nationalistic gesture toward indeterminacy, to be "just American," certainly helps to explain the shared reactions of (male) critics to the false soprano of his racially neutered and mystical works, such as *Essentials.*[17]

Here Gates elaborates on the analogy between race and gender that guides his analysis: black is to masculine as white is to feminine; to reject either category is to fall somewhere in between, repeating the logic of late-nineteenth-century sexologists and their notion of a "third sex." Moreover, black and white become privileged sites of an authentic voice, in contrast to a "false soprano." By characterizing as "racial castration" Toomer's refusal to identify as black, this interpretation also disturbingly mobilizes cultural stereotypes that link the black male body with hypersexuality. Gates equates a "deep black bass" with an authentic black masculinity and suggests that any resistance to this racial identification calls masculinity into question. Toomer, a writer who is considered by many to have "betrayed" the race by refusing to identify as black, is marked by that act also as having betrayed his gender. Race treachery becomes gender treachery. Toomer's work is "racially neutered."

To be fair, I emphasize that the passage quoted from Gates is not necessarily representative of his other work on gender and sexuality.[18] It is worth attention, however, because it serves as a useful index to the kinds of responses that Toomer and his work provoke, even among critics as careful as Gates. Gates's analogy between race and gender results in a perhaps unintentionally punitive characterization that mobilizes an unconsciously homophobic and sexist logic. But what if we refuse the characterization of Toomer as emasculated yet retain the underlying point that racial and sexual boundary making are deeply intertwined? What if we understand Toomer's gesture not through a simple analogy between gender and race but rather through an expanded lens that allows us to see race, gender, and sexuality as mutually embedded categories?

In doing so, we need to pay close attention to the language that Toomer himself invoked to express his profound alienation from identity categories. For instance, in an unpublished autobiographical text, Toomer wrote:

> People see me and ask questions, though they are usually inhibited from asking outright. What race, what nationality, where did I come from, what do I do? I see myself and ask questions, for, when I really see myself, I am as strange, odd, queer to myself as I am to you.[19]

Does Toomer's self-characterization as "strange, odd, queer" have any connection to the current political and theoretical meanings of "queer"? If so, how might the insights of so-called queer theory give us a way to understand Toomer's refusal to be classified as "Negro"? Is it possible to see this gesture as an articulation of resistance partly but not only to a discourse of naturalized racial identity? Can we, and do we want to, see Toomer's disidentification as "queer"?

On its own, Toomer's declaration would seem to have little to do with the guiding questions of queer theory, which has tended to define itself as revolving around the axis of sexuality.[20] To "queer" becomes a way to denaturalize categories such as "lesbian" and "gay" (not to mention "heterosexual"), revealing them as socially and historically constructed identities that have worked to establish and police the line between the "normal" and the "abnormal" since the late nineteenth century. Moving away from the underlying assumptions of identity politics, queer theory has tended not toward locating stable "queer" subjects but rather toward understanding the very process of deviant subject formation that results from a refusal or "failure" to adhere to the proscriptions of compulsory heterosexuality. If part of queer theory's project is defined broadly as an attempt to critique identity categories that are presented as stable, transhistorical, or authentic, then Toomer's refusal to position himself according to the available categories of "black" or "white" may be linked to this antinormative project of queer theory. To reiterate my guiding argument, compulsory heterosexuality in the twentieth-century United States has drawn much of its ideological power from the ways in which it buttresses as well as depends on naturalized categories of racial difference. Compulsory heterosexuality has been not simply parallel to discourses of racial segregation but integral to its logic; to disrupt naturalized constructions of racial difference involves simultaneously unsettling one's relationship to normative constructions of gender and sexuality as well.

As I take this discussion forward, I am aware that my own (constructed) position as a white lesbian, a late-twentieth-century queer academic, has potentially problematic implications. There may be risks here of a kind of expansionist and imperialist appropriation of Toomer for this theoretical project. To be clear, I am not attempting to retrieve Toomer as a long lost ancestral hero for some queer hall of fame. Nor am I calling for a method of reading that might be termed "queering Jean Toomer," a project of simply seeking and marking homoerotic presences in his texts. (Those resonances do exist in his work, however, as will become clear hereafter.) My aim is not to defend or criticize either Toomer's racial ambivalence or critics' disapproval of such ambivalence. Rather, I am interested in the ways in which Toomer's racial ambivalence has been connected implicitly to cultural proscriptions against gender ambiguity and homosexuality. By directly interrogating these constructions (along with Toomer's participation in them) in this chapter, I raise what I see as crucial questions about the position of discourses of race and racialization in queer reading and theorizing.[21]

At stake in this discussion is the extent to which "race" and "racialization" are seen as constitutive of sexuality in current attempts to mobilize "queer" approaches. It is not that attention to race has been absent in recent work consolidating itself under this rubric. Two theorists whose work is most often cited as generating and sustaining queer theory, Eve Sedgwick and Judith Butler, have both called attention to the importance of thinking about the position of race in the landscape of queer scholarship. Sedgwick, for instance, has noted that a lot of the most exciting recent work around "queer" spins the term outward along dimensions that can't be subsumed under gender and sexuality at all: the ways that race, ethnicity, postcolonial nationality criss-cross with these *and other* identity-constituting, identity-fracturing discourses, for example. Intellectuals and artists of color whose sexual self-definition includes "queer"—I think of an Isaac Julien, a Gloria Anzaldúa, a Richard Fung—are using the leverage of "queer" to do a new kind of justice to the fractal intricacies of language, skin, migration, state. Thereby, the gravity (I mean the *gravitas,* the meaning, but also the *center* of gravity) of the term "queer" itself deepens and shifts.[22]

Sedgwick's suggestion that the fulcrum of "queer" might be located precisely in race, ethnicity, and nationality is the trajectory that my own work seeks to address more specifically. I would point out, though, that shifting the weight of race and racialization in our understandings of "queer" will not occur unless the burden for that thinking is redistributed and made central to the intellectual labor of "white" queers, as well as those "of color."

Like Sedgwick, Butler has also addressed the ways in which queer theory might engage the questions central to recent work in critical race theory. In the course of her own analyses, however, she demonstrates the very difficulty of doing so. Drawing on Michael Omi and Howard Winant's emphasis on analyzing the process of racialization, rather than static notions of "race" or "racism," Butler asserts:

> The point may be taken for queer studies as well, such that "queering" might signal an inquiry into (a) the *formation* of homosexualities . . . and (b) the *deformative* and *misappropriative* power that the term currently enjoys. At stake in such a history will be the differential formation of homosexuality across racial boundaries, including the question of how racial and reproductive relations become articulated through one another.[23]

In her adaptation of Omi and Winant's model, Butler reveals an understanding of "queer studies" as a field analogous to (and therefore separate from) the field of critical race theory. Ironically, this analogy between "queering" and "racialization" draws on a logic that recalls Gates's

"metaphorical substitution" of race and "sex" to produce Toomer as "cas-
trato." Such an analogy constitutes racialization and queering as separable, rather than part of the same mechanism. Further, Butler privileges
the "differential formation of homosexuality across racial boundaries"
as central to the analysis of "queering." Yet it may be the case that emphasizing the formation of homosexualities cannot adequately address
the ways in which racialized identities and sexualities might be understood through the lens of "queer." This is not to say that it is necessary to
abandon the specificity of same-sex sexual object choice in queer analysis. There are risks in de-centering homosexuality within queer studies,
as Sedgwick has pointed out:

> And given the historical and contemporary force of the prohibitions
> against *every* same-sex sexual expression, for anyone to disavow those
> meanings, or to displace them from the term's definitional center,
> would be to dematerialize any possibility of queerness itself.[24]

Yet it is equally true that the privileging of same-sex sexual expression
limits the possibility of understanding a whole range of sexual practices and identity formation that historically and theoretically can be
understood as having been arranged and articulated under the purview
of "queer."

I will return to these larger theoretical concerns and the question of
Toomer's racial disidentification as "queer" at the end of this chapter.
But first I want to turn my attention to what has been largely responsible
for spurring my consideration of the connection between Toomer and
queer theory in the first place: that is, how Toomer's work, both published and unpublished, so insistently pushes the very word "queer" to
the foreground. Toomer's repeated use of the term seems to complicate
and enrich available genealogies of "queer" and demands to be situated
in relation to historical and literary contexts, as well as our own current theoretical understandings of the term. In the following section, I
address how "queer" is quite literally invoked by Toomer in his writing
from the 1920s. I focus on three works: "Kabnis" and "Bona and Paul"
(two stories from *Cane,* published in 1923) and "Withered Skin of Berries," published posthumously in 1980. It is important to pay attention
to the ways in which the vocabulary of "queer" emerged in Toomer's
texts as a way to mark figures who disrupted or scrambled the bound-

ary logics of race and gender, figures who indirectly included Toomer himself. Recognizing the need to distinguish current usage of this word from its meanings in the 1920s, I argue that understanding the force of "queer" in Toomer's writing and his historical context allows us to see this term in ways that dislodge it from models that have either privileged the analysis of sexuality over race or attempted to detach processes of sexualization from those of racialization.

"A Queer Feller"

"Kabnis," the final story of *Cane,* is set in the fictional town of Sempter, Georgia, where Ralph Kabnis, a northern African American man, has come to work as a schoolteacher. "Kabnis" was originally written as a closet drama (that is, a play for voices, not actual staging), and the story retains this structure. It begins with a meditation on Kabnis's feeling of restlessness in the South. This anxiety is fueled in the second section when a rock bearing an anonymous threatening note crashes through a window of the room where Kabnis and his friends are visiting. The note reads, "You northern nigger, its time fer y t leave. Git along now." [25] As an outsider, Kabnis assumes that the warning is directed at him and fears that he is about to be lynched. The warning, we discover later, is intended not for Kabnis but for another character, Lewis, instead. After Kabnis is caught drinking in his room at the school where he teaches, he loses his job and begins a new one in a repair shop. The final scene of the story takes place in an underground room, where Kabnis encounters Father John, a living embodiment of a southern African American past. At the end of the story, Kabnis emerges from the cellar, somewhat hopefully, into daylight.

Although the story centers on Kabnis, its events seem to be put into motion by another character, Lewis, also from the North, who simultaneously mirrors and shadows Kabnis. An elusive figure, Lewis disrupts the familiar routines and alliances in the town, eliciting suspicion from white and black townspeople alike. It is this character, Lewis, around whom the term "queer" accumulates. One character, Halsey, for example, calls him "a queer cuss" (91), "a damn queer feller" (91), "a queer one" (101), "a queer feller" (109), "queer as hell" (109), and "queer as y are" (110). Likewise, another character says, "Cant make heads or tails of [Lewis], an I've seen lots o queer possums in my day. Everybody's wonderin about him. White folks too" (91). At one point, Toomer calls attention to the multiple meanings of "queer." Halsey tells Lewis that

> A feller dropped in here tother day an said he knew what you was about. Said you had queer opinions. Well, I could have told him you was a queer one, myself. But not th way he was driftin. Didnt mean anything by it, but just let drop he thought you was a little wrong up here—crazy, y'know. (Laughs.) (101)

Lewis answers that "what he found queer, I think, was not my opinions, but my lack of them" (101), suggesting that Lewis's inscrutability sets him dangerously apart from the townspeople of Sempter.

Significantly, Toomer also used the term "queer" to mark out lines of identification between Kabnis and Lewis. The stage notes in the text introduce Lewis as "the queer fellow who has been referred to. A tall wiry copper-coloured man, thirty perhaps. . . . He is what a stronger Kabnis might have been, and in an odd faint way resembles him" (97). Halsey reinforces the identification between Kabnis and Lewis later in the story when he says, "One queer bird ought t know another, seems like t me" (110).[26] In fact, Toomer describes the initial meeting between these two "queer bird[s]," Kabnis and Lewis, as a powerful mix of attraction and repulsion:

> [Lewis's] eyes turn to Kabnis. In the instant of their shifting, a vision of the life they are to meet. Kabnis, a promise of a soil-soaked beauty; uprooted, thinning out. Suspended a few feet above the soil whose touch would resurrect him. Arm's length removed from him whose will to help . . . There is a swift intuitive interchange of consciousness. Kabnis has a sudden need to rush into the arms of this man. His eyes call, "Brother." And then a savage, cynical twist-about within him mocks his impulse and strengthens him to repulse Lewis. His lips curl cruelly. His eyes laugh. They are glittering needles, stitching. With a throbbing ache they draw Lewis to. (98, Toomer's ellipses)

This description centers on the men's exchange of gazes, which combine both attraction and aggression. Kabnis, it seems, undergoes a moment of homosexual panic, in which his initial "need to rush into the arms of this man" is quickly countered by a "twist-about" that disavows his

initial desire and transforms it into hatred.[27] Toomer's construction of
point of view in this scene reinforces a confusion between erotic identification and objectification that often characterizes representations of
same-sex desire.[28] Through a "swift intuitive interchange of consciousness," the passage shifts from Lewis's to Kabnis's point of view, a slippage
reinforced by the ambiguity of the pronouns.

This curious mixture of attraction and repulsion seems to figure
Toomer's own relationship to these characters. As Darwin Turner suggests, "Lewis resembles the self-portrait Toomer sometimes created in
his fiction and drama" (*Cane,* 91 n. 7). Although "Kabnis" is by no
means straightforwardly autobiographical, its setting and characters do
have connections to Toomer's life: in 1921 he served temporarily as
the head of an industrial and agricultural school for African American
students in Sparta, Georgia. Toomer himself explicitly identified with
Kabnis, writing to Waldo Frank in the early 1920s that "Kabnis is *Me.*"[29]
In fact, as mentioned earlier, in his autobiographical writing, Toomer
echoes his characterizations of Lewis and Kabnis, invoking "queer" to
describe his own physical illegibility and to signal his alienation from
conventional narratives of racial difference. Elsewhere the word takes
on stronger sexual connotations. Describing his return to his Washington, D.C., neighborhood after attending college, Toomer writes: "I got
the reputation of being a very queer fellow. Those, even those who
once upon a time had said what a fine dancer and what a sweet lover I
was, gave me a sufficiently wide berth."[30] Echoing his characterization
of Lewis as a "queer fellow," Toomer's use of "queer" in this instance
takes on connotations of danger and is linked with sexuality through
the comparisons with his former status as a "fine dancer" and "sweet
lover." Further, Toomer implies that this danger is transferable by association or proximity: the "very queer fellow" is both imagined and
avoided through his onlookers' careful construction and control of the
space around him, through "a sufficiently wide berth."

As a way to understand some of the resonances of Toomer's invocation of "queer," it is useful to consider contemporary usage in the 1920s.
Pursuing the historical significance of the term, George Chauncey has
recently suggested that "queer" circulated widely in New York City
during this period to describe men who engaged in same-sex sexual activity. According to Chauncey, "By the 1910s and 1920s, the men who

identified themselves as part of a distinct category of men primarily on the basis of their homosexual interest rather than their womanlike gender status usually called themselves queer. . . . *Queer* did not presume that the men it denoted were effeminate, for many queers were repelled by the style of the fairy and his loss of manly status, and almost all were careful to distinguish themselves from such men."[31] Further, explains Chauncey, the distinction between "queer" and "fairy" also signaled class differences: effeminate "fairies" were associated with working-class culture, but the queer was linked with middle-class communities, such as those in Greenwich Village, and the more well-to-do sections of Harlem and Times Square. According to Chauncey, "The cultural stance of the queer embodied the general middle-class preference for privacy, self-restraint, and lack of self-disclosure, and for many men this constituted part of its appeal."[32] In the 1920s, then, "queer" was not generally regarded as derogatory, according to Chauncey. It was not until the 1940s that "gay" became a term around which a later generation consolidated a new understanding of their identity against an older and now negative model of the "queer." Taking into account Toomer's own participation in bohemian and middle-class culture in Greenwich Village in the early 1920s, not to mention his friendship with gay writers such as Hart Crane during that period, it is likely that he was aware to some extent of the sexual meanings of "queer" when he wrote *Cane*.

Given the powerful presence of Lewis (and perhaps Kabnis's revealing resistance to him) and the sexual connotations of "queer," it would be a mistake, however, to say simply that Lewis is a gay character (as it would be to describe him as heterosexual or straight). Lewis also expresses and elicits desire toward Carrie K., the central female character of "Kabnis." The scene in which Lewis first meets Carrie K. parallels that of his first encounter with Kabnis:

[Lewis] draws her unwitting attention. Their meeting is a swift sunburst. Lewis impulsively moves towards her. His mind flashes images of her life in the southern town. He sees the nascent woman, her flesh already stiffening to cartilage, drying to bone. Her spirit-bloom, even now touched sullen, bitter. Her rich beauty fading . . . He wants to—He stretches forth his hands to hers. He takes them. They feel like warm cheeks against his palms. The sun-burst from her eyes floods up and haloes him. Christ-eyes, his eyes look at her. Fearlessly she loves into them. And then something happens. Her face blanches. Awkwardly she draws away. (103, Toomer's ellipses)

The similarity of this description to that of the first meeting between Lewis and Kabnis is striking. Just as the earlier scene focuses on the exchange of gazes between Kabnis and Lewis, so Toomer foregrounds "the sun-burst from her eyes." Likewise, although the passage marks the distinction between subject and object more clearly through gendered pronouns, Toomer nevertheless leaves the referent of "Christ-eyes" ambiguous: given Toomer's sentence construction, either Carrie K. or Lewis could be the possessor of the "Christ-eyes." The structure of desire and repulsion in this passage also parallels the earlier scene with Kabnis, although Carrie K.'s reaction to Lewis seems marked less by aggression than by fear. Like Kabnis, after she initially "loves" Lewis, she suddenly resists the attraction and instead rejects him. Toomer attributes Carrie's withdrawal to her internalization of "the sin-bogies of respectable colored folks" whose imagined voices caution her to "Look out! Be a *good* girl. A *good* girl. Look out!" (103, Toomer's italics). In both of these scenes, Toomer suggests that codes of sexual respectability block both Kabnis's and Carrie K.'s access to the erotic (and saviorlike) Lewis.

Toomer also invokes "queer" in "Bona and Paul," the story that precedes "Kabnis" in *Cane*. This story follows the relationship between Bona, a young white woman, and Paul, her schoolmate, whose racial identity is puzzling to those around him. Described as "red-brown," Paul is rumored at school to be a "nigger." As in "Kabnis," "queer" circulates through the relationship between two male characters, Paul and his white roommate Art. In a description of Paul watching Art prepare for an evening out, for example, Toomer writes: "He sees Art, curiously. Art is a purple fluid, carbon-charged, that effervesces beside him. He loves Art. But is it not queer, this pale purple facsimile of a red-blooded Norwegian friend of his?" (75). When Art notices Paul's distraction in a nightclub later that evening, he muses, "Paul's a queer fish. . . . Queer about him. I could stick up for him if he'd only come out, one way or the other, and tell a feller. Besides, a room-mate has a right to know. Thinks I wont understand. Said so" (77). Although this train of thought ostensibly is about Paul hiding his racial identity from Art, it can be read as referring to a sexual secret as well. In fact, Paul's refusal to name his racial identity is at the same time a refusal to expose his relationship to Bona as interracial or not. The possibility of a sexual meaning is reinforced when Art's girlfriend Helen becomes jealous of the bond between Paul and Art: "She tries to get Art to break with him, saying, that if Paul, whom the whole dormitory calls a nigger, is more to him than she is, well, she's through" (78). Here it is difficult to say whether Helen protests against the homoerotic or the interracial bonds between the two men.

The imbrication of homoerotic and interracial attraction surfaces through the language of "queer" in another text that has achieved canonical status among "Harlem Renaissance" writings, Nella Larsen's novella *Passing* (1929), whose author, like Toomer, has been constructed as an elusive and somewhat tragic figure. *Passing* is ostensibly a story about racial passing, but as Deborah McDowell has shown, Larsen enfolds within the narrative a simultaneous plot about sexual attraction and identification between two African American women, Irene Redfield and Clare Kendry.[33] The term "queer" appears at a number of crucial moments in the story, such as the scene in which the light-complexioned Irene and her darker-complexioned friend Felise literally bump into Clare's white husband, who does not know that Irene is African American. After the encounter, Felise exclaims to Irene, "Aha! Been 'passing,' have you? Well, I've queered that" (227). Attempting to rethink the ways in which psychoanalytic theories have positioned sexual difference as separable from processes of racialization, Butler has discussed the sense of exposure that is invoked by Larsen with the word "queer." According to Butler, "as a term for betraying what ought to remain concealed, 'queering' works as the exposure within language—an exposure that disrupts the repressive surface of language—of both sexuality and race."[34] Butler's comment is useful for understanding the resonances of "queer" in Toomer's writing: a similar sense of dangerous exposure also circulates in "Kabnis" and "Bona and Paul." Lewis's reason for being in Sempter is to collect information, apparently about lynchings that have taken place in the town. The character Layman remarks that Lewis is "always askin questions . . . pokin round an notin somethin" (91). The things that Lewis wants to know, he adds ominously, "werent for notin down" (91). Toomer implies that the African American townspeople, including the preacher Layman and the school principal Hanby, have as much at stake in keeping the lynchings quiet as do the white residents. Out of fear or complacency, they are deeply skeptical about openly revealing the circumstances of the lynchings. At one point in the story, Lewis and Halsey tease Kabnis by referring to a hidden truth about him. When Kabnis asks, "What about me?" Halsey insists that Lewis reveal the truth. When Kabnis repeats his desire to hear this truth spoken, Lewis responds, "Life has already told [Kabnis] more than he is capable of knowing. It has given him in excess of what he can receive. I have been offered. Stuff in his stomach curdled, and he vomited me" (101). This elusive response disturbs Kabnis, whose "face twitches" and whose "body writhes" (101). What Lewis knows about Kabnis is never revealed in the text, but the scene points out how the "queer" Lewis is positioned: he roots out knowledge whose revelation is both feared and desired.

Toomer leaves unclear whose interests the "queer" Lewis serves by collecting and recording information. As in *Passing,* the threat of exposure elicits an attempt to violently eliminate the transgressive figure. In *Passing,* Clare falls from a window to her death, but Larsen never resolves whether it is a murder or a suicide; in "Kabnis," the threat of lynching is real, but Toomer does not clearly identify the origins of, or the reasons for, the threat. Although Lewis does not come to a violent end, Toomer seems to expel him from the story without resolving his position in the narrative. Just as the "queer" Lewis remains an outsider to the community in Sempter, so he remains an outsider to the narrative itself. When the group in the cellar begins to divide into heterosexual couples, Kabnis with Cora, Halsey with Stella, Lewis "finds himself completely cut out" and "plunges . . . into the night" (112). In fact, it seems that to resolve the story, Toomer must remove Lewis and his ability to ignite so many directions of identification, desire, and repulsion.

The conflicted and multiple vectors of desire and identification mobilized by the "queer" Lewis in "Kabnis" reemerge at the center of Toomer's short story "Withered Skin of Berries," probably written in the 1920s around the time that *Cane* was published.[35] This story comes closer than perhaps any of Toomer's fiction to addressing directly the topic of same-sex desire (which may be part of the reason it was not published in his lifetime). Set in Washington, D.C., the story revolves around Vera, an African American woman who is passing for white at her job as a typist. The story presents a series of scenes of Vera's thwarted sexual relationships with three men: Carl, her coworker, an unself-consciously racist white man who has colonialist fantasies of "the conquest of the Argentine" (140); Art, an African American friend; and David Teyy, an elusive and poetic African American man. In a series of episodes set on the Potomac River, Vera rejects both Art and Carl, who, in her eyes, are either too sexually aggressive or sexually undesirable, respectively. Vera, however, is drawn to David and somewhat ambivalently has a sexual encounter with him.

This story is the subject of the only published critical discussion of homoeroticism in Toomer's work. In an article that characterizes this story as "a celebration of the redeeming power of love and sex" in a racist culture, Peter Christensen notes that "the only happy and mutual, if muted, sexual experience of the story is a homosexual one."[36] He refers to an incident narrated by Carl, who, while on a date with Vera, rhapsodizes about an encounter that he had with another man while attending college. We subsequently find out that this man is David Teyy, described by Carl as "an odd sort of chap. Peculiar, and most of the fellows resented it" (146). The responses to David's "peculiarity" are contradictory. Later, Carl says to David, "Like the fellows used to say, you were a queer duck, but they couldnt help liking you. Damn" (163). Carl recalls to Vera that while he and David were on an evening boat ride on Lake Mendota, "something like a warm finger seemed to touch my heart" (146). He remembers his moment of intimacy with David: "He closed his hand over mine. Me, a football man, holding hands with a man on the lake. If that had ever got out it would have done for me. But it never did. I could never tell it. Only to you" (147). Carl's chagrin ("Me, a football man") and his shame ("If that had ever got out it would have done for me") signal that Carl self-consciously acknowledges the implications of this homoerotic moment. He is clearly admitting his capacity to feel sexual desire for another man, which does not necessarily preclude his desire for women, but also registers his fear that his reputation might be damaged if he were labeled a "homosexual."

Importantly, Toomer builds into this encounter explicit acknowledgment of a cross-racial fantasy between the two men, in which the black/white dichotomy is displaced onto an Indian/white axis.[37] As the white Carl tries to move closer to David (whom we later learn to be African American), David says, "Come on, dont be afraid, youre with an Indian, pale-face friend" (146). This statement, Carl admits, made him "feel strange and queer, you bet" (147). The question of David's racial identity is part of what draws Carl to him and part of what makes him feel "queer." This curiosity recalls Art's wish in "Bona and Paul" that Paul would "only come out, one way or the other." As Carl settles next to David, he asks, "Are you an Indian, really?" (147). The confusion and fascination that Carl feels is heightened when David sings "a negro folk song" and invokes Native Americans ("vanished people") who died near lake Mendota. Carl is moved by David's words and admits to his chagrin, "God if he hadnt stirred me" (147).

Although Christensen does not address it in his discussion of "Withered Skin of Berries," this story includes another significant homoerotic moment, this time narrated by Art, the second of Vera's lovers. When Vera asks Art to tell her one of his dreams, he begins a story about the "syrup man," a figure who comes to boil cane at harvest time. The dream culminates in the following scene:

> I saw my body there, seated with the other men. As I looked, it seemed to dissolve, and melt with the others that were dissolving too. They were a stream. They flowed up-stream from Africa and way up to a height where the light was so bright I could hardly see, burst into a multi-colored spraying fountain. My throat got tight. (151)

Although it is more metaphoric than Carl's encounter with David Teyy on the boat, Art's dream is clearly homoerotic, with its orgasmic imagery and language of "dissolving" and "melting" with other men. The desire that Art describes, however, depends as much on racial identification and (perhaps interracial) mingling as it does on homoeroticism. The "stream" begins in Africa and, through its blending with other men, becomes a "multi-colored spraying fountain." This description also ties Art's dream to the figure of David Teyy, who is referred to as the "man of the multi-colored leaves" (160, 163).[38]

Even though the narrative ostensibly centers on Vera and her relationships with these three men, these two homoerotic scenes are presented as more ecstatic and satisfying than any of the heterosexual encounters of the story, which tend to be conflicted and aborted. In his discussion of the significance of the scene between Carl and David, Christensen speculates that Carl is "really a repressed homosexual."[39] Although I agree that the scene in the boat is clearly one of same-sex desire, Christensen's interpretation tends to flatten the very instability of sexuality and race that Toomer seems so fascinated by in this story. The scene in the boat, as well as Art's dream, has the most potent implications, it seems, for understanding not Carl but David, a character whose depiction resonates with other heroic and spiritual figures in Toomer's fiction. Clearly, David Teyy, not Vera, is the erotic center of this story, the figure who mediates sexual desire for all the characters. For example, traveling in a car with Carl, Vera finds that her attention is interrupted: "Curious for her, lines of a poem came unbidden to her mind" (141), lines that turn out to be some of David's poetry. Similarly, after Carl recalls his experience with David, he uses it as a model of his feelings for Vera: "I feel like that with you, here by the falls, in the shadow of a boulder where some Indian made love" (148). Likewise, Vera later tells David, "I knew it was you Carl dreamed about. I seemed to love him when the dreams he poured into me were you" (160). This "queer duck" (163), as David is described by Carl, and self-proclaimed "Indian" (146) seems an irresistible object of desire and a model lover across lines of either race or gender.

To analyze "Withered Skin of Berries" only for its significance in terms of sexual orientation is to simplify the contradictions that Toomer builds into the story. Fixing either David or Carl as "homosexual" not only reproduces a model of naturalized lesbian/gay identity but also minimizes questions of racial identity, which in fact are crucial for understanding the erotic force of the central figure David Teyy. Like Lewis in "Kabnis," David serves as a catalyst for the events of the story; his presence serves to expose the other characters' unpredictable and unconventional desires, manifested simultaneously in cross-racial and same-sex attraction.

"Sheik and Anti-Sheik": Popular Culture and Racialized Erotics

Toomer's fascination with these mediating, eroticized "queer" male figures—Lewis in "Kabnis," Paul in "Bona and Paul," and David Teyy in

"Withered Skin of Berries"—is central to another of his unpublished manuscripts, an intriguing uncompleted work entitled "Sheik and Anti-Sheik."[40] Although this work exists only as an unpublished and incomplete manuscript, I discuss it here because it lends insight into Toomer's fascination with these boundary-crossing figures. This fascination was not merely a reflection of Toomer's individual concerns but rather was shaped by and participated in larger cultural developments in the construction of race, masculinity, and homosexuality, particularly as represented in popular culture, a context that has been largely ignored in scholarship on Toomer.

"Sheik and Anti-Sheik" concerns another love triangle, involving the characters Dave Gordon, Lillian Williams, and John "Bone" Walker. Although the story seems to explore the rivalry between the two men for the attention of Lillian, it can be read as being centrally concerned with the homoerotic bonds between them.[41] Detailing what the two men have in common, for instance, Toomer writes, "And they were both in love with Lillian. Not really, either."[42] This ambivalent rendering of heterosexual desire contrasts strikingly with Toomer's depiction of the relationship between the two men. The story begins:

> Sheik and Anti-Sheik are that pair of opposites to be found in all races, nations, and conditions of peoples, the world over.
>
> Sheik and Anti-Sheik are everywhere. And they are everybody, split in twos. Of two men going down the street, one is, and one isnt.[43] It makes no difference if they are farmers, miners, laborers, undertakers, grocerymen, salesmen, druggists, artists, scientists, professors . . . Sheik and Anti-Sheik are that pair of opposites to be found in all conditions, the world over. You know them. One has a flare [sic] with women, and with life in general. One hasnt. But wishes that he had, though you couldnt pay him to exchange his sober gifts for the glitter of the other. He wants himself, and he wants the other. He wants two in one. The Sheik most often doesnt need a single thing to complete himself. Can you imagine a tom-cat yearning for the one he's just sent lick-spitting down the alley? Neither can I. The thing usually doesnt happen. But Sheik and Anti rub shoulders all the time. Given a third party, the friction that they generate is electric. Doubtless you yourself have been shocked by it. So much then, for generalities.[44]

One intriguing aspect of this opening passage is the way in which it overturns conventional oppositions. Toomer does not draw out a dialectic between male and female, or black and white, but rather establishes an opposition between two types of masculinity. Like the homoerotic scenes in "Withered Skin of Berries" and "Kabnis," Toomer's description here also foregrounds a confusion or blurring of subject and object: "He wants himself, and he wants the other. He wants two in one." These "opposites" are revealed to be not at all symmetrical, but defined instead through presence and lack: "One is, and one isnt." . . . One has a flare [sic] with women, and with life in general. One hasnt."

The relationship between "Sheik" and "Anti-Sheik" is marked as a powerful tension between attraction and resistance, echoing Toomer's other portrayals of relationships between men. Their "friction" is "electric" and generates "a slight itching for the outstanding features of the other." In the third version of the manuscript, Toomer describes the two men "rubbing shoulders, and, sometimes friendly, sometimes hostile." In contrast to the "electric" eroticism between the two men, the heterosexual relationship between the characters Lillian and Bone in the story is decidedly de-eroticized, described in terms of mother and child: "Bone was wistful enough to be mothered. Beneath his rather stiff and set exterior maturity, there existed something soft and helpless as a child, constantly in need of a mother's ministrations. . . . Unconsciously, Lillian was pulled to fulfill them. Their really personal contact was established on this basis."[45] Like Bone, Dave also de-eroticizes Lillian. His desire for her is based on her middle-class status and respectability, not on her erotic appeal: "She was the wifey type. Good to look on, but not in other ways desirable for fast life. For one thing, she was just a little bit too chunky."

In contrast to this negative rendering of Lillian's body, the two men are described through a much more eroticizing gaze at the beginning of the story. Consider this description of Dave:

I had no sooner heard the word ["Sheik"] and had a pretty little thing define it for me, than I knew Dave Gordon would be called the Sheik. His build was perfect. Fine head, sharp eyes, lips that made the women envy him, jealous to love him. A chest and back that Kuppenheimer clothes fit snug on. Thig[h]s and calves that could give a really graceful hang to French trow[s]ers. (Some limbs, I'll say!) And feet that took a J and M, brogue or patent-leather, like an aristocrat. Enough for Dave.[46]

The narrator of this passage unmistakably objectifies and eroticizes Dave Gordon's body as he catalogs its features from his "fine head" down to his feet. Nor can the narrator mask his enthusiastic visual pleasure at the sight of Dave's body: he gushes, parenthetically, "Some limbs, I'll say!" Interestingly, the narrator suggests that women both identify with and objectify Dave. As if they want to be as beautiful as this man, "women envy him." Yet they are also "jealous," presumably vying with other men for the opportunity "to love him," to take him as their object of desire.[47]

The narrator's focus on brand-name clothing ("Kuppenheimer clothes" and "J and M" shoes) also suggests an envy for the way Dave's body literally fits manufactured constructions of the male physique. He emphasizes how Dave's body fits the clothes, not the other way around, as one might expect. The tone of envy suggests that the narrator himself has a body that does not fit cultural standards of male beauty. Indeed, he is later described in contrast to Dave's mannequin-perfect proportions:

Too tall for the ready-mades to fit. Too serious and thin for women to gomadd [sic] over. Too much out of the run of things generally. And when the craze for Sheiks began, I could see him loose [sic] even what little pull he had with the more puritanical young women.[48]

The narrator is literally a misfit, a body out of sync with the cultural ideals represented by "ready-made" clothing.

The connection between clothing and "aristocratic" style returns in the story, but oddly in a description of the narrator, Bone, who begins to fulfill the role of the ideal male body as he prepares for a dinner party:

Once there, took his bath, got out his full dress clothes. There was delight in this. He liked himself in evening clothes. Had circumstances been favorable, he would have worn them every evening. They gave him a sense of well being, of life, aristocracy, wealth, all things that a certain portion of his nature longed for. In fact, on these evenings when he wore them, he quite naturally assumed the role, really lived the part of a gentleman of wealth. He looked it. The evening suit, the stiff white shirt, high color [*sic*], quite transformed him. Even Lillian had to admit that he was rather handsome on such occasions.[49]

In contrast to the first characterization of Bone as "too tall," "too serious and thin," and "too much out of the run of things generally," this passage differs dramatically in its emphasis on ease and plenitude. Bone here experiences a kind of narcissistic pleasure and, in fact, describes himself in language that identifies him with the earlier description of the Sheik. He is "all things that a certain portion of his nature longed for," just as the Sheik has everything that the Anti-Sheik lacks. When Bone sees the literal reflection of himself in evening clothes, he sees an image like Dave Gordon, a fuller projection of himself, a wholeness that answers his previous inadequacy. Further, this sense of fullness and presence is clearly expressed in class terms: his "sense of well being" is equated with "aristocracy" and "wealth."

Unfortunately Toomer never completed "Sheik and Anti-Sheik," but it is clear that the story explores two versions of masculinity and male desire. Interestingly, whereas in "Withered Skin of Berries" and "Kabnis" he uses race as an explicit part of his characterizations of male characters, in the existing parts of "Sheik and Anti-Sheik," Toomer does not refer directly to racial difference. Yet within popular culture in the United States during the 1920s, the term "sheik" itself was racialized and seems to have been used to characterize a specific type of sexualized masculinity, an eroticized and ironically somewhat feminized object of desire, but one who also enacted unbridled sexuality. The "sheik" figure might have appealed to Toomer because it troubled the larger cultural insistence on a bifurcation of "white" and "black" identities. The "sheik" did not fit neatly into either category, and that was, in part, the source of his fascination.

The word most obviously referred to the enormously popular film *The Sheik* (Paramount, 1921) starring Rudolph Valentino.[50] *The Sheik* took up the story of Diana Mayo, a young, wealthy British "new woman" (played by Agnes Ayres) traveling alone in the Sahara. She is captured by Sheik Ahmed (Valentino), who, the film suggests, forces her to submit sexually to him. Although Diana initially resists him, she gradually begins also to desire him. When a rival bandit captures her, Sheik Ahmed rescues her and is wounded in the process. Diana nurses him back to health, but when he recovers, the sheik is filled with remorse about his treatment of her and wants to release her. By the end of the story, Diana learns that Ahmed is in fact not an Arab but rather the son of an English lord. The two are reunited as lovers at the end of the movie. A device frequently employed in the conventional romance novel, the revelation of the Sheik's true ancestry means that the audience can both fantasize about but ultimately avoid confronting the possibility of interracial sexuality.

By the mid-1920s, as Patricia Raub has noted, "sheik" had become a slang expression in the United States for a type of eroticized male.[51] Other writers, including Claude McKay and Frank Norris, used the sheik as a character type in the early twentieth century.[52] The "sheik" persona popularized by Valentino is a useful reference point for understanding the popular cultural context surrounding Toomer's use of this figure and his fascination with racially and sexually "queer" figures. Feminist film critic Gaylyn Studlar has suggested that Valentino's popularity as the sheik erupted at a time when "the sexual discourses that combined the beauty of the male body with ethnic/racial otherness were already being inscribed in popular culture aimed at women."[53] Valentino, according to Studlar, was the highly visible articulation of disruptions of a Victorian model of masculinity that was "*already* destabilized, that was, in actuality, cracking apart at the seams."[54] In her discussion of the sheik persona's appeal to female audiences, she writes, "*The Sheik,* like all ideal romance narratives, acts as an exercise 'in the imaginative transformation of masculinity to conform with female standards.'"[55] Yet in addition to his catalytic effect on female audiences, Valentino also appealed to male audiences, or at least he aroused intense responses from them. Studlar quotes an interview with *Collier's* magazine, in which Valentino said,

> I had to pose as a sheik for five years! . . . A lot of the perfumed bally-
> hooing was my own fault. I wanted to make a lot of money, and so I
> let them play me up as a lounge lizard, a soft, handsome devil whose
> only sin in life was to sit around and be admired by women. . . . 5,000
> letters that have come in this week. . . . More than half of them *are
> from men.*[56]

Miriam Hansen likewise understands Valentino as a figure who especially articulated this period's cultural anxieties and fantasies, particularly those of (white) women: "He seems to have combined the projections of ethnic and sexual otherness in such a manner that the defensive strategies mobilized around each one of these terms actually fed into the threat of the other." [57] Hansen confirms the role that emerging notions of sexual orientation might have played in the widespread fascination with Valentino, who

> called into question the very idea of a stable sexual identity. Beckoning with the promise of sexual—and ethnic-racial—mobility, the Valentino figure appealed to those who most keenly felt the need, yet also the anxiety, of such mobility, who themselves were caught between the hopes fanned by the phantasmagoria of consumption and an awareness of the impossibility of realizing them within existing social and sexual structures. [58]

These are precisely the effects that Toomer seems to have been drawn to in his characterizations of "queer" figures such as the "sheik." Gay filmmaker and critic Kenneth Anger has discussed the ways in which, to some audiences, Valentino seemed to embody an attack on American notions of manhood that was linked to the emerging visibility of gay men. He cites the *Chicago Tribune*'s famous "pink powder puff" attack, a panicky broadside against everything that Valentino seemed to represent:

> Is this degeneration into effeminacy a cognate reaction with pacifism to the virilities and realities of the war? Are pink powder and parlor pinks in any way related? How does one reconcile masculine cosmetics, sheiks, floppy pants, and slave bracelets with a disregard for law and an aptitude for crime more in keeping with the frontier of half a century ago than a twentieth-century metropolis? [59]

Anger points out the irony that although Valentino's image could elicit this kind of outrage, it also appealed even to "the most straight of men," including H. L. Mencken and D. W. Griffith. [60]

The frequent appearance of "queer" figures such as Paul in "Bona and Paul," Lewis in "Kabnis," David Teyy in "Withered Skin of Berries," and

Dave Gordon in "Sheik and Anti-Sheik" suggests that Toomer's work participated in the larger popular cultural fascination with male figures who embodied racial and sexual mobility during the 1920s. At stake were the ways in which conventions of masculinity and race shaped and responded to emerging forms of desire and identification. These cultural contestations and Toomer's own autobiographical struggles fueled his writing and his drive toward modernist innovations in form and language during this period.

"What a Man!": Toomer's Autobiographical Portraits

At the beginning of this chapter, I noted that critical accounts of Toomer's authorship have tended to privilege a narrative of racial passing to explain his resistance to identifying as either "black" or "white." Further, these narratives of passing have often constructed Toomer's seeming racial ambivalence through analogies with sexual or gender ambiguity. In what follows, I return to the question of the construction of narratives about Toomer, with particular attention to those that he himself authored. I emphasize that my goal in analyzing these texts is not to "prove" Toomer's sexual orientation or racial identification but rather to show how "queer" figures such as the "sheik" appear repeatedly in Toomer's texts, whether autobiographical or not, to throw into question normative categories of race and masculinity. Toomer's characterizations of these figures can be understood as attempts to articulate subjectivities that had begun to appear in the larger landscape of American culture, particularly in popular representations. In Toomer's autobiographical writing and fiction, these queer figures evoke both desire and fear, but seem necessary for his construction of and exploration of the meanings of race, masculinity, and modernism in the 1920s.

Biographies of Toomer give only scant explicit attention to questions about his fascination with male figures, apparently attempting to skirt altogether issues of homoeroticism and homosexuality. In *The Lives of Jean Toomer,* Cynthia Earl Kerman and Richard Eldridge mention homosexuality explicitly only once, in a discussion of Toomer's sessions with a psychoanalyst. According to Kerman and Eldridge, the analyst apparently suggested that Toomer had "a slight leaning toward homosexuality," which "was a surprise to Jean, but he recognized it as a true part of his personality."[61] Despite the possibilities for further analysis of how this "true part of his personality" might be important in understanding Toomer and his writing, this one sentence is the extent of the volume's attention to homosexuality. In his recent biographical study of Toomer and Nella Larsen, Charles Larson also notes that the question of homosexuality came up during Toomer's analysis. Larson writes that "several dreams also suggest veiled homosexual tendencies or at least a fascination with observing homosexual acts."[62] Rather than considering the implications of homosexuality specifically, however, Larson instead lumps it with what he perceives as a negative part of Toomer's life: "Jean's sexuality, if ambivalent, can only be described as voracious."[63] John Chandler Griffin's *Jean Toomer: American Writer (A Biography)* gives much more attention to the presence and importance of homoeroticism in Toomer's life, but without explicitly engaging the possibility of homosexual attachments. For instance, in a footnote, Griffin writes, "Jean was always fascinated with powerful, ultra-masculine males," but Griffin never deals directly with a connection between this fascination and Toomer's fiction.[64] Although his book includes a number of innuendos about Toomer's sexual attraction to men, Griffin never pauses to discuss it directly as a critical question.

What emerges from the biographies and Toomer's own autobiographical writing, however, *is* a serial fascination with male figures who had transformative effects on Toomer. Four men in particular seem to have been powerful influences as well as figures of erotic fascination in Toomer's life: his uncle Bismarck ("Bis"), who lived with Toomer, his mother, and his grandparents in Washington; fellow writer Waldo Frank, founder of *Seven Arts;* George Gurdjieff, philosopher and spiritual leader; and Nathan Toomer, Toomer's father, who existed only in an imaginary realm for Toomer through photographs and other people's reminiscences.

In his autobiography, *Earth-Being,* Toomer recorded the beginning of his "special relationship" with his uncle Bismarck, who was one of the numerous family members living in the Washington, D.C., house in which Toomer spent most of his childhood. "Bis," as Toomer affectionately referred to his uncle, was remembered by Toomer as characteristically "in bed surrounded by the materials of a literary man."[65] Toomer noted a marked shift in their relationship just before he reached adolescence:

> Then something happened which swiftly transferred my interests from the world of things to the world of ideas and imagination. Uncle Bis and I suddenly discovered each other. He had been there all along, and his sensitivity and affection had drawn me to him. I had been there all along, and he had loved me. He had probably been aware that despite the difference of our ages and my restless activity our temperaments were similar. He had certainly noticed that the minute he spoke to me of interesting things I became attentive, pensive, and even grave — save when some particularly fine thing made my eyes flash or glow and caused a flush of eagerness, curiosity, thrill or enthusiasm to irradiate my face. All the years of my young life we had been there together. He had been my uncle and I his kid. But now the time was ripe for a special relationship. All at once the veils of familiarity dropped from our eyes and each in his own way beheld the wonder of the other.[66]

Toomer describes this awakening and bonding through visual metaphors: he notes that Bis often made his "eyes flash or glow" and that what marked his new intimacy with Bis was when "the veils of familiarity dropped from our eyes" and they "beheld the wonder of each other." These images, of course, recall the exchange of gazes that Lewis elicits in "Kabnis" with Kabnis and Carrie K. Toomer continues this passage by describing his intellectual awakening with Bis as one of unconditional devotion: "I held him in the highest regard. I was devoted to him as to one beyond doubt wise and knowing, one capable of holding my complete faith and trust."[67]

This tableau of a sudden recognition of kinship with another man repeats itself in Toomer's account of his first impression of white writer Waldo Frank, who would later play an important part in Toomer's literary career. In 1919 they were brought together at a party in New York, at which, as Toomer reminisced, they did not speak to each other. Even so, Toomer was immediately attracted to Frank: "One man stood out. He had a fine animated face and a pair of lively active eyes. I felt there could be something between him and myself. I didn't know his name, but I marked him."[68] Although the two men did not speak during this first encounter, they made contact again during the following week. While Toomer was walking alone in Central Park in New York, a man who seemed familiar walked toward him. They passed each other without speaking, but then, as Toomer recalled, "suddenly drawn by some force, I stopped and turned around. At the same moment he stopped and glared back at me. It was Waldo Frank."[69] They sat down on a bench and began to talk, and according to Griffin, "immediately became the best of friends."[70] The aggression and eroticism that characterize this scene of recognition also characterize scenes of "cruising," no "strange quirk of chance," as Griffin describes it, but a stylized and highly conscious exchange between men.

In a discussion of Frank and Toomer's relationship, Mark Helbling has described the two writers as "something like surrogate brothers."[71] Helblings's sibling analogy is one way to make sense of the intimate relationship between them, but it also tends to dismiss any discussion of homoeroticism. Toomer and Frank traveled together in the South, a trip during which Frank wrote his novel *Holiday* and Toomer completed *Cane*. Before the trip, Toomer explained to Frank that he must travel as a "Negro" in order to get the most out of the trip. Frank replied in a way that reveals a great deal about the function of racial difference in the volatile mix of objectification and envy that characterized their relationship.

> If you go as a Negro, cant I also? What is a Negro? Doubtless, if the Southerner could see in my heart my feeling for "the Negro," my love of his great qualities, my profound sympathy for his trials and respect for the great way he bears them, that southerner would say, "Why you're worse than a nigger! . . . so if you go as a Negro so go I![72]

Frank's romanticization of both African Americans and his own relationship to them suggests a profound naïveté, which shaped his understanding of Toomer's own complicated racial identity and its implications for Toomer's position within the literary market. Frank once told Toomer that "the important thing which has at length released you to the creating of literature is that you do not write as a Negro,"[73] a statement that revealed Frank's own racism toward African American writers. At the same time, Frank had a considerable stake in construct-

ing Toomer as African American. Frank's own racial envy and desire
later shaped his representation of Toomer as a "Negro" writer to publishers and other writers, an emphasis on racial identity that Toomer
resisted and that brought irreparable tension to the surface of their relationship.

That both Toomer and Frank presented themselves as African Americans in their trip to the South suggests that they bonded in a relationship of identification, transgression, and envy. Toomer and Frank
collaborated on the editing and revision of each of their manuscripts,
and Toomer acknowledged his relationship with Frank by dedicating
"Kabnis" to him. Yet Toomer had anxieties about their professional relationship and wrote to Gorham Munson, a mutual friend of his and
Frank's, that

> I cannot *will* out of Waldo. With the exception of Sherwood Ander-
> son some years ago (and to a less extent, Frost and Sandburg) Waldo
> is the only modern writer who has immediately influenced me. He
> is so powerful and close, he has so many elements that I need, that I
> would be afraid of downright imitation if I were not so sure of my-
> self. But I know my own rhythm . . . and I feel with you that I will
> "eventually make a successful amalgamation with (my) own special
> contribution." I must *grow* out of him.[74]

This letter, with its emphatic resolve, suggests that Toomer acknowledged at the same time that he resisted the ways in which his and Frank's
identities had become interwoven in their intense literary collaboration.
Like the homoerotic confusion of subject and object relationships that
Toomer portrayed in his fiction, his attachment to Frank was conflicted,
simultaneously affirming and threatening his sense of a unique identity, literary or otherwise. Tellingly, if one draws on Sedgwick's model
of homoerotic triangles, Toomer became involved sexually with Frank's
wife, Margaret Naumberg, who mediated Toomer's relationship not
only with Frank but also with the man who was to influence Toomer's
life in a similarly powerful way, Russian mystic George Gurdjieff.[75]

The homoerotic gaze that structures Toomer's description of his first
encounter with Frank returns in a passage recounting his first glimpse
of Gurdjieff, to whose spiritual movement Toomer would devote more

than a decade of his life.[76] Toomer recalled his first sight of Gurdjieff from the vantage point of an audience member:

> Presently I saw an unforgettable figure of a man walking down one of the aisles, looking at people in the audience as he moved along, looking for what? His head was shaven. He wore a tuxedo. But what a monk! And, I might add, as I did at the time, what a man! My first impression was of the whole body of this man, and something of the individual in the body. . . .
>
> His complexion was swarthy, his dark eyes wide-spread, his nose finely modelled and even delicate compared with the rugged four-square lower face, and he had a tigerish black moustache. I was fascinated by the way the man walked. As his feet touched the floor there seemed to be no weight on them at all.[77]

This passage's eroticism and close attention to the body recall Toomer's description of Dave Gordon in "Sheik and Anti-Sheik." Likewise, his enthusiastic eruptions, "what a monk!" and "what a man!", echo his breathless "Some limbs, I'll say!" in that same story.

Two aspects of Toomer's description of Gurdjieff—his "swarthy" complexion and his "dark eyes wide-spread"—link it to an even more idolizing description of Toomer's father, Nathan Toomer, whom he knew most intimately through a photograph. In his autobiographical writings, Toomer recalled the "distinctly swarthy tinge" of his father's complexion, echoing his description of Gurdjieff as well as the racially and sexually ambiguous hero that "the sheik" embodied. Yet the aspect "that struck [Toomer] more [than] any thing else" about his father's photograph was the intensity of his eyes:

> The eyes were large, brooding, far-seeing, as if they held in view a dream or vision away and beyond the things of the every day world. They might have been the eyes of a very creative person, for that matter of a genius. They were amazing eyes. They made you look at them, even though they were not looking at you or even aware of your presence.[78]

Toomer's fixation on his father's mesmerizing eyes fits into the pattern established by his other fictional and autobiographical writing about magnetic male figures. As in his other portraits of attraction between men, Toomer here also invokes his father's aristocratic qualities:

> The pose of the body was relaxed, nonchalant, self-assured, with a suggestion of daring and a feeling of natural superiority. There was something regal about that body and its pose, a suggestion of carnal elegance. It was very well groomed yet carelessly so. Nathan Toomer, by all reports, wore the finest clothes selected with excellent taste. This I know. The only worldly possessions that came to me from him were some beautiful large silk handkerchiefs, a set of small diamond shirt studs, and a slender ebony cane with a gold head. His liking of fine things and his good taste in dress were perhaps the only traits he had in common with P.B.S. Pinchback [Toomer's grandfather].[79]

Toomer's description of this photograph rearticulates the qualities he found so attractive in the most compelling male figures in his life and fiction. The description's emphasis on "natural superiority," "something regal about that body and its pose," "carnal elegance," "finest clothes," "excellent taste," "silk," "diamond[s]," "ebony," "gold," "fine things," and "good taste" suggests again Toomer's fascination with the aura, textures, and aesthetics of aristocracy and wealth. It is difficult to say whether this image of Toomer's father shaped his characters, or whether his characters shaped Toomer's construction of this photographic image of his father. Both, it seems, reflected both Toomer's and the larger popular cultural interest and eroticization of "sheik"-like figures of masculinity.

The eroticized, often aristocratic, and racially ambiguous male figure became a repeated trope in Toomer's fictional and autobiographical writing. The "queer" presence of this figure in Toomer's writing suggests that his conflicted and fluid position toward racial difference resonated with, as much as it structured, his representation of his own and his characters' homoerotic bonds. The aristocratic status of this figure may also be read as a fantasy of privilege, where class status might immunize one against the risks attached to racial and sexual classification. Toomer's strategies for attempting to evade the stigmatizing gaze of a segregated culture ironically made him and his post-*Cane* writing culturally and literally unreadable for decades. By attempting to refuse being claimed as African American within the publishing industry and the larger culture, he was rendered unclassifiable and therefore uncommodifiable as an author.

"Simply an American"

I return now to my initial questions: How might Toomer's gesture of racial disidentification, his refusal to adhere to a system of naturalized racial difference, be connected to the proliferation of "queer" in his writing? And does this connection relate to the current work of queer reading? Having raised these questions, I admit that they remain difficult to resolve. Frankly, it may not be useful to call Toomer's racial disidentification "queer." His attempt to replace the racial fictions of black and white with the nationalistic vocabulary of "American" is surely as potentially problematic as any narrative of passing would be. It is difficult, after all, to extricate "American" from a history of racialized hierarchies and imperialism. However, it is important to consider what work this insistence on an abstract "American" identity accomplishes. In a discussion of the function of discourses of race, nation, and citizenship in Larsen's *Passing,* Lauren Berlant notes the character Irene's insistence that "she was an American," adding that "Irene's embrace of the nation seems a pathetic misrecognition."[80] Berlant's questions about this misrecognition are also applicable to Toomer: "What kind of body does American national identity give her, and how does the idea of this body solve or salve the pain that the colonized body experiences? And if a desire to be fundamentally American marks one field of fantasy for Irene, how does this intersect [with] her other desire, to be incorporated in another woman's body?"[81] Berlant's discussion serves as a point from which to untangle some of the possible valences of Toomer's assertion that he was "simply an American" and his disidentification as either African American or "white." Following Berlant, it is also possible to read this fantasy of disembodied citizenship as one that belies Toomer's own internalized notions of the racialized male body as the spectacularized site of pleasure and fear, a dialectic that recurred repeatedly in his writing and tended to be named as "queer." The sheer accumulation of "queer" around characters such as Lewis and around Toomer himself points to a need to take further account of "queer" in the context of epistemologies of race and national identity in the United States.

In a recent article demonstrating Toomer's involvement in black literary circles before the publication of *Cane,* George B. Hutchinson writes
that "one of the great ironies of Toomer's career is that he matured during the very period in which black as well as white Americans became
most insistent upon maintaining 'racial integrity.'"[82] It is worth remembering that there were, of course, crucial differences in motivation and
power between white and black attempts to draw racial boundaries. I
would agree, however, that it is important to situate Toomer's work
and authorship within the historical context of increasingly solidified
distinctions between "white" and "black," and add that, as I have emphasized, this was also an era characterized by an increasing interest
in distinguishing between homo- and heterosexual bodies. Hutchinson
points out that Toomer's fiction countered the more prevalent image
of the tragic "mulatto" represented by white and African American authors alike. It is true that Toomer's "queer," racially ambiguous male
characters are in fact idealized figures, godlike rather than tragic. Unlike
James Weldon Johnson, who incorporated anxieties about the border
between male and female (and implicitly, between "normal" and "deviant" sexuality) as a way to question the ex-coloured man's character,
Toomer approached the blurring of these oppositions in male figures
with a kind of longing and even romanticization.

If, in the characterizations of Toomer that I quoted at the beginning of this chapter, Gates repeats James Weldon Johnson's strategy of
critiquing the ex-coloured man through a portrait of "gender trouble,"
in my own analysis, I want to resist reproducing Toomer's tendency
to romanticize the figure who blurs racial and gender boundaries. A
useful touchstone for this point is Martha Umphrey's recent discussion
of the relationship between queer theory and lesbian/gay history. In
her analysis, Umphrey warns against any queer project that would too
easily recuperate its subjects:

> In other words, queer history can queer the celebratory politics of
> lesbian/gay history; out of that queering can come a hard-boiled his-
> tory, one with no *necessary* moral center, posing new questions and
> revealing different sexual practices in the name of exploding com-
> pulsory heterosexuality.[83]

Although, as I have argued, part of this project also means not limiting analysis to "sexual practices," Umphrey's warning against the tendency toward celebratory politics and histories is well taken. In this way, one would not have to applaud Toomer's disidentification to see how it exposes the normalizing discourses of race and sexuality that came to circumscribe his authorship.

Finally, what emerges from this discussion is that queer reading is perhaps most useful in resisting any attempt to see race and sexuality as metaphoric substitutes; instead it might insist on marking the ways in which racialization is constitutive of sexuality, and vice versa, in specific historical contexts. But it must also resist the expectation that such reading will be reassuring or celebratory. Just as it is difficult to say whose interests are served by Lewis's presence in "Kabnis" or by Toomer's racial disidentification, so we cannot predict what alliances or antagonisms will be unsettled in the process.

Conclusion

Through it all I discerned one clear and certain truth: in the core of the heart
of the American race problem the sex factor is rooted; rooted so deeply that
it is not always recognized when it shows at the surface. Other factors are
obvious and are the ones we dare to deal with; but, regardless of how we
deal with these, the race situation will continue to be acute as long as the
sex factor persists.

—James Weldon Johnson, *Along This Way*

This book has attempted to demonstrate a range of approaches for
understanding the ways in which representations of supposed differences between "black" and "white" and "heterosexual" and "homosexual" bodies summoned and shaped one another in late-nineteenth-
and early-twentieth-century American culture. These representations
often performed contradictory ideological work depending on the specific context of their production and reception and thus require a diverse range of interpretive strategies.

Although my argument and methodology are grounded in a particular historical moment, that of the late nineteenth and early twentieth
centuries, they do have implications for questioning the imbrication
of racial and sexual discourses in other historical contexts. Given that
my work is a product of our own historical moment, we might consider how current discourses of race and sexuality are shaped by residual
effects of the earlier period and how they provide a context for making
visible the very interconnections that I have explored. In the last decade
alone, for example, recent scientific research into sexual orientation has
demonstrated a reenergized determination to discover a biological key
to the origins of homosexuality. Highly publicized new studies have
attempted to locate indicators of sexual orientation in discrete niches
of the human body, ranging from a particular gene on the X chromo-
some, to the hypothalamus, to the ridges of fingertips.[1] In an updated

and more technologically sophisticated form, comparative anatomy is again being granted a peculiar cultural authority in the construction of sexual identity, even though the current discourses disguise their histories. These studies, of course, have not gone uncontested, arriving as they have within a moment characterized not only by the development of poststructuralist theories of sexuality but also, in the face of AIDS, by a profound ambivalence toward prevailing scientific methods and institutions. At the same time, some gay-affirmative activists see political efficacy in these new scientific studies, arguing that gay men and lesbians might gain greater access to civil rights if sexual orientation could be proven an immutable biological difference. Such arguments make an obvious analogy to historical precedents for understanding race as immutable difference. The absence of any acknowledgment of histories of racialization in these studies, however, is startling when placed within a context of the history of scientific racism. Urgent questions remain about how current efforts to rebiologize sexual orientation might reflect or influence existing cultural anxieties and discourses about racialized bodies. As a way of pointing toward the implications of this book's argument for other contexts and periods, while still being aware of the need to reformulate its terms, I want to step out of the period of my study and turn briefly to two other sites of cultural contestation over identity categories, the 2000 census and a founding text of the transgender movement, Leslie Feinberg's semiautobiographical novel *Stone Butch Blues*.

Body Counts

At the turn into the twenty-first century, racial categories are being contested explicitly and fiercely in the United States census, demonstrating the ways in which discursive constructions of race are inseparable from the material status of bodies. In spite of the claims of its administrators, the United States census serves not as an objective measurement of self-evident categories of people but rather as a representation of dominant ideologies. The racial categories measured by the census have regularly been revised to reflect concurrent understandings of identity, but also, less intentionally, to enforce those dominant understandings. The differences between the 1890 and 1920 censuses, for instance, reveal an increasingly bifurcated understanding of race as Jim Crow segregation became more pervasive in the early part of the century. In 1890 the available categories included "black," "white," "mulatto," "quadroon," and "octoroon," demonstrating an ideological emphasis on more subtle distinctions of racial mixture. In 1920, however, these distinctions were removed, leaving "black" and "white" as the only possible categories of racial identification, effectively asserting a national fiction of racial purity that reinforced the logic of institutionalized segregation. Since 1920 the census has moved toward dismantling this bifurcated system of racial identity, and in 1977, under Directive 15, the census provided four categories of race: "American Indian or Alaskan Native," "Asian or Pacific Islander," "Black," and "White," with the addition of an ethnic marker, "Hispanic Origin or Not of Hispanic Origin." This apparent progression from a bifurcated system to a model of multiple racial identities seems to be continuing in the design of the 2000 census. More specifically, policy makers and activists have considered a number of options for revising the document: offer a new "multiracial" category, eliminate the measurement of race and ethnicity altogether, or allow respondents to select more than one racial and ethnic identification. The Office of Management and Budget, which provided recommendations for the implementation of the census, eventually chose to allow respondents to select more than one racial category from the following groups: "White," "Black or African American," "American Indian and Alaska Native," "Asian," "Native Hawaiian and other Pacific Islander," or "Some other race."[2]

In the controversy over racial and ethnic categories in the 2000 census, questions of language and its interpellation of racialized subjects cannot be separated from their material effects. For instance, the Association of Multiethnic Americans lobbied to add a multiracial category to the census questionnaire because the association seeks redress for the lack of official acknowledgment of mixed-heritage people in the United States. According to the president of that group, Ramona Douglass, who is the daughter of a Sicilian American mother and an African American–Ogalala Sioux father, the group is frustrated with the cultural invisibility of multiracial and multiethnic people.[3] These epistemological questions of visibility and invisibility are tied to material effects: the mapping provided by the census is used to monitor and enforce civil rights legislation, as well as major entitlement and affirmative action programs.

Although the 2000 census itself will do little (if anything) to transform long-entrenched fictions of racial identity, in the most optimistic
reading of the current debate, it is at least possible to see the potential
for a public conversation that might expose the material effects of these
discursive formations. However, it is important to be alert to the ways
in which this debate obscures other boundary-making logics at work,
such as gender and sexual orientation. When Susan Graham, a white
woman married to an African American man, filled out the 1990 census, there was no category that reflected the biracial status of her children. Not knowing what box to check, she asked the Census Bureau,
which responded that the children should take the race of their mother.
When she objected and asked why they should be classified according
to her race only, a Census Bureau administrator answered, "Because, in
cases like these, we always know who the mother is and not always the
father." [4] Thus while racial categories are contested, the epistemological
status of maternity versus paternity is reinforced but left unmarked in
the official record. Troublingly, categories of gender seem to be taken
for granted in this debate, as evidenced also in the opening of a recent
article by sociologists Ivan Light and Cathie Lee concerning the census
controversy:

> Asked what sex they are, Americans give consistent answers. They
> are the same sex one year that they were the year before. This consis-
> tency carries over to age, which reliably increases by one every year.
> However, Americans do not demonstrate the same consistency in the
> ethnic or racial identity they report to census takers.[5]

In effect, although Light and Lee take as their subject the instability of
categories of ethnic and racial identity, they do so by fixing "sex" as a
natural, transhistorical, and self-evident aspect of bodies. Whereas those
who admit inconsistency in their racial or ethnic identifications are included in Light and Lee's construction of "Americans," those whose "sex"
is mutable apparently are unimaginable in the context of this construction of the national body. What the census debate obscures in this instance is the existence of other movements afoot that fiercely contest the
notion that "sex" is an immutable or binary category of identity. In the
next section, I look briefly at one site of this contest, Leslie Feinberg's
Stone Butch Blues, a founding text in the current transgender movement.

I attend not only to its destabilization of "natural" categories of sex and gender but, importantly, to the ways in which racial discourses simultaneously shape and are shaped by the terms of that contestation.

Stone Butch Blues and Other Sorrow Songs

"Transgender" emerged in the early 1990s as a term to describe a subject position that did not rely on stable categories of sexual orientation or gender. Terms such as "male," "female," "lesbian," "gay," "heterosexual," or "bisexual" could not account for the specific ways in which some subjects embodied their alienation from normative categories of identity. Transgender, as defined recently by Susan Stryker, refers not

> to one particular identity or way of being embodied but rather as an umbrella term for a wide variety of bodily effects that disrupt or denaturalize heteronormatively constructed linkages between an individual's anatomy at birth, a nonconsensually assigned gender category, psychical identifications with sexed body images and/or gendered subject positions, and the performance of specifically gendered social, sexual, or kinship functions.[6]

Stryker's necessarily broad statement reflects the fluidity and imprecision of notions of transgender subjectivity at this historical moment, which is witnessing the attempt to forge a new model of gender identity, one that self-consciously defines itself in relation to (and sometimes against) a model of sexual orientation. In the ongoing discursive formation of this transgendered subject, Leslie Feinberg's semiautobiographical novel *Stone Butch Blues* has become a founding text for the political and theoretical mobilization of a model of transgendered subjectivity.

Through scenes of excruciating violence and physical pain, *Stone Butch Blues* demonstrates relentlessly what is at stake when no language is available for expressing one's own subjectivity and identity. A century after the emergence of discourses of homo- and heterosexuality in the United States, Feinberg's novel chronicles the ways in which those discourses, as well as normative constructions of gender (like those invoked by the census), are inadequate for representing her protagonist's sexual and gendered subjectivity. As Jess states at one point: "I can't hear

my own voice say the words out loud. I've got no language."[7] Retro-
actively, as expressed in Feinberg's subsequent book *Transgender Warriors,*
the film documentary *Outlaw,* and her speeches and pamphlets, we can
see that a model of "transgender" identity describes Jess's subjectivity at
the end of the novel, even though this actual term is never used in the
novel itself.[8] In one of its final scenes, Jess literally emerges as a speaking subject, ascending from a subway to a stage platform at a rally on
Christopher Street, where she stands to voice her existence as a transgendered subject publicly for the first time. What I want to show briefly
is how the emergence of this transgendered voice and subjectivity is
mediated through racial discourses in the text, specifically, for Feinberg, through repeated invocations of analogies to Native American and
African American culture and identity. In this account of transgendered
subject formation exists a residual logic echoing the historical emergence of discourses of homo- and heterosexuality in the United States
through a mediating discourse of racialization.

Throughout *Stone Butch Blues,* Feinberg uses Native American culture
as the site of an alternative system of gender, one that offers the possibility of nurturing Jess's resistance to normative categories of gender,
in contrast to mainstream, middle-class culture, which would prefer to
discard those whose bodies and subjectivities "fail" to be interpellated
into categories of "male" and "female." The instrumental role of Native
American culture is perhaps no more powerful in the book than in the
very scene of Jess's birth. When her mother begins labor during a violent storm that prevents her from going to a hospital, her neighbors,
some Dineh women, act as impromptu midwives to the birth. The different responses of Jess's mother and the Dineh women foreshadow Jess's
later treatment in life:

> "Put the baby over there," [my mother] told them, pointing to a bas-
> sinet near the sink. *Put the baby over there.* The words chilled the Indian
> women. My mother could see that. The story was retold many times
> as I was growing up, as though the frost that bearded those words
> could be melted by repeating them in a humorous, ironic way. (14)

Later, the Indian women offer refuge for the baby and toddler Jess by
baby-sitting her and providing a nurturing context, in contrast to the

mother who fears touching this child: "And so I grew in two worlds, immersed in the music of two languages. One world was Wheaties and Milton Berle. The other was fry bread and sage. One was cold, but it was mine; the other was warm, but it wasn't" (14). When Jess comes too close to forging a hybrid identity based in both white middle-class and Dineh cultures by claiming the women's native languages as her own, her parents forbid her from participating in this alternative world altogether. Her father overhears Jess speak "with words he'd never heard before," and drawing on the enduring trope of the captivity narrative, he "rescues" his daughter, asserting that "he couldn't stand by and watch his own flesh and blood be kidnapped by Indians" (14).[9] Although Jess is removed physically from contact with Native American culture, these Dineh women continue to populate her utopian visions. One recurring motif is a dream in which Jess inhabits spaces—the desert or a hut— within Native American culture in which she is affirmed and accepted. Nor is Jess the only character for whom the acquisition of an affirmative transgendered identity is mediated racially. The instrumental status of Native American culture in Jess's formation as a subject is echoed in the experience of her transgendered best friend, Ruth, who narrates a story about a Senecan "spirit" who tells her uncle simply to "let the child be" (262). These motifs of an affirming Native American culture perform a legitimating function in the text, authorizing and encouraging the existence of the transgendered subject in the face of the normalizing forces of the dominant culture, which constantly seeks either to transform or to annihilate the subject who is not rendered legible through the standards of a normative "male" or "female" body.[10]

If Native American culture provides Jess with an enabling fantasy of an alternative gender system, African American culture and identity figure for her a model of a colonized subject unassimilable into the national body, a model that will become both instrumental and discouraging in her attempt to find language for her own experience as a transgendered subject. The particular relationship between African American and transgender identity, however, is more conflicted and ambiguous than is the position of Native American identity in the text. Jess's engagement with African American culture is figured through her friendship with Ed, an African American "he-she" whom she befriends in the bars.[11] Ed attempts to forge an intellectual context for their experiences as "he-shes" by giving Jess books significant to the history of African American political struggles, such as Malcolm X's *The Ballot and the Bullet,* W. E. B. Du Bois's *The Souls of Black Folk,* as well as texts by James Baldwin (57). Du Bois's writing becomes the most significant of these texts and reappears at two key points in the narrative: when Ed admits that she has begun hormone therapy and after Jess learns that Ed has committed suicide.

Significantly, it is when Ed has begun to take hormones that she reiterates her initial suggestion that Jess read Du Bois. Feinberg leaves unspecified why Du Bois's text is relevant to this moment in Ed's transformation, but the novel implies that in the absence of her own ability to articulate her sense of pain and alienation, Ed borrows Du Bois's theory of "double consciousness" to express how she feels, insisting "I couldn't say it any better" (147). Without the existence of representations of an African American transgendered subjectivity, then, in Feinberg's text, Du Bois's words mediate Ed's self-understanding. Her reference to Du Bois at the moment when she has admitted taking hormones suggests that she is making an analogy between her double consciousness as a "Negro"/"American" and the split subjectivity that she experiences as a he-she, or transgendered subject. Yet it is also possible that Ed is expressing not her shared transgendered subjectivity with Jess but rather her very distance from Jess's position: it is precisely Ed's racial identity as African American that precludes her ever finding a resolution between the two "souls"—"American" and "Negro"—that abide within her, a resolution for which Jess, through the privilege of whiteness, holds out optimism.

Jess, however, does not actually read Du Bois's theory of double consciousness until later in the text, after she has learned of Ed's suicide. At this point, Feinberg quotes the Du Bois paragraph that Ed has carried in her wallet:

It is a peculiar sensation, this double-consciousness, this sense of always looking at one's self through the eyes of others, of measuring one's soul by the tape of a world that looks on in amused contempt and pity. One ever feels his twoness—an American, a Negro; two souls, two thoughts, two unreconciled strivings; two warring ideals in one dark body, whose dogged strength alone keeps it from being torn asunder.[12]

Narratively, the juxtaposition of Jess's knowledge of Ed's suicide and her reading of the Du Bois passage comes at a significant moment in the text: it occurs just after a scene in which Jess has undergone surgery for removal of her breasts, a moment when Jess's "twoness" has been reconciled, if only temporarily, in her body. This is the stage at which Jess has come closest to assimilating to a (white) male identity and to her idealized version of her own body:

> I stood up carefully. When I opened the closet door, I saw myself reflected in the full-length mirror mounted inside. I could tell from my beard growth I had slept for days. My chest was bandaged. There it was—the body I'd wanted. I wondered why it had to have been so hard. (177)

Immediately after this scene, Jess tries to telephone Ed but gets no answer. When she reaches Ed's sister, Jess learns that Ed shot herself weeks ago. The effect on Jess is a complete loss of her own subjectivity: "I went back to the bedroom and lost consciousness. When I woke, I hoped Edwin's death was just a dream" (177). We might consider why Jess's achievement of this idealized body image coincides with the demise of Ed and her removal from the narrative. Their coincidence seems even more weighty when we take into account Jess's expressions of guilt: " 'Ed,' I cried out loud. 'Please come back. Give me another chance to understand. I'll be a better friend if you'll just come back' " (178). According to the logic of this narrative, Jess's access to a position of normative white masculinity is achieved at the expense of her friend Ed, whose African American identity ensures that she will never be able to obtain the same position of privilege. Further, via her suicide, Ed is positioned in a conventionally tragic narrative, one that, by implication, racializes Jess's own seemingly heroic attainment of masculinity.[13] Jess's guilt, therefore, might be born of her implicit awareness that, in her own search for a stable, normative position of power, she has disaffiliated from Ed and her seemingly inevitable alienation from racially unmarked categories of masculine privilege.

Jess, of course, eventually refuses the cultural imperatives to become either a man or a woman: she stops taking hormones and gradually extricates herself from her own narrative of passing (as a man). It is no coincidence that the figure of Ed returns to the narrative one last time at the moment of Jess's affirmative emergence into public space and language as a transgendered subject. After Jess leaves the stage at the public rally, she is approached by a "young butch" who "reminded me so much of my old friend Edwin that for just a split second I thought Ed had come back to life to give me another shot at friendship" (297). The fantasized figure of Ed thus reemerges at a moment when Jess presumably renounces the privileges attached to dominant white masculinity and instead seeks to reidentify with the "double-consciousness" embodied by Ed. Jess misrecognizes a reincarnated Ed in the figure of the "young butch," a fantasy that expresses Jess's wish that, through her own affirmation of her transgendered status, she might transform Ed's tragic narrative into a heroic one. This spectral return of Ed reveals the ways in which an embodied racialized subject becomes constitutive of Jess's (and Feinberg's) ability to imagine and articulate a transgendered subject. Feinberg's novel is only one of a number of recent texts attempting to narrate and theorize transgendered subjectivity and is not necessarily representative of all this work. As one of the most powerful attempts to articulate transgender identity, however, it demonstrates how discourses of race have been available and indeed instrumental in providing a language and conceptual framework for this relatively recent model of embodied subjectivity.

The previous chapters of this book have shown that emerging models of homo- and heterosexuality at the turn of the twentieth century were embedded within discourses of race and racialization, particularly bifurcated constructions of "black" and "white" bodies. At our own century's turn, speaking optimistically, public contestations of identity, such as the 2000 census or Feinberg's novel, suggest that we live in a moment of vigorous suspicion about naturalized categories of bodies. However, as I have emphasized, it is important to note that the denaturalization of one identity category is often achieved through a renaturalization of another category. Current contestations over race, gender, and sexuality enact a productive search for new language and models of subjectivity. At the same time, the affirmative potential of these debates may be at risk if the analogies that enable that denaturalization are left uninterrogated.

The specific ways in which constructions of race and sexuality are linked and deployed are unpredictable and contradictory within any particular text or historical context. At the risk of unraveling the careful historicization that I have pursued throughout this book, I offer these concluding speculations as a gesture toward the kinds of readings and analyses that my guiding questions make possible. My purpose has been to shift critical attention and practices of reading toward a methodology that foregrounds the inextricability of constructions of race and sexuality, and that places both at the focus of inquiry, rather than at the periphery of our critical vision.

Appendix

A Florida Enchantment (Vitagraph, 1914)
CAST

The text of the cast list is taken from the film's title captions.

Dr. Fred Cassadene, young doctor
for summer and winter hotels . . . . Sidney Drew

Miss Lillian Travers, a young northern heiress . . . . Edith Storey

Major Horton, who believes in the New South, civilly . . . . Charles Kent

Bessie Horton, a Florida flower who
does not wish to blush unseen . . . . Jane Morrow[1]

Mrs. Stella Lovejoy, a fashionable New York widow . . . . Ada Gifford

Jane, Miss Travers' mulatto maid . . . . Ethel Lloyd[2]

Malvina, colored maid to Constancia . . . . Lillian Burns

Miss Constancia Oglethorpe, Miss Travers' aunt,
a Florida maiden of mature years . . . . Grace Stevens

Mr. Stockton Remington, a hunter after
fossils and phosphates . . . . Allan Campbell

Charley Wilkes, an orange grower . . . . Cortland van Deusen

Gustavus Duncan, porter at hotel . . . . Frank O'Neil

1 Jane Morrow was the stage name of Lucille McVey, who was married to actor and director Sidney Drew.
2 The black characters—Jane, as well as two other servants, Malvina and Gus—are played by white actors in black makeup. In his brief criticism of *A Florida Enchantment* in *Slow Fade to Black: The Negro in American Film, 1900–1942* (New York: Oxford University Press, 1977; reprint, 1993), Thomas Cripps states that the film included "a single actual Negro" (24) but has been unable to identify this character or actor's name. Personal correspondence with the author, August, 1994.

SYNOPSIS

The movie begins in St. Augustine, Florida, with the arrival of Lillian Travers (played by Edith Storey), a New York heiress who has just received her inheritance. She arrives at her aunt's house along with her "mulatto maid" Jane (Ethel Lloyd). Lillian has come to Florida to make a surprise visit to her fiancé, Fred Cassadene (Sidney Drew), the house doctor at the luxurious Ponce de León Hotel. When she arrives at the hotel, however, Lillian's surprise is ruined: she catches Fred flirting with another woman and becomes furious. After exchanging a few passionate words, however, Fred and Lillian quickly make up, and he promises to visit her later that day.

In the meantime, Lillian goes shopping with her best friend, Bessie (Jane Morrow). In an old curiosity shop, Lillian discovers a mysterious hundred-year-old wooden box that looks very familiar to her. It turns out to be an exact duplicate of one owned by Lillian's aunt. Happily, she buys the box and carries it home. Waiting carefully until she is alone, Lillian opens the box and finds inside a note and a vial containing four mysterious seeds. The vial is labeled simply "For Women Who Suffer." Written by Hauser Oglethorpe, who happens to be one of Lillian's ancestors, the note explains how he carried these magical seeds back from a "Sex-Change Tree" in Africa.

Meanwhile, Lillian receives note after note from Fred postponing their date. Exasperated, she eyes the old wooden box, throws back her head in defiance, and swallows one of the seeds. Immediately she feels its effects and begins to swagger around the house, brusquely discarding the flowers that Fred had sent to appease her. Lillian thus begins the first stage of her transformation: she continues to dress as a woman but ostensibly is becoming biologically male. This biological change becomes physically visible the following morning, when Lillian discovers that she has grown a mustache overnight. After her initial shock, she sits down before her mirror, lathers up, and shaves off the telltale stubble. Although Lillian still dresses in women's clothes, she has trouble controlling the new desires that have accompanied her sex change. Fred finally comes to visit that morning, but Lillian ignores him, preferring instead to flirt with her friend Bessie, whom she eagerly and romantically kisses hello and good-bye.

Now that Lillian is becoming a man, she decides that she will need a male valet instead of a maid. She corners Jane and forces her to eat one of the seeds also. The seed's effect is more exaggerated on Jane than on Lillian: Jane at once becomes violent and begins to tear through the house. Her explosive behavior alarms the white family; Bessie's father nearly shoots Jane, but Lillian instead knocks her out temporarily with chloroform.

When things calm down, Lillian decides to take a trip back to New York and to return to Florida as a man. On the evening of her farewell party, Lillian, still dressed in women's clothes, dances and flirts passionately with Bessie. Behind the scenes, Jane is also flirting, rivaling Gus Duncan for the attention of the maid Malvina. Unlike Bessie, though, who adores Lillian, Malvina has no intention of returning Jane's desire. She runs from Jane and calls the police for help. Making her getaway, Jane disguises herself in men's clothes and successfully evades the police.

The next morning, Lillian and Jane return to New York, where they quickly purchase men's clothes and transform themselves completely. The film titles reintroduce them as "Mr. Lawrence Talbot" and his valet "Jack." Soon they return as men to Florida and reintroduce themselves to their previous circle of friends. Lawrence and Bessie seem to fall immediately in love, and after some ardent flirting, Lawrence proposes marriage.

Fred, suspicious of this new bachelor, begins to link Lawrence to the mysterious disappearance of Lillian. When Fred accuses Lawrence of murdering her to get her money, Bessie's father suggests that the only way to resolve the matter is through a duel. Alarmed that the game has spiraled out of control, Lawrence privately confesses "the secret of the seeds" to Fred. In disbelief, Fred himself eats one of the seeds and begins to experience his own sex change: he suddenly becomes effeminate, curling his hair and shyly averting his eyes. Lawrence merely laughs at the results.

The movie accelerates toward its ending at the scene of the duel, which turns into a full-blown farce when Fred shows up in a dress. When he tries to charm the male bystanders, they respond violently and chase Fred through the city and off a pier into the ocean. Just as Fred begins to sink into the water and drown, the film cuts back to Lillian fast asleep in her aunt's house. She awakens with a start to discover that the entire farce has been a dream. Her fiancé arrives at that very moment, and the film ends with their embrace.

Notes

Introduction

1   Otto Olsen, *The Thin Disguise: Turning Point in Negro History* (New York: AIMS, 1967), 14, 69.

2   For a compelling discussion of this case, see Eric Sundquist, "Mark Twain and Homer Plessy," *Representations* 24 (fall 1988): 102–28.

3   On imperialism, see Hazel Carby, " 'On the Threshold of Woman's Era': Lynching, Empire, and Sexuality in Black Feminist Theory," *Critical Inquiry* 12 (autumn 1985): 262–77; and George Fredrickson, *The Black Image in the White Mind: The Debate on Afro-American Character and Destiny, 1817–1914* (New York: Harper and Row, 1971), 311. See also Amy Kaplan and Donald E. Pease, eds., *Cultures of United States Imperialism* (Durham, N.C.: Duke University Press, 1993). In *The Tragedy of Lynching* (Chapel Hill: University of North Carolina Press, 1933), Arthur F. Raper estimated that 3,724 lynchings occurred during this period (1).

4   On segregation, see C. Vann Woodward, *The Strange Career of Jim Crow,* 2d rev. ed. (New York: Oxford University Press, 1966). For a discussion of the states' efforts to strengthen antimiscegenation legislation and its culmination in laws such as Virginia's so-called Racial Integrity Act of 1924, see Walter Wadlington, "The *Loving* Case: Virginia's Anti-Miscegenation Statute in Historical Perspective," *Virginia Law Review* 52 (1966): 1195–1202.

5   For an excellent discussion of the Mitchell-Ward case, see Lisa Duggan, "The Trials of Alice Mitchell: Sensationalism, Sexology, and the Lesbian Subject in Turn-of-the-Century America," *Signs* 18 (summer 1993): 791–814.

6   Wilde was prosecuted under clause 9, section xi of the Criminal Law Amendment Act of 1885: "Any male person who, in public or private, commits, or is a party to the commission of, or procures or attempts to procure the commission by any male person of, any act of gross indecency with another male person, shall be guilty of a misdemeanour, and being convicted thereof, shall be liable, at the discretion of the Court,

to be imprisoned for any term not exceeding two years with or without hard labour" (quoted in *Oscar Wilde: Three Times Tried* [London: Ferrestone Press, n.d.], 136). An attempt to prohibit "acts of gross indecency" between "female persons" did not occur until 1921 in the English Parliament, but it was rejected by the House of Lords (Denise Thompson, *Flaws in the Social Fabric: Homosexuals and Society in Sydney* [Boston: George Allen and Unwin, 1985], 78).

7   Richard Ellman, *Oscar Wilde* (New York: Vintage, 1987), 438. Wilde died in 1900 soon after completing this sentence, which left him physically and psychologically debilitated.

8   Thomas Beer, *The Mauve Decade* (1926), 129. Cited in Richard Ellman, *Oscar Wilde,* 548.

9   See, for instance, Michel Foucault, *The History of Sexuality,* vol. 1 (New York: Vintage, 1980); George Chauncey, "From Sexual Inversion to Homosexuality: Medicine and the Changing Conceptualization of Female Deviance," *Salmagundi* 58–59 (fall–winter 1982): 114–46; Jeffrey Weeks, *Sex, Politics, and Society: The Regulation of Sexuality since 1800* (London: Longman, 1981); and David Halperin, "Is There a History of Sexuality?" in *The Lesbian and Gay Studies Reader,* ed. Henry Abelove, Michèle Aina Barale, and David M. Halperin (New York: Routledge, 1993), 416–31. On the invention of the classification of heterosexuality, see Jonathan Katz, "The Invention of Heterosexuality," *Socialist Review* 20 (1990): 17–34. For a related and intriguing argument that locates the earlier emergence of hierarchies of reproductive over nonreproductive sexual activity, see Henry Abelove, "Some Speculations on the History of 'Sexual Intercourse' during the 'Long Eighteenth Century' in England," *Genders* 6 (1989): 125–30.

10 Foucault, *The History of Sexuality,* vol. 1, 43.

11 Eve Sedgwick, *Epistemology of the Closet* (Berkeley: University of California Press, 1990), 1.

12 W. E. B. Du Bois, *The Souls of Black Folk* (1903; reprint, New York: Penguin, 1989), 1.

13 Biddy Martin, "Sexualities without Gender and Other Queer Utopias," *Diacritics* 24 (summer–fall 1994): 110.

14 A few examples of this extensive body of scholarship include bell hooks, *Ain't I a Woman: Black Women and Feminism* (Boston: South End Press, 1981); Hazel V. Carby, *Reconstructing Womanhood: The Emergence of the Afro-American Woman Novelist* (New York: Oxford University Press, 1987); Valerie Smith, "Reading the Intersection of Race and Gender in Narratives of Passing," *Diacritics* 24 (1994): 43–57; Gail Bederman, *Manliness and Civilization: A*

Cultural History of Gender and Race in the United States, 1880–1917 (Chicago: University of Chicago Press, 1995); and Robyn Wiegman, *American Anatomies: Theorizing Race and Gender* (Durham, N.C.: Duke University Press, 1995).

15 Kobena Mercer and Isaac Julien, "Race, Sexual Politics, and Black Masculinity: A Dossier," in *Male Order: Unwrapping Masculinity,* ed. Rowena Chapman and Jonathan Rutherford (London: Lawrence and Wishart, 1988), 106. Other scholars, such as Abdul R. JanMohamed and Ann Stoler, have offered useful analyses and critiques of the position of racial discourses in Foucault's formulations of the history of sexuality. See Abdul R. Jan-Mohamed, "Sexuality on/of the Racial Border: Foucault, Wright, and the Articulation of 'Racialized Sexuality,' " in *Discourses of Sexuality: From Aristotle to AIDS,* ed. Domna C. Stanton (Ann Arbor: University of Michigan Press, 1992), 94–116; and Ann Laura Stoler, *Race and the Education of Desire: Foucault's History of Sexuality and the Colonial Order of Things* (Durham, N.C.: Duke University Press, 1995).

16 Houston Baker has written that when Black studies was initially formulated in the academy, it was committed "to undoing all prevalent 'authentic' notions of such disciplines as history and English" (*Black Studies, Rap, and the Academy* [Chicago: University of Chicago Press, 1993], 13). Baker's statement is useful because it challenges the usual view that Black studies was concerned primarily with establishing its *own* authenticity. Instead Baker points to the ways in which Black studies' very existence implicitly challenged the seemingly "natural" status of epistemological assumptions of established disciplines.

17 I borrow this phrase from Willa Cather's essay "The Novel Démeublé," in *Not Under Forty* (New York: Knopf, 1922), 50.

18 On interpellation, see Louis Althusser, "Ideology and Ideological State Apparatuses (Notes towards an Investigation) (1969)," in *Lenin and Philosophy and Other Essays,* trans. Ben Brewster (New York: Monthly Review Press, 1971), 121–73.

19 See Carl Degler, *Neither Black nor White: Slavery and Race Relations in Brazil and the United States* (New York: Macmillan, 1971; reprint, Madison: University of Wisconsin Press, 1986).

20 On the production of "whiteness," see, among others, David R. Roediger, *The Wages of Whiteness: Race and the Making of the American Working Class* (New York: Verso, 1991); Ruth Frankenberg, *White Women, Race Matters: The Social Construction of Whiteness* (Minneapolis: University of Minnesota Press, 1993); Michael Rogin, *Blackface, White Noise: Jewish Immigrants and*

the Hollywood Melting Pot (Berkeley: University of California Press, 1995); and Richard Dyer, *White* (New York: Routledge, 1997).

21   Michael Omi and Howard Winant, *Racial Formation in the United States: From the 1960s to the 1980s* (New York: Routledge, 1986), 64.

22   See, for example, Lowell Tong, "Comparing Mixed-Race and Same-Sex Marriage," in *On the Road to Same-Sex Marriage: A Supportive Guide to Psychological, Political, and Legal Issues,* ed. Robert P. Cabaj and David W. Purcell (San Francisco: Josey-Bass, 1998), 109–27; and Andrew Koppelman, "The Miscegenation Precedents," in *Same-Sex Marriage: Pro and Con,* ed. Andrew Sullivan (New York: Vintage, 1997), 335–42.

23   bell hooks, *Talking Back: Thinking Feminist, Thinking Black* (Boston: South End Press, 1989), 125.

24   Albion Tourgée, "Brief for Homer A. Plessy" (1895), in Olsen, *The Thin Disguise,* 98, Tourgée's italics.

25   This famous line originated in a poem written by Lord Alfred Douglas to Wilde, quoted in *Oscar Wilde: Three Times Tried,* 271.

26   Neil Bartlett, *Who Was That Man? A Present for Mr. Oscar Wilde* (London: Serpent's Tail, 1988), 149, Bartlett's italics.

27   Ellman, *Oscar Wilde,* 476.

28   Tourgée, "Brief for Homer A. Plessy" (1895), 83. In a recent discussion of the case, Amy Robinson has deftly unpacked Tourgée's mistaken logic of identity as property. See her "Forms of Appearance of Value: Homer Plessy and the Politics of Privacy," in *Performance and Cultural Politics,* ed. Elin Diamond (New York: Routledge, 1996), 237–61.

29   Stuart Hall, "Race, Articulation, and Societies Structured in Dominance," in *Sociological Theories: Race and Colonialism* (Paris: UNESCO, 1980), 342.

30   For the most important feminist analyses of Hopkins, see Carby, *Reconstructing Womanhood;* Ann duCille, *The Coupling Convention: Sex, Text, and Tradition in Black Women's Fiction* (New York: Oxford University Press, 1993); and Claudia Tate, *Domestic Allegories of Political Desire: The Black Heroine's Text at the Turn of the Century* (New York: Oxford University Press, 1992). See also *The Unruly Voice: Rediscovering Pauline Elizabeth Hopkins,* ed. John Cullen Gruesser (Urbana and Chicago: University of Illinois Press, 1996).

31   Joel Williamson, *New People: Miscegenation and Mulattoes in the United States* (New York: Free Press, 1980), 103.

32   See Lisa Lowe, *Immigrant Acts: On Asian American Cultural Politics* (Durham, N.C.: Duke University Press, 1996); and Sander L. Gilman, *Freud, Race, and Gender* (Princeton, N.J.: Princeton University Press, 1993).

1 Scientific Racism and the Invention of the Homosexual Body

1 Havelock Ellis and John Addington Symonds, *Studies in the Psychology of Sex,* vol. 1, *Sexual Inversion* (London: Wilson and Macmillan, 1897; reprint, New York: Arno, 1975), x, italics mine. Ellis originally coauthored *Sexual Inversion* with John Addington Symonds. For a discussion of their collaboration and the eventual erasure of Symonds from the text, see Wayne Koestenbaum, *Double Talk: The Erotics of Male Literary Collaboration* (New York: Routledge, 1989), 43–67.

2 See Michel Foucault, *The History of Sexuality,* vol. 1 (New York: Vintage, 1980); George Chauncey, "From Sexual Inversion to Homosexuality: Medicine and the Changing Conceptualization of Female Deviance," *Salmagundi* 58–59 (fall–winter 1982): 114–46; and Vernon A. Rosario, ed. *Science and Homosexualities* (New York: Routledge, 1997).

3 Chauncey, "From Sexual Inversion to Homosexuality."

4 David Halperin has briefly and provocatively suggested that "all scientific inquiries into the aetiology of sexual orientation, after all, spring from a more or less implicit theory of sexual races, from the notion that there exist broad general divisions between types of human beings corresponding, respectively, to those who make a homosexual and those who make a heterosexual object-choice. When the sexual racism underlying such inquiries is more plainly exposed, their rationale will suffer proportionately—or so one may hope" ("Homosexuality: A Cultural Construct," in *One Hundred Years of Homosexuality: And Other Essays on Greek Love* [New York: Routledge, 1990], 50).

5 In *Disorders of Desire: Sex and Gender in Modern American Sexology* (Philadelphia: Temple University Press, 1990), Janice Irvine notes that for example, "the invisibility of Black people in sexology as subjects or researchers has undermined our understanding of the sexuality of Black Americans and continues to be a major problem in modern sexology." She adds that Kinsey, the other major sexologist of the twentieth century, planned to include a significant proportion of African American case histories in his *Sexual Behavior in the Human Male* (1948) and *Sexual Behavior in the Human Female* (1953) but failed to gather a sufficient number of them, and so "unwittingly colluded in the racial exclusion so pervasive in sex research" (43).

6 My use of the concept of ideology draws on Barbara Fields, "Slavery, Race, and Ideology in the United States of America," *New Left Review* 181 (1990): 95–118; Louis Althusser, "Ideology and Ideological State Apparatuses (Notes towards an Investigation)," in *Lenin and Philosophy and Other*

Essays, trans. Ben Brewster (New York: Monthly Review Press, 1971), 121–73; and Teresa de Lauretis, "The Technology of Gender," in *Technologies of Gender: Essays on Theory, Film, and Fiction* (Bloomington: Indiana University Press, 1987), 1–30.

7   John D'Emilio, *Sexual Politics, Sexual Communities: The Making of a Homosexual Minority in the United States, 1940–1970* (Chicago: University of Chicago Press, 1983), 18–19.

8   [Dr. Richard] von Krafft-Ebing, "Perversion of the Sexual Instinct: Report of Cases," translated by H. M. Jewett, *Alienist and Neurologist* 9, no. 4 (October 1888): 565–81. For an extract of this article, see Jonathan Ned Katz, *Gay/Lesbian Almanac: A New Documentary* (1983; reprint, New York: Carroll and Graf, 1994), 205–8.

9   See Katz, *Gay/Lesbian Almanac,* 146–47.

10 Ibid., 147.

11 Phyllis Grosskurth, *Havelock Ellis: A Biography* (New York: Knopf, 1980), 196–97.

12 Havelock Ellis, "Sexual Inversion in Women," *Alienist and Neurologist* 16, no. 2 (April 1895): 141–58.

13 Havelock Ellis, *Studies in the Psychology of Sex,* vol. 2, *Sexual Inversion,* 3d ed. (Philadelphia: F. A. Davis, 1915). Hereafter cited in the text unless otherwise stated. Although *Sexual Inversion* was published originally as volume 1, Ellis changed its position to volume 2 in the second and third editions, published in the United States in 1901 and 1915, respectively. In the later editions, volume 1 became *The Evolution of Modesty.*

14 In "Sex and the Emergence of Sexuality," *Critical Inquiry* 14 (autumn 1987): 16–48, Arnold I. Davidson characterizes Ellis's method as "psychiatric" (as opposed to "anatomical") reasoning.

15 Ellis, *Sexual Inversion* (1900), xi.

16 For further discussion of Ellis's similarity to Charles Darwin as a naturalist and their mutual interest in "natural" modesty, see Ruth Bernard Yeazell, "Nature's Courtship Plot in Darwin and Ellis," *Yale Journal of Criticism* 2 (1989): 33–53.

17 See Jeffrey Weeks, "Havelock Ellis and the Politics of Sex Reform," in Sheila Rowbotham and Jeffrey Weeks, *Socialism and the New Life: The Personal and Sexual Politics of Edward Carpenter and Havelock Ellis* (London: Pluto Press, 1977), 154; and Grosskurth, *Havelock Ellis,* 191–204.

18 Grosskurth, *Havelock Ellis,* 186.

19 F. O. Matthiessen to Russell Cheney, 5 November 1924. Reprinted in Katz, *Gay/Lesbian Almanac,* 414.

20 Reprinted in Katz, *Gay/Lesbian Almanac,* 414–15. Katz provides consider-

able evidence of the range of Carpenter's influence in the United States. He quotes responses to Carpenter's writing from novelist Jack London, a university language instructor, a music teacher, and anonymous readers in Detroit, as well as reviews in medical and academic publications. See Katz, *Gay/Lesbian Almanac*, 349, 430, 433, 395–97, 429, 354.

21 Edward Carpenter, "The Homogenic Attachment," in *Selected Writings*, vol. 1, *Sex* (London: GMP, 1984), 209.

22 Katz, *Gay/Lesbian Almanac*, 414.

23 Chauncey, "From Sexual Inversion to Homosexuality."

24 On the reception of Freud's theories of homosexuality in the United States, see Henry Abelove, "Freud, Male Homosexuality, and the Americans," in *The Lesbian and Gay Studies Reader*, ed. Henry Abelove, Michèle Aina Barale, and David M. Halperin (New York: Routledge, 1993), 381–93; and Erin G. Carlston, "'A Finer Differentiation': Female Homosexuality and the American Medical Community, 1926–1940," in Rosario, *Science and Homosexualities*, 177–96.

25 Eve Sedgwick, *Epistemology of the Closet* (Berkeley: University of California Press, 1990), 44–48, 86–87.

26 Sander Gilman, *Freud, Race, and Gender* (Princeton, N.J.: Princeton University Press, 1993), 6.

27 Lisa Duggan, "The Trials of Alice Mitchell: Sensationalism, Sexology, and the Lesbian Subject in Turn-of-the-Century America," *Signs* 18 (summer 1993): 791–814.

28 Classic discussions of the term's history include Peter I. Rose, *The Subject Is Race* (New York: Oxford University Press, 1968), 30–43; and Thomas F. Gossett, *Race: The History of an Idea in America* (Dallas: Southern Methodist University Press, 1963). For a history of various forms and theories of biological determinism, see Stephen Jay Gould, *The Mismeasure of Man* (New York: W. W. Norton, 1981).

29 My discussion of monogeny and polygeny draws heavily on George M. Fredrickson, *The Black Image in the White Mind: The Debate on Afro-American Character and Destiny, 1817–1914* (1971; reprint, Hanover, N.H.: Wesleyan University Press, 1987), 71–96; and Gould, *The Mismeasure of Man*, 30–72.

30 Fredrickson, *The Black Image*, 74.

31 John S. Haller Jr., *Outcasts from Evolution: Scientific Attitudes of Racial Inferiority, 1859–1900* (Urbana: University of Illinois Press, 1971), 4.

32 Quoted in Haller, *Outcasts*, 196. On Cope, see also Gould, *The Mismeasure of Man*, 115–18.

33 Nancy Leys Stepan and Sander Gilman, "Appropriating the Idioms of Science: The Rejection of Scientific Racism," in *The Bounds of Race: Perspectives*

on Hegemony and Resistance, ed. Dominick LaCapra (Ithaca, N.Y.: Cornell University Press, 1991), 74.

34   Fields, "Slavery, Race, and Ideology," 97 n. 3.

35   Haller, *Outcasts,* 48.

36   See Nancy Stepan, *The Idea of Race in Science: Great Britain, 1800–1960* (Hamden, Conn.: Archon Books, 1982), 53.

37   Gould, *The Mismeasure of Man,* 114.

38   Ibid., 115.

39   *Lectures on Man* (1864); quoted in Gould, *The Mismeasure of Man,* 103.

40   Robyn Wiegman, *American Anatomies: Theorizing Race and Gender* (Durham, N.C.: Duke University Press, 1995), 53.

41   Elsewhere in *Sexual Inversion,* Ellis entertained the idea that certain races or nationalities had a "special proclivity" to homosexuality (4), but he seemed to recognize the nationalistic impulse behind this argument and chided those who wielded it: "The people of every country have always been eager to associate sexual perversions with some other country than their own" (57–58).

42   Sander Gilman, *Difference and Pathology: Stereotypes of Sexuality, Race, and Madness* (Ithaca, N.Y.: Cornell University Press, 1985); Nancy Stepan, "Race and Gender: The Role of Analogy in Science," in *The Anatomy of Racism,* ed. David Theo Goldberg (Minneapolis: University of Minnesota Press, 1990), 38–57; and Londa Schiebinger, *Nature's Body: Gender in the Making of Modern Science* (Boston: Beacon, 1993).

43   Gilman, *Difference and Pathology,* 112.

44   According to Gilman, "When one turns to autopsies of black males from [the late nineteenth century], what is striking is the absence of any discussion of the male genitalia" (89).

45   The *American Journal of Obstetrics* (*AJO*) was a frequent forum for these debates. On the position of the hymen, for example, see C. H. Fort, "Some Corroborative Facts in Regard to the Anatomical Difference between the Negro and White Races," *AJO* 10 (1877): 258–59; H. Otis Hyatt, "Note on the Normal Anatomy of the Vulvo-Vaginal Orifice," *AJO* 10 (1877): 253–58; A. G. Smythe, "The Position of the Hymen in the Negro Race," *AJO* 10 (1877): 638–39; Edward Turnipseed, "Some Facts in Regard to the Anatomical Differences between the Negro and White Races," *AJO* 10 (1877): 32–33. On the birth canal, see Joseph Taber Johnson, "On Some of the Apparent Peculiarities of Parturition in the Negro Race, with Remarks on Race Pelves in General," *AJO* 8 (1875): 88–123.

      This focus on women's bodies apparently differed from earlier studies. See Schiebinger, *Nature's Body,* esp. 143–83.

46 W. H. Flower and James Murie, "Account of the Dissection of a Bush-woman," *Journal of Anatomy and Physiology* 1 (1867): 208. Hereafter cited in the text. For brief discussions of this account, see Gilman, *Difference and Pathology*, 88–89; and Anita Levy, *Other Women: The Writing of Class, Race, and Gender, 1832–1898* (Princeton, N.J.: Princeton University Press, 1991), 70–72.

47 Georges Cuvier, "Extraits d'observations faites sur le cadavre d'une femme connue à Paris et à Londres sous le nom de Vénus Hottentote," *Mémoires du Musée d'histoire naturelle* 3 (1817): 259–74. On Baartman, see Schiebinger, *Nature's Body*, 160–72, and Stephen Jay Gould, *The Flamingo's Smile* (New York: Norton, 1985), 291–305.

48 Richard von Krafft-Ebing, *Psychopathia Sexualis*, 12th ed., trans. Franklin S. Klaf (1902; reprint, New York: Putnam, 1965).

49 This practice continued well into the twentieth century. See, for example, Jennifer Terry, "Lesbians under the Medical Gaze: Scientists Search for Re-markable Differences," *Journal of Sex Research* 27 (August 1990): 317–39; and "Theorizing Deviant Historiography," *Differences* 3 (summer 1991): 55–74.

50 On the history of this association, see Valerie Traub, "The Psychomorph-ology of the Clitoris," *GLQ* 2 (1995): 81–113; and Margaret Gibson, "Cli-toral Corruption: Body Metaphors and American Doctors' Constructions of Female Homosexuality, 1870–1900," in Rosario, *Science and Homosexu-alities*, 108–32.

  In the first edition of *Sexual Inversion*, Ellis, who did search the lesbian body for masculine characteristics, nevertheless refuted this claim about the clitoris: "There is no connection, as was once supposed, between sexual inversion in women and an enlarged clitoris" (98).

51 Perry M. Lichtenstein, "The 'Fairy' and the Lady Lover," *Medical Review of Reviews* 27 (1921): 372.

52 Morris, "Is Evolution Trying to Do Away with the Clitoris?" paper pre-sented at the meeting of the American Association of Obstetricians and Gynecologists, St. Louis, 21 September 1892, Yale University Medical Li-brary, New Haven, Conn.

53 See Hazel V. Carby, *Reconstructing Womanhood: The Emergence of the Afro-American Woman Novelist* (reprint, New York: Oxford University Press, 1987), 20–39; and Barbara Welter, "The Cult of True Womanhood, 1820–1860," in her *Dimity Convictions: The American Woman in the Nineteenth Cen-tury* (Columbus: University of Ohio Press, 1976), 21–41.

54 Havelock Ellis, *Man and Woman: A Study of Human Secondary Sexual Char-acters*, 4th ed. (1894; reprint, New York: Scribner's, 1911), 13. Of course, the "beginnings of industrialism" coincided with the late eighteenth century,

the period during which, as Schiebinger has shown, anatomists began looking for more subtle marks of differentiation. See Londa Schiebinger, *The Mind Has No Sex? Women in the Origins of Modern Science* (Cambridge: Harvard University Press, 1989), 189–212.

55   Patrick Geddes and J. Arthur Thomson, *The Evolution of Sex* (London: W. Scott, 1889; New York: Scribner, 1890), 80. Ellis no doubt read this volume closely, for he had chosen it to inaugurate a series of popular scientific books (the Contemporary Science Series) that he edited for the Walter Scott company. For more on this series, see Grosskurth, *Havelock Ellis*, 114–17.

56   Francis Galton, *Inquiries into Human Faculty and Its Development* (1883; reprint, New York: AMS Press, 1973), 17.

57   For a discussion of Roosevelt's place within the racial ideology of the period, see Thomas G. Dyer, *Theodore Roosevelt and the Idea of Race* (Baton Rouge: Louisiana State University Press, 1980). See also John Higham, *Strangers in the Land: Patterns of American Nativism, 1860–1925* (New Brunswick: Rutgers University Press, 1955; reprint, New York: Atheneum, 1963), 146–57.

58   Mark H. Haller, *Eugenics: Hereditarian Attitudes in American Thought* (New Brunswick, N.J.: Rutgers University Press, 1963), 144.

59   Edward Byron Reuter, *The Mulatto in the United States: Including a Study of the Role of Mixed-Blood Races throughout the World* (Boston: Gorham Press, 1918), 338.

60   Cited in *Eugenical News* 3 (February 1918): 14–15. Quoted in Haller, *Eugenics,* 148.

61   William Robinson, "My Views on Homosexuality," *American Journal of Urology* 10 (1914): 550–52. Quoted in Katz, *Gay/Lesbian Almanac,* 357–58.

62   See Vern Bullough, *Science in the Bedroom: A History of Sex Research* (New York: Basic Books, 1994), 49–62.

63   Jeffrey Weeks, *Sexuality and Its Discontents: Meanings, Myths, and Modern Sexualities* (Boston: Routledge and Kegan Paul, 1985), 76; Grosskurth, *Havelock Ellis,* 410. See also Havelock Ellis, "The Sterilization of the Unfit," *Eugenics Review* (October 1909): 203–6.

64   Haller, *Eugenics,* 18.

65   Quoted in Grosskurth, *Havelock Ellis,* 410.

66   Ellis and Symonds, *Sexual Inversion* (1897), 1 n.

67   Edward Carpenter, "The Homogenic Attachment," in *The Intermediate Sex: A Study of Some Transitional Types of Men and Women,* 5th ed. (London: George Allen and Unwin, 1918), 40 n.

68   Xavier Mayne [Edward Irenaeus Prime Stevenson], *The Intersexes: A History of Similisexualism as a Problem in Social Life* ([Naples?], ca. 1908; reprint, New York: Arno, 1975), 14.

69   Ibid., 15, 17.

70   Quoted in Carpenter, *The Intermediate Sex*, 133, 170. Carpenter gives the following citations for these quotations: Dr. James Burnet, *Medical Times and Hospital Gazette* 34, no. 1497 (London, 10 November 1906); and Charles G. Leland, *The Alternate Sex* (London: William Rider and Son, 1904), 57.

71   In *New People: Miscegenation and Mulattoes in the United States* (New York: Free Press, 1980), Joel Williamson suggests that a similar psychologization of race was underway by 1900 (108). See also Elazar Barkan, *The Retreat of Scientific Racism: Changing Concepts of Race in Britain and the United States between the World Wars* (New York: Cambridge University Press, 1992). On legal analogies between sodomy and miscegenation, see Andrew Koppelman, "The Miscegenation Analogy: Sodomy Law as Sex Discrimination," *Yale Law Journal* 98 (November 1988): 145–64; and Janet Halley, "The Politics of the Closet: Towards Equal Protection for Gay, Lesbian, and Bisexual Identity," *UCLA Law Review* 36 (1989): 915–76. I am grateful to Julia Friedlander for bringing this legal scholarship to my attention.

72   Margaret Otis, "A Perversion Not Commonly Noted," *Journal of Abnormal Psychology* 8 (June–July 1913): 113. Hereafter cited in the text.

73   Chauncey, in "From Sexual Inversion to Homosexuality," notes that "by the early teens the number of articles or abstracts concerning homosexuality regularly available to the American medical profession had grown enormously" (115 n. 3).

74   Kathryn Hinojosa Baker, "Delinquent Desire: Race, Sex, and Ritual in Reform Schools for Girls," *Discourse* 15, no. 1 (fall 1992): 53.

75   Editorial, *New Orleans Times Democrat,* 9 July 1890. Reprinted in Otto Olsen, *The Thin Disguise: Turning Point in Negro History* (New York: Humanities Press, 1967), 53.

76   Rich originally made these comments in a discussion following a conference paper by Teresa de Lauretis. See Teresa de Lauretis, "Film and the Visible," in *How Do I Look? Queer Film and Video,* ed. Bad Object-Choices (Seattle: Bay Press, 1991), 274–75.

77   B. Ruby Rich, "When Difference Is (More than) Skin Deep," in *Queer Looks: Perspectives on Lesbian and Gay Film and Video,* ed. Martha Gever, John Greyson, and Pratibha Parmar (New York: Routledge, 1993), 321.

78   Biddy Martin, "Sexualities without Genders and Other Queer Utopias," *Diacritics* 24 (summer–fall 1994): 114.

79 Ibid., 115.

80 Linda Nochlin, "The Imaginary Orient," *Art in America* 71 (May 1983): 126. Quoted in Rich, "When Difference Is (More than) Skin Deep," 321.

81 W. T. English, "The Negro Problem from the Physician's Point of View," *Atlanta Journal-Record of Medicine* 5 (October 1903): 468.

82 On the other hand, antilynching campaigns could also invoke the language of sexology. Although the analogy invoked sadism, rather than homosexuality, in 1935 a psychologist characterized lynching as a kind of "Dixie sex perversion . . . much that is commonly stigmatized as cruelty is a perversion of the sex instinct." Quoted in Phyllis Klotman, " 'Tearing a Hole in History': Lynching as Theme and Motif," *Black American Literature Forum* 19 (1985): 57. The original quote appeared in the *Baltimore Afro-American,* 16 March 1935.

83 "Edison's Vitascope Cheered," *New York Times,* 24 April 1896, 5. Quoted in Charles Musser, *Before the Nickelodeon: Edwin S. Porter and the Edison Manufacturing Company* (Berkeley: University of California Press, 1991), 60–61.

2   The Queer Career of Jim Crow: Racial and Sexual Transformation in Early Cinema

1 "Archibald Clavering Gunter," *The Bookman* 16 (October 1902): 103. This same critic admitted that although "[Gunter's] novels abound in anachronism, blunders, absurdities of every kind . . . he used to know what a good story was and the way to write one" (104–5).

2 Archibald Clavering Gunter and Fergus Redmond, *A Florida Enchantment* (New York: Hurst and Company, 1891). Hereafter cited in the text. A year later, in 1892, the Home Publishing Company, owned by Gunter himself, published the book.

Gunter (1847–1907), born in England and raised in the United States, began his career as a writer in the 1870s, after working for some time as a chemist, mine superintendent, and stockbroker. Gunter's early works included plays entitled *Found the True Vein* (1872) and *Prince Karl* (1886), which were produced in San Francisco and New York, respectively. In 1887 Gunter published his first and most famous novel, *Mr. Barnes of New York,* which was produced as a stage play a year later in New York. The novel, which follows the adventures of a wealthy young American in Europe, was immensely successful on publication by Gunter's own Home Publishing Company; it sold more than one million copies in the United States. Although Gunter and his best-seller have faded into obscurity, the character Mr. Barnes was described as "the most talked-of and sensational hero of a decade" by a reviewer in 1907.

Gunter wrote at least thirty-eight novels between 1887 and 1907, including *Mr. Potter of Texas* (1888), *That Frenchman* (1889), *Miss Nobody of Nowhere* (1890), *Baron Montez of Panama and Paris* (1893), *Don Balasco of Key West* (1896), and *The Power of Woman* (1897). The books were sold at $1.25 for hardcover and 50¢ for paperback. Despite (or perhaps because of) the books' disposability, Gunter was a successful entrepreneur in publishing. For a contemporary review of his books, see "The Return of Burton Barnes," *The Bookman* 25 (March 1907): 234–36. For biographical information on Gunter, see *Dictionary of American Biography,* ed. Dumas Malone, vol. 8 (New York: Charles Scribner's Sons, 1932), 54; and *National Cyclopaedia of American Biography,* vol. 15 (New York: James T. White and Co., 1916), 247. For information on Gunter's publishing company, see Jane I. Thesing, "Home Publishing Company," *Dictionary of Literary Biography,* vol. 49 (Detroit: Bruccoli Clark, 1986), 209.

Virtually no information is available on Fergus Redmond, Gunter's coauthor. There is no evidence that he ever collaborated again with Gunter after *A Florida Enchantment.*

3   I provide a full plot summary of the film version of *A Florida Enchantment* in the appendix.

4   Scott Simon, "Sex Change and Cross-Dressing in the Early Silent Film," program, San Francisco International Lesbian and Gay Film Festival (16–25 June 1989), 13.

5   James Robert Parish, *Gays and Lesbians in Mainstream Cinema: Plots, Critiques, Casts, and Credits for 272 Theatrical and Made-for-Television Hollywood Releases* (Jefferson, N.C.: McFarland and Company, 1993), viii.

6   Vito Russo, *The Celluloid Closet: Homosexuality in the Movies* (New York: Harper and Rowe, 1981), 11–13.

7   I borrow this phrase from Judith Butler, *Gender Trouble: Feminism and the Subversion of Identity* (New York: Routledge, 1990), a key text in discussions of gender and performativity.

8   See Thomas Cripps, *Slow Fade to Black: The Negro in American Film, 1900–1942* (New York: Oxford University Press, 1977), 24; and Daniel J. Leab, *From Sambo to Superspade: The Black Experience in Motion Pictures* (Boston: Houghton Mifflin, 1975), 16.

9   See Stuart Hall, "New Ethnicities," in *Black Film/British Cinema,* ed. Kobena Mercer (London: ICA, 1988); Homi K. Bhabha, "The 'Other' Question: The Stereotype and Colonial Discourse," *Screen* 24, no. 6 (winter

1983): 18–36; and Eric Lott, *Love and Theft: Blackface Minstrelsy and the American Working Class* (New York: Oxford University Press, 1993).

10   Hall, "New Ethnicities," 27.

11   My summary of this transition period relies on work by film historians, including Eileen Bowser, *The Transformation of Cinema* (New York: Scribner, 1990); David Bordwell, Janet Staiger, and Kristin Thompson, *The Classical Hollywood Cinema: Film Style and Mode of Production to 1960* (New York: Columbia University Press, 1985); and William Uricchio and Roberta E. Pearson, *Reframing Culture: The Case of the Vitagraph Quality Films* (Princeton, N.J.: Princeton University Press, 1993).

12   Tom Gunning, "Weaving a Narrative: Style and Economic Background in Griffith's Biograph Films," in *Early Cinema: Space, Frame, Narrative,* ed. Thomas Elsaesser (London: BFI, 1990), 338–39. Gunning's italics.

13   Ibid.

14   Anthony Slide, *The Big V: A History of the Vitagraph Company* (Metuchen, N.J.: Scarecrow Press, 1976), 8. One tactic in this attempt to attract middle-class audiences was Vitagraph's production of "quality films," which were based on biblical stories and literature by authors such as Shakespeare and Dante. For a full discussion of these films, see Uricchio and Pearson, *Reframing Culture.*

15   Cripps, *Slow Fade to Black,* 118.

16   Henry Jenkins, *What Made Pistachio Nuts? Early Sound Comedy and the Vaudeville Aesthetic* (New York: Columbia University Press, 1992), 81.

17   See "Sidney Drew One of First Actors of Established Reputation to Quit Legitimate Stage for Vaudeville," 16 September 1912, Sidney Drew scrapbook, ser. 2, vol. 135, Robinson Locke Collection, Billy Rose Theatre Collection, New York Public Library. A well-known instance of this practice was the formation of Famous Players in Famous Plays by Adolph Zukor, Jesse Lasky, and Cecil B. DeMille in 1914, which brought such famous stage actors as Sarah Bernhardt, Douglas Fairbanks, and Mary Pickford to film. See Lary May, *Screening Out the Past: The Birth of Mass Culture and the Motion Picture Industry* (New York: Oxford University Press, 1980), 175–76.

18   On the popularity of cross-dressing acts during this period, see Sharon Ullman, " 'The Twentieth Century Way': Female Impersonation and Sexual Practice in Turn-of-the-Century America," *Journal of the History of Sexuality* 5, no. 4 (1995): 577.

19   Richard Alan Nelson, "Movie Mecca of the South: Jacksonville, Florida, as an Early Rival to Hollywood," *Journal of Popular Film and Television* 8 (fall 1980): 40, 50–51.

20   Ibid., 43.

21   Ibid., 50–51.

22   Ibid.

23   "The Octoroon" [advertisement], *Moving Picture World* 4 (23 January 1909): 100.

24   "Made in Jacksonville Motion Picture Films," *Florida Times-Union,* 6 May 1914, sec. 4, p. 23.

25   Mark Derr, *Some Kind of Paradise: A Chronicle of Man and the Land in Florida* (New York: William Morrow, 1989), 22–23, 319.

26   William Foster, generally held to have been the first African American to establish a film production company, attempted to appeal to black audiences with films such as *The Railroad Porter* (1912) and *The Fall Guy* (1913). On Foster and the beginnings of African American film companies, see Mark A. Reid, *Redefining Black Film* (Berkeley: University of California Press, 1993), 7–18; Cripps, *Slow Fade to Black,* 70–89; and Henry T. Sampson, *Blacks in Black and White: A Source Book on Black Films* (Metuchen, N.J.: Scarecrow Press, 1977). The two other major African American film companies during the silent period were the Lincoln Motion Picture Company, established in 1916 in Los Angeles, and the film production company founded by novelist Oscar Micheaux in 1918. These early attempts, however successful initially, were unfortunately short-lived, and according to Reid, "black independent filmmaking was almost nonexistent by the late 1920s," because of a combination of higher production costs for sound films, white consolidation of control over distribution markets, and the effects of the Great Depression (*Redefining Black Film,* 15). Reid notes that although Oscar Micheaux retained his name in the Micheaux Film Corporation into the 1940s, in 1929 the company was bought by two white men (18).

　　　Other black-owned film companies during this period included Afro-American Film Company in New York City, Haynes Photoplay Company, Unique Film Company in Chicago, Barlett Film Company, Historical Feature Film Company, and the Jones Photoplay Company. See Gregory A. Waller, "Another Audience: Black Moviegoing, 1907–1916," *Cinema Journal* 31 (winter 1992): 2–25; and Reid, *Redefining Black Film,* 7–18.

27   Nelson, "Movie Mecca," 42.

28   Ibid.

29   "Colored Lubin Comedies," *Moving Picture World* 16 (10 May 1913): 600.

30   See Uricchio and Pearson, *Reframing Culture;* Slide, *The Big V;* Jenkins, *What Made Pistachio Nuts?;* and Peter Kramer, "Vitagraph, Slapstick, and Early Cinema," *Screen* 29, no. 2 (1988): 9–104.

31   F. H. Richardson, "The Home of the Vitagraph," *Moving Picture World* 19, no. 4 (24 January 1914): 401–2.

32   Quoted in May, *Screening Out the Past,* 186.

33   Einar Lauritzen and Gunnar Lundquist, eds., *American Film Index, 1908–1915* (Stockholm, Sweden: Film-Index, 1976).

34   Marguerite Bertsch, *How to Write for Moving Pictures: A Manual of Instruction and Information* (New York: George H. Doran, 1917). Hereafter cited in the text.

35   Slide, *The Big V,* 17. This characterization of the slippage between popular visual representations of Jews and African Americans is an early instance of a phenomenon discussed expertly and at length by Michael Rogin in "Blackface, White Noise: The Jewish Jazz Singer Finds His Voice," *Critical Inquiry* 18 (spring 1992): 417–53.

Blackton seems to have been particularly fascinated by physical transformation. In *Two Reels and a Crank* (Garden City, N.Y.: Doubleday, 1952), his partner Albert E. Smith recalled one of Blackton's early performances for the "elite citizenry" of White Plains, New York:

> Blackton's "Chalk Talk"—cartoons and black-and-white drawings at a large easel—was received with restrained courtesy but a surprised murmur greeted his appearance in the next number, programmed as "Mademoiselle Stuart" in "Lightning Landscape Painting." Blackton, a man of chesty physique, was neither decorative nor poised. He was encased in white tights and wore a morbid black wig fringed with a row of delicate rosebuds. More unfortunate still, little clusters of flesh-colored sequins formed at the points where Blackton's knotty arm and leg muscles bulged most, giving the effect of something conceived by a diabolical impressionist with a weakness for misplaced bosoms. The dowagers of White Plains viewed Blackton with cold contemptuous silence, found him particularly lacking in virility and charm despite his emotional gyrations at the easel. (29–30)

36   William Basil Courtney, "History of Vitagraph," *Motion Picture News* 31 (7 February 1925), 342c.

37   See May, *Screening Out the Past,* 167–99, 253. In fact, 1925 was the very year in which Warner Brothers would buy out Vitagraph studios.

38   *Athenaeum* 3745 (5 August 1899): 189.

39   The play was performed at Hoyt's Theatre and the Columbia Theatre. See programs dated 9 November 1896, 23 November 1896, and 30 November 1896, in clipping file, Billy Rose Theatre Collection, New York Public Library, Lincoln Center. In *"We Can Always Call Them Bulgarians": The*

Emergence of Lesbians and Gay Men on the American Stage (Boston: Alyson Publications, 1987), Kaier Curtin dates the debut to April 1896 (20).

40 Annie Russell, "The Theaters," *New York Times* (supplement), 18 October 1896, 10; "The Drama," *Critic* 765 (17 October 1896): 234; and "A Silly and Vulgar Play," *New York Times,* 13 October 1896, 5.

41 *Critic,* 234.

42 Gunter is quoted in "Mr. Gunter Can't See It," *New York Herald,* 14 October 1896, 14.

43 Laurence Senelick, "The Evolution of the Male Impersonator on the Nineteenth-Century Stage," *Essays in Theatre* 1 (1982): 38.

44 Lisa Duggan, "The Trials of Alice Mitchell: Sensationalism, Sexology, and the Lesbian Subject in Turn-of-the-Century America," *Signs* 18, no. 4 (summer 1993): 791–814.

45 Andrea Weiss, *Vampires and Violets: Lesbians in the Cinema* (London: Jonathan Cape, 1992), 17.

46 Ullman, "The Twentieth Century Way," 578 n. 9, 587.

47 Ibid., 577 n. 8. On the ideological uses of a negative portrayal of lesbians, see George Chauncey, "From Sexual Inversion to Homosexuality: Medicine and the Changing Conceptualization of Female Deviance," *Salmagundi* 58–59 (1982): 114–46; and Christina Simmons, "Companionate Marriage and the Lesbian Threat," *Frontiers* 4 (1979): 54–59.

48 Vitagraph Company of America, *Vitagraph Bulletin of Life Portrayals* 4 (1–30 September 1914): 6.

49 Justus Dickinson, "Putting One's Best Face Forward," *Green Book Magazine,* December 1914, 1016.

50 Ibid.

51 Edith Storey, "My Theories of Physical Culture," *Physical Culture* (September 1916): 76. See also "Queen of the Wild West Films," *St. Louis Globe Democrat,* 14 December 1913, n.p., in New York Public Library, Robinson Locke Collection, ser. 2 (Stevens-Stuart), 180–82.

52 Julian Johnson, "The Story of Storey," *Photoplay Magazine,* January 1920, 114.

53 "A Florida Enchantment," *New York Dramatic Mirror,* 19 August 1914, 26.

54 Sime, "A Florida Enchantment," *Variety,* 14 August 1914, 21.

55 Ibid., 22.

56 See Esther Newton, "The Mythic Mannish Lesbian: Radclyffe Hall and the New Woman," *Signs* 9, no. 4 (summer 1984): 557–75.

57 For contemporary descriptions of the dime museum, see J. G. Wood, "Dime Museums from a Naturalist's Point of View," *Atlantic Monthly* 55 (June 1885): 759–65; and William Dean Howells, "At a Dime Museum," in

Literature and Life: Studies (New York: Harper and Brothers, 1902), 193–201.
For more recent discussions, see Robert Bogdan, *Freak Show: Presenting
Human Oddities for Amusement and Profit* (Chicago: University of Chicago
Press, 1988), 35–39; Neil Harris, *Humbug: The Art of P. T. Barnum* (Chi-
cago: University of Chicago Press, 1973); Lott, *Love and Theft,* 75–78; and
Robert C. Allen, *Vaudeville and Film, 1895–1915: A Study in Media Interaction*
(Ph.D. diss., University of Iowa, 1977; reprint, New York: Arno Press,
1980), 32–34.

58   The Rothschild anecdote is reported in Harris, *Humbug,* 95. Bogdan includes a photo of J. W. Coffey, also known as "the Skeleton Dude," perhaps
not surprisingly posed with his black "valet." See Bogdan, *Freak Show,* 232.
See also the photo of Annie Jones, "the Bearded Lady," looking at her
reflection in a mirror, a pose echoed in the movie version of *A Florida
Enchantment* when Lillian first sees her mustache (225).
  Wood identifies "the Missing Link" as "Krao the little Burmese hairy
girl . . . another example of an abnormal race." See Wood, "The Dime
Museum," 762. Harris writes that "the Missing Link" (who was also marketed as "What Is It?") was played by William Henry Johnson, described
by Harris as "a deformed black dwarf called 'Zip' " (*Humbug,* 167).

59   Morris Robert Werner, *Barnum* (New York: Harcourt, Brace, 1923), 204.
Werner is cited in Lott, *Love and Theft,* 254 n. 29. Barnum promoted this
exhibit to take full advantage of the political controversies of the day; he
apparently "hailed this negro and his weed as the solution of the slavery
problem, contending in his advertisements that if all the negroes could be
turned white the problem of slavery would disappear with their color."
According to Werner, "the newspapers reported daily the progress of the
negro's change in color" (204).

60   Gunter eagerly participated in the business side of authorship. In an article
written for the *Writer,* a trade journal for "literary workers," Gunter outlined his strategies for developing his own publishing company. See Archibald C. Gunter, "Authors as Publishers," the *Writer* 14.10 (October 1901):
145–46.

61   In 1885, when the famous team of Edward Harrigan and Tony Hart dis-
solved, Collyer replaced Hart, regularly appearing in blackface and drag
roles. See William Torbert Leonard, *Masquerade in Black* (Metuchen, N.J.:
Scarecrow Press, 1986), 258, 285. Robert Toll, in *On with the Show: The First
Century of Show Business in America* (New York: Oxford University Press,
1976), includes an illustration of Collyer in blackface and drag as "Clara"
in Edward Harrigan's *McNooney's Visit* (188).

62   For a discussion of the interplay of blackface and drag on the minstrel stage, see Lott, *Love and Theft,* 159–68.

63   Robert C. Allen, *Horrible Prettiness: Burlesque and American Culture* (Chapel Hill: University of North Carolina Press, 1991), 165, 311 n. 10.

64   Ibid., 165.

65   Ibid., 16.

66   Ibid., 165.

67   Ibid., 292–93 n. 21.

68   For a useful attempt to theorize representations of whiteness in film, see Richard Dyer, *White* (New York: Routledge, 1997) and "White," *Screen* 29 (1988): 44–64. See also his perceptive discussion of Marilyn Monroe's racialized image in his *Heavenly Bodies* (London: Macmillan, 1986), 42–45.

69   On Tilley, see Sara Maitland, *Vesta Tilley* (London: Virago, 1986); and Senelick, "The Evolution of the Male Impersonator," 39–40. On Clifford, see "The Gentle Art of Being a Man: A Chat with Kathleen Clifford, 'The Smartest Chap in Town,'" *New York Dramatic Mirror,* 4 March 1914, 23. On both performers, see also *Selected Vaudeville Criticism,* ed. Anthony Slide (Metuchen, N.J.: Scarecrow Press, 1988), 52–53, 183–85.

70   See Slide, *Selected Vaudeville Criticism,* 63–71. The Duncan Sisters' performance is preserved on film: *Topsy and Eva* (1927), Library of Congress, Motion Picture, Broadcasting, and Recorded Sound Division, Washington, D.C.

71   Sophie Tucker, *Some of These Days: The Autobiography of Sophie Tucker* (Garden City, N.Y.: Doubleday, Doran, 1945), 33–42. On Tanguay, see Douglas Gilbert, *American Vaudeville: Its Life and Times* (1940; reprint, New York: Dover, 1963), 329.

72   Cripps, *Slow Fade to Black,* 12, 393 n. 16.

73   Tom Gunning, "The Cinema of Attractions: Early Film, Its Spectator and the Avant-Garde," *Wide Angle* 8 (1986): 63–70; reprinted in *Early Cinema: Space, Frame, Narrative,* ed. Thomas Elsaesser with Adam Barker (London: BFI, 1990), 56–62. Gunning explains that the "cinema of attractions directly solicits spectator attention, inciting visual curiosity, and supplying pleasure through an exciting spectacle—a unique event, whether fictional or documentary, that is of interest in itself" (58).

74   Ibid., 60.

75   May, *Screening Out the Past,* 83. Gender seems to have circumscribed filmic conventions for the use of blackface as well. Although this area needs further research, it is suggestive that in Leonard's list of 145 white actors and actresses who appeared in blackface in film, only one of the blackface roles

was also a cross-dressed performance (*Masquerade in Black,* 371). The actor was Nick Cogley, who played "Aunt Mandy" in *Boys Will Be Boys* (1921).

76   Cripps, *Slow Fade to Black,* 118.

77   Norma Talmadge, "Close-Ups" (1927), in *The American Film Industry,* ed. Tino Balio (Madison: University of Wisconsin Press, 1976), 98–99.

78   For a discussion of early-twentieth-century stereotypes of black masculinity, see Jacquelyn Dowd Hall, *Revolt against Chivalry: Jessie Daniel Ames and the Women's Campaign against Chivalry* (New York: Columbia University Press, 1979).

79   Alice Guy-Blaché, "Woman's Place in Photoplay Production," *Moving Picture World,* 11 July 1914, reprinted in Karyn Kay and Gerald Peary, eds., *Women and the Cinema: A Critical Anthology* (New York: Dutton, 1977), 337–40.

80   Miriam Hansen, *Babel and Babylon: Spectatorship in American Silent Film* (Cambridge: Harvard University Press, 1991), 119. See also Kathy Peiss, *Cheap Amusements: Working Women and Leisure in Turn-of-the-Century New York* (Philadelphia: Temple University Press, 1986), 148–53.

81   Hansen, *Babel and Babylon,* 120.

82   William Leach, "Transformations in a Culture of Consumption: Women and Department Stores, 1890–1925," *Journal of American History* 71, no. 2 (September 1984): 333.

83   Paul K. Edwards, *The Southern Urban Negro as a Consumer* (New York: Prentice Hall, 1932), 184. Edwards's suggestion that sitting "all classes together" was a drawback reveals that class stratification was as much an issue for African American audiences as it was for white audiences.

84   Waller, "Another Audience." Waller cites Juli Jones (the pen name of pioneer black filmmaker William Foster) writing in the *Indianapolis Freeman,* 13 March 1909, 5.

85   Mary Carbine, " 'The Finest outside the Loop': Motion Picture Exhibition in Chicago's Black Metropolis, 1905–1928," *Camera Obscura* 23 (May 1990): 9–41. These theaters exhibited a range of movies, some produced by African American film companies, others the standard fare of movie theaters catering to white audiences. In the silent era, African American filmmakers had relatively more (though still very few) opportunities for establishing their own production companies compared with the later period.

86   Michael Rogin, " 'Make My Day!' Spectacle as Amnesia in Imperial Politics [and] the Sequel," in *Cultures of United States Imperialism,* ed. Amy Kaplan and Donald E. Pease (Durham, N.C.: Duke University Press, 1993), 506.

87   Rogin, "Make My Day!" 506–7.

88   The film spells the name "Quasi," but the novel spells it "Quassi."

89   Derr, *Some Kind of Paradise,* 298.
90   Lott, *Love and Theft,* 59.

3   Inverting the Tragic Mulatta Tradition: Race and Homosexuality in Pauline E. Hopkins's Fiction

1   After 1904 Hopkins continued to publish her writing, but on a much smaller scale, and eventually returned to her job as a stenographer at the Massachusetts Institute of Technology, where she worked until her death in 1930. For further discussion of the history of *Colored American Magazine,* see Hazel V. Carby, *Reconstructing Womanhood: The Emergence of the Afro-American Woman Novelist* (New York: Oxford University Press, 1987), 121–27; and Ann Allen Shockley, "Pauline Elizabeth Hopkins: A Biographical Excursion into Obscurity," *Phylon* 33, no. 1 (spring 1972): 22–26.
2   Elizabeth Ammons, "Afterword: *Winona,* Bakhtin, and Hopkins in the Twenty-first Century," in *The Unruly Voice: Rediscovering Pauline Elizabeth Hopkins,* ed. John Cullen Gruesser (Urbana: University of Illinois Press, 1996), 214.
3   Pauline E. Hopkins, *Contending Forces: A Romance Illustrative of Negro Life North and South* (1900; reprint, New York: Oxford University Press, 1988), 13–14. Hereafter cited in the text.
4   For a key discussion of Hopkins's efforts to reshape the political landscape through literary production, see Carby, *Reconstructing Womanhood,* 121–44.
5   See Hazel V. Carby, introduction to *The Magazine Novels of Pauline Hopkins* (New York: Oxford University Press, 1988), xxxi; and Richard Yarborough, introduction to *Contending Forces: A Romance Illustrative of Negro Life North and South* (1900; reprint, New York: Oxford University Press, 1988), xlii–xliii.
6   Cornelia Condict, letter to the editor, *Colored American Magazine,* March 1903, 398–99.
7   Ibid., 399.
8   Pauline Hopkins, reply to Condict, *Colored American Magazine,* March 1903, 399.
9   Ibid.; Hopkins's italics.
10 For a critique of Hopkins's internalization of racial hierarchies and of the broader imperialist assumptions of ideologies of "racial uplift," see Kevin Gaines, "Black Americans' Racial Uplift Ideology as 'Civilizing Mission': Pauline E. Hopkins on Race and Imperialism," in *Cultures of United States Imperialism,* ed. Amy Kaplan and Donald E. Pease (Durham, N.C.: Duke University Press, 1993), 433–55.

11 See, for instance, Houston Baker, *Workings of the Spirit: The Poetics of Afro-American Women's Writing* (Chicago: University of Chicago Press, 1991), 24.

12 Carby, *Reconstructing Womanhood,* 89.

13 Ibid., 89, 90.

14 Deborah McDowell, introduction to *"Quicksand" and "Passing,"* by Nella Larsen (New Brunswick: Rutgers University Press, 1986), ix–xxxv.

15 See Baker, *Workings of the Spirit,* 25.

16 Claudia Tate, *Domestic Allegories of Political Desire: The Black Heroine's Text at the Turn of the Century* (New York: Oxford University Press, 1992), 9.

17 Ann duCille, *The Coupling Convention: Sex, Text, and Tradition in Black Women's Fiction* (New York: Oxford University Press, 1993), 3.

18 DuCille's question is highly relevant for our own historical moment, within the context of current efforts to legalize gay and lesbian marriage and the corresponding backlash against these efforts, perhaps most tellingly demonstrated by the proposed "Defense of Marriage Act," which would attempt to renaturalize the connection between legal marriage and heterosexuality.

19 DuCille, *Coupling Convention,* 14.

20 On African American lesbian identities and subcultures, see, for instance, Thadious M. Davis, *Nella Larsen, Novelist of the Harlem Renaissance: A Woman's Life Unveiled* (Baton Rouge: Louisiana State University Press, 1994); and Hazel Carby, " 'It Jus Be's Dat Way Sometime': The Sexual Politics of Women's Blues," in *Unequal Sisters: A Multicultural Reader in U.S. Women's History,* ed. Ellen Carol DuBois and Vicki L. Ruiz (New York: Routledge, 1990), 238–49. On gay and lesbian communities in Harlem, see Eric Garber, "A Spectacle in Color: The Lesbian and Gay Subculture of Jazz Age Harlem," in *Hidden from History: Reclaiming the Gay and Lesbian Past,* ed. Martin Duberman, Martha Vicinus, and George Chauncey Jr. (New York: Meridian, 1989), 318–31; and George Chauncey, *Gay New York: Gender, Urban Culture, and the Making of the Gay Male World, 1890–1940* (New York: Basic Books, 1994).

21 The legal prohibition against marriage, of course, did not prevent slaves from marrying without legal recognition. As historians have shown, extralegal and religious ceremonies frequently formalized sexual and affectional unions between slaves. See Herbert Gutman, *The Black Family in Slavery and Freedom, 1750–1925* (New York: Pantheon, 1976).

22 Both African American and Euro-American authors wrote novels about passing during the nineteenth century, but they often had different reasons for exploring this theme. See, for example, Frank Webb, *The Garies and Their Friends* (1857); William Wells Brown, *Clotel* (1853); William Dean

Howells, *An Imperative Duty* (1892); Mark Twain, *Pudd'nhead Wilson* (1894); Charles Chesnutt, *The House behind the Cedars* (1900); and Gertrude Atherton, *Senator North* (1900).

23   Judith Berzon, *Neither White nor Black: The Mulatto Character in American Fiction* (New York: New York University Press, 1978), 74. Berzon also makes a distinction between white and African American writers' portrayals of mulatta characters; in particular, she notes that in fiction by black novelists between 1908 and 1920, black women are portrayed as "beautiful (in Caucasian terms), morally upstanding, prim, and wealthy (or at least comfortable)" (62).

24   Mary Dearborn, *Pocahontas's Daughters: Gender and Ethnicity in American Culture* (New York: Oxford University Press, 1986), 139–40, italics mine. In a recent discussion of the mulatto figure in American race melodrama, Susan Gillman concurs that in the conventions of the tragic mulatto tale, the protagonist is most often a woman; see her "The Mulatto, Tragic or Triumphant? The Nineteenth-Century American Race Melodrama," in *The Culture of Sentiment: Race, Gender, and Sentimentality in Nineteenth-Century America,* ed. Shirley Samuels (New York: Oxford University Press, 1992), 221–43.

25   Werner Sollors, " 'Never Was Born': The Mulatto, an American Tragedy?" *Massachusetts Review* 27 (summer 1986): 302.

26   See, for instance, Elizabeth Ammons, *Conflicting Stories: American Women Writers at the Turn into the Twentieth Century* (New York: Oxford University Press, 1991), 80; and Tate, *Domestic Allegories,* 148–49.

27   Baker, *Workings of the Spirit,* 24.

28   Elaine Marks writes that "Sappho and her island Lesbos are omnipresent in literature about women loving women, whatever the gender or sexual preference of the writer and whether or not Sappho and her island are explicitly named" ("Lesbian Intertextuality," in *Homosexualities and French Literature,* ed. George Stambolian and Elaine Marks [Ithaca, N.Y.: Cornell University Press, 1978], 356).

29   Joan DeJean, *Fictions of Sappho, 1546–1937* (Chicago: University of Chicago Press, 1989), 202.

30   Thomas Wentworth Higginson, "Sappho," *Atlantic Monthly* 28 (July 1871): 83. Although there is no proof that Hopkins ever saw this article on Sappho, she did draw explicitly on Higginson as a literary influence: the subtitle of her short story "A Dash for Liberty" states that it was "Founded on an article written by Col. T. W. Higginson for the *Atlantic Monthly* June 1861" (*Colored American Magazine,* August 1901, 243).

31   Higginson, "Sappho," 88.

32 According to the *Oxford English Dictionary,* the first English reference to "sapphism" in print occurs in 1890 in the *National Medical Dictionary.* It dates the first appearance of "lesbianism" (as the female equivalent to "sodomy") to 1870. Nonprint usage probably antedated these instances. DeJean writes that "French usage of 'sapphisme' and 'lesbienne' preceded and probably inspired English terminology, whereas the reverse implantation occurred with the vocabulary of 'homosexual.' . . . Prior to the complex nineteenth-century situation, the dominant French terms were 'tribade,' 'tribadisme' " (*Fictions of Sappho,* 350 n. 51).

33 Havelock Ellis, *Studies in the Psychology of Sex,* vol. 2, *Sexual Inversion,* 3d ed., (Philadelphia: F. A. Davis Company, 1915), 197.

34 DeJean, *Fictions of Sappho,* xiv–xv, 200, 280.

35 Susan Gubar, "Sapphistries," *Signs* 10 (autumn 1984): 55. See also Willis Barnstone, *Sappho: Lyrics in the Original Greek* (New York: New York University Press, 1965), xxii–xxiii.

36 John Addington Symonds, quoted in Henry Thornton Wharton, *Sappho: Memoir, Text, Selected Renderings, and a Literal Translation* (1885; reprint, Chicago: A. C. McClurg, 1895), 13. The comment originally appeared in Symonds, *Studies of Greek Poets,* first series (New York: Harper and Brothers, 1880), 127. Symonds played a significant role in articulating emergent models of homosexuality. With Havelock Ellis, he cowrote *Sexual Inversion,* originally published as the first volume of Ellis's *Studies in the Psychology of Sex.* For a discussion of their collaboration and the eventual erasure of Symonds from the text, see Wayne Koestenbaum, *Double Talk: The Erotics of Male Literary Collaboration* (New York: Routledge, 1989), 43–67.

37 Quoted in Wharton, *Sappho,* 13.

38 That Sappho's poetry fragments were preserved through Egyptian remains could have provided Hopkins with a link to Egypt, an important symbol of ancient African civilization for Hopkins.

   Hopkins claimed ancient figures as models for her characters in other works. Her first serialized novel, *Hagar's Daughter: A Story of Southern Caste Prejudice,* took its heroine's name from the Bible. "Hagar and Ishmael," an article in the series entitled "Fascinating Bible Stories," appeared in *Colored American Magazine* one month before the first installment of *Hagar's Daughter* (Charles Winslow Hall, "Fascinating Bible Stories IV: Hagar and Ishmael," *Colored American Magazine,* February 1901, 302–6). In this retelling of the story, Hall related how Hagar, "the stately and passionate Egyptian" and the female slave of Sarah, was chosen to bear a child for Sarah's husband, Abraham (306). Hagar's son, Ishmael, was described as "the son of a Caucasian father and African mother," just as Jewel, the daughter of

Hopkins's Hagar, was the daughter of an African American woman and a white man (304). The article presented Ishmael, disowned by Abraham and Sarah, as a hero and forefather who built "a race unconquerable" (306).

Of One Blood; or, the Hidden Self (1902–1903) is Hopkins's most explicit exploration of Ethiopianism; the novel travels back in time to the city of Meroe, the ancient capital of Ethiopia.

39 J[ohn] E. Bruce, "Some Famous Negroes," Voice of the Negro 2 (December 1905): 876.

40 Bruce quotes from Alexander Pope's 1712 translation of Ovid's "Sappho to Phaon" in Ovid's Epistles: "To me what nature has in charms denied / Is well by wit's more lasting flames supplied, / Though short my stature, yet my name extends / To heaven itself and earth's remotest ends. / Brown as I am an Ethiopian dame / Inspired young Perseus with a generous flame. / Turtles and doves of different hues unite, / And glossy jet is paired with shining white" (876). According to John Butt in The Poems of Alexander Pope (London: Methuen, 1963), the "Ethiopian dame" refers to Andromeda, daughter of Cepheus and Cassiopeia, king and queen of Egypt (30 n. 41). I have not found other references to Sappho's African origins, although as Higginson noted, "Tradition represents her as having been 'little and dark'" ("Sappho," 84).

41 See Carroll Smith-Rosenberg, "The Female World of Love and Ritual: Relations between Women in Nineteenth-Century America," Signs 1 (autumn 1975): 1–29.

42 Lillian Faderman, "Lesbian Magazine Fiction in the Early Twentieth Century," Journal of Popular Culture 11 (1978): 802.

43 Marylynne Diggs, "Romantic Friends or a 'Different Race of Creatures'? The Representation of Lesbian Pathology in Nineteenth-Century America," Feminist Studies 21, no. 2 (summer 1995): 321.

44 For discussions of how Hopkins employs the marriage plot, see duCille, The Coupling Convention, 36–43; and Tate, Domestic Allegories, 124–25.

45 The Oxford English Dictionary defines "unsex" as "to deprive or divest of sex, or of the typical qualities of one or other (esp. the female) sex."

46 James G. Kiernan, "Inversion and Dreams," Urologic and Cutaneous Review 19 (June 1915): 352.

47 It also suggests a link to Sappho, who is described elsewhere in identical language. When Sappho sneaks out of the Smith boardinghouse after she has been blackmailed by John Langley, Hopkins writes: "A form attired in black, closely veiled, . . . was swallowed up in the heart of the metropolis" (321–22, italics mine).

48 Eve Kosofsky Sedgwick, *Epistemology of the Closet* (Berkeley and Los Angeles: University of California Press, 1990), 71.

49 *Oxford English Dictionary,* 2d ed., s.v. "skeleton in the closet."

50 For brief discussions of this scene, see Claudia Tate, "Allegories of Black Female Desire: Or, Rereading Nineteenth-Century Sentimental Narratives of Black Female Authority," in *Changing Our Own Words: Essays on Criticism, Theory, and Writing by Black Women,* ed. Cheryl Wall (New Brunswick: Rutgers University Press, 1989), 122–23; and Mary Helen Washington, "Uplifting the Women and the Race," in *Invented Lives: Narratives of Black Women, 1860–1960* (Garden City, N.Y.: Anchor Press, 1987), 81.

51 See Carby, *Reconstructing Womanhood,* 23–34; duCille, *Coupling Convention,* 30–47; and Tate, *Domestic Allegories,* 97–98, 152–53.

52 Nancy F. Cott, "Passionlessness: An Interpretation of Victorian Sexual Ideology, 1790–1850," in Nancy F. Cott and Elizabeth H. Pleck, *A Heritage of Her Own: Toward a New Social History of American Women* (New York: Simon and Schuster, 1979), 168–69.

53 Ibid., 173.

54 Richard Yarborough, introduction to *Contending Forces: A Romance Illustrative of Negro Life North and South,* by Pauline E. Hopkins (Boston: Colored Co-operative Publishing, 1900; reprint, New York: Oxford University Press, 1988), xl. Yarborough suggests that Willis may have been modeled after Josephine St. Pierre Ruffin, president of the Women's Era Club in Boston during the late nineteenth century.

55 Tate, *Domestic Allegories,* 164.

56 Sedgwick, *Epistemology of the Closet,* 100, 222.

57 "The Adventures of a Near-White," *Independent,* 14 August 1913, 375.

58 Yarborough, introduction to *Contending Forces,* xli.

59 Pauline E. Hopkins, *Winona: A Tale of Negro Life in the South and Southwest, Colored American Magazine* 5 (May–October 1902): 287. Reprinted in *The Magazine Novels of Pauline Hopkins,* with an introduction by Hazel V. Carby (New York: Oxford University Press, 1988), 287–437. Hereafter cited in the text; subsequent references are to the Oxford edition. For readers who are unfamiliar with this text, I provide a plot synopsis hereafter.

This historical novel takes place in the 1850s within a number of different geographic and political settings, including the United States–Canada border, a slaveholding plantation in Missouri, and the frontier state of Kansas. The title character, Winona, is the biracial daughter of an unnamed fugitive slave woman and White Eagle, the chief of a community of Seneca Indians in Canada. Winona's mother dies in childbirth, and when White Eagle is murdered by slave rustlers, Winona and her step-brother Judah are sold into slavery. A new character, the British lawyer Warren Maxwell, enters the text by arriving in North America in search of heirs to the estate of a wealthy English aristocrat, Lord Carlingford. Through a series of complicated plot twists, Maxwell befriends Judah and Winona and eventually helps them escape the slaveholders. Soon all three join forces with the radical abolitionist John Brown on behalf of the Free-Soil movement in Kansas. During this time, Winona falls in love with Maxwell. After a number of suspenseful captures and escapes, the novel concludes with revelations about the characters' origins, including Winona's identity as the lawful heir to the Carlingford estate. In the novel's final scenes, Winona and Maxwell plan their marriage and set sail to live permanently in England.

60   See Chauncey, *Gay New York*, 120–21.

61   James Kiernan, "Invert Marriages," *Urologic and Cutaneous Review* 18 (1914): 550. Quoted in Jonathan Ned Katz, *Gay American History: Lesbians and Gay Men in the USA* (New York: Crowell, 1976).

62   Ironically, Anderson's case "inverted" the masquerades that had originally brought about the imposition of the "masking" laws under which she was prosecuted. According to Thomas B. Stoddard et al., under "New York's former cross-dressing statute, individuals were not able to wear disguises, or have painted faces in public. That statute was adopted in the nineteenth century in response to the actions of farmers who, during anti-rent riots, murdered law-enforcement officers *while disguised as Indians, or while wearing dresses*" (italics mine). See Thomas B. Stoddard et al., *The Rights of Gay People* (1975; reprint, New York: Bantam Books, 1983), 119. Cross-dressing is still a criminal act in many cities and states in the United States.

63   Kiernan, "Invert Marriages," 550.

64   For a discussion of Hopkins's use of popular fiction genres in her serialized novels, see Carby, *Reconstructing Womanhood*, 145–62; and Tate, *Domestic Allegories*, 195–96.

65   Elizabeth Ammons, "Afterword," 217–18.

66   Jonathan Goldberg, *Sodometries: Renaissance Text, Modern Sexualities* (Stanford, Calif.: Stanford University Press, 1992), 19.

67   For further discussion of anal rape and homophobia, see Eve Sedgwick, *Between Men: English Literature and Male Homosocial Desire* (New York: Columbia University Press, 1985).

68   Hopkins's strategy is similar to the intricate interweaving of authorial power and knowledge that D. A. Miller discusses in *The Novel and the Police* (Berkeley: University of California Press, 1988): " 'Poor Dorothea,' 'poor Lydgate,' 'poor Rosamond,' the narrator of *Middlemarch* frequently

exclaims, and the lament is credible only in an arrangement that keeps the function of narration separate from the causalities operating in the narrative. The *knowledge* commanded in omniscient narration is thus opposed to the *power* that inheres in the circumstances of the novelistic world" (25).

69   See Tate, *Domestic Allegories,* 194–208.

4   Double Lives on the Color Line: "Perverse" Desire in *The Autobiography of an Ex-Coloured Man*

1   James Weldon Johnson, *Along This Way: The Autobiography of James Weldon Johnson* (1933; reprint, New York: Penguin, 1990), 238.

2   For a discussion of fictional representations of this "crisis experience," see Judith Berzon, *Neither White nor Black: The Mulatto Character in American Fiction* (New York: New York University Press, 1978), 119–39.

3   See Louis Althusser, "Ideology and Ideological State Apparatuses (Notes Towards an Investigation)," in *Lenin and Philosophy and Other Essays,* trans. Ben Brewster (New York: Monthly Review Press, 1971), 121–73.

4   James Weldon Johnson, *The Autobiography of an Ex-Coloured Man* (1912; 1927; reprint, New York: Vintage, 1989), 17. Hereafter cited in the text.

5   For discussions of the conventional emphasis on the mulatta figure's beauty, see Berzon, *Neither White nor Black,* 99–116; John G. Mencke, *Mulattoes and Race Mixture: American Attitudes and Images, 1865–1918* (Ann Arbor, Mich.: UMI Research Press, 1979), 154–55; and Anna Shannon Elfenbein, *Women on the Color Line: Evolving Stereotypes and the Writings of George Washington Cable, Grace King, Kate Chopin* (Charlottesville: University Press of Virginia, 1989), 1–24. Claudia Tate, among others, has made the important point that these standards of beauty were also associated with upwardly mobile or elite social status within African American culture in the late nineteenth century. See her *Domestic Allegories of Political Desire: The Black Heroine's Text at the Turn of the Century* (New York: Oxford University Press, 1992), 59–64. As I will discuss, this fascination with aristocracy, or at least aristocratic style, also has a hold on the ex-coloured man's erotic attachments.

6   Charles Chesnutt, *The House Behind the Cedars* (1900; reprint, Athens: University of Georgia Press, 1988).

7   Philip Brian Harper, *Are We Not Men? Masculine Anxiety and the Problem of African-American Identity* (New York: Oxford University Press, 1996), 103.

8   Ibid., 110.

9   See Marlon Riggs's film documentary *Ethnic Notions* (1987) for a survey of these stereotypes in American popular culture.

10   Although it is situated in early-twentieth-century American culture rather than Victorian England, the association of this scene with decadence suggests affinities with the kind of aristocratic gay subculture and aesthetics discussed by Eve Kosofsky Sedgwick in a brief overview of the class-inflected parameters of homosocial and homosexual identities. Groups of aristocratic men and small groups of their friends, according to Eve Sedgwick, formed a "genuine subculture, facilitated in the face of an ideologically hostile dominant culture by money, privilege, internationalism, and, for the most part, the ability to command secrecy. . . . Its strongest associations . . . are with effeminacy, transvestitism, promiscuity, prostitution, continental European culture, and the arts." See her *Between Men: English Literature and Male Homosocial Desire* (New York: Columbia University Press, 1985), 173.

11   See Robert B. Stepto, "Lost in a Quest: James Weldon Johnson's *The Autobiography of an Ex-Coloured Man,*" in *From behind the Veil: A Study of Afro-American Narrative* (Chicago: University of Illinois Press, 1979), 103.

12   In a reading of *The Autobiography of an Ex-Coloured Man* that also marks the centrality of homoerotic desire in the text, Cheryl Clarke refers to this relationship as one of "homosexual interracial concubinage." See Cheryl Clarke, "Race, Homosocial Desire, and 'Mammon' in *Autobiography of an Ex-Coloured Man,*" in *Professions of Desire: Lesbian and Gay Studies in Literature,* ed. George E. Haggerty and Bonnie Zimmerman (New York: Modern Language Association, 1995), 89.

13   Harper, *Are We Not Men,* 110.

14   For an intriguing discussion of historically racialized and sexualized proscriptions against "the right to look," see Jane Gaines, "White Privilege and Looking Relations: Race and Gender in Feminist Film Theory," *Cultural Critique* 4 (fall 1986): 59–79.

15   The title of this section alludes to black lyricist Andy Razaf's 1930 hit song "Go Harlem," quoted in Barry Singer, *Black and Blue: The Life and Lyrics of Andy Razaf* (New York: Schirmer, 1992), 239.

16   I use the term "Harlem Renaissance" loosely here, following the important and enabling critiques of critics such as Hazel Carby and Ann duCille, who have drawn attention to both the problematic periodization and lack of attention to women writers in most characterizations of the "Harlem Renaissance." See Hazel Carby, *Reconstructing Womanhood: The Emergence of the Afro-American Woman Novelist* (New York: Oxford University Press, 1987), 163–75; and Ann duCille, *The Coupling Convention: Sex, Text, and Tradition in Black Women's Fiction* (New York: Oxford University Press, 1993), 82–85.

17   Bruce Kellner, *Carl Van Vechten and the Irreverent Decades* (Norman: University of Oklahoma Press, 1968), 197–98.

18   See Harriet A. Jacobs, *Incidents in the Life of a Slave Girl, Written by Herself* (1861; reprint, Cambridge: Harvard University Press, 1987); and *Narrative of the Life of Frederick Douglass, an American Slave, Written by Himself* (1845; reprint, New York: Signet, 1968).

19   See Eric Lott, *Love and Theft: Blackface Minstrelsy and the American Working Class* (New York: Oxford University Press, 1995), for a useful discussion of the ways in which blackface has circulated historically as a vehicle for white male bohemianism in the United States. Lott suggests that nineteenth-century "blackface stars inaugurated an American tradition of class abdication through gendered cross-racial immersion which persists, in historically differentiated ways, to our own day" (51).

20   Jonathan Weinberg, "'Boy Crazy': Carl Van Vechten's Queer Collection," *Yale Journal of Criticism* 7, no. 2 (1994): 25–49.

21   Ibid., 31.

22   Ibid.

23   See Eric Garber, "A Spectacle in Color: the Lesbian and Gay Subculture of Jazz Age Harlem," in *Hidden from History: Reclaiming the Gay and Lesbian Past,* ed. Martin Duberman, Martha Vicinus, and George Chauncey Jr. (New York: Meridian, 1989), 318–31; George Chauncey, *Gay New York: Gender, Urban Culture, and the Making of the Gay Male World, 1890–1940* (New York: Basic Books, 1994), 227–67; and Kevin Mumford, *Interzones: Black/White Sex Districts in Chicago and New York in the Early Twentieth Century* (New York: Columbia University Press, 1997), 73–92.

24   See Garber, "A Spectacle in Color," 326–31; Thadious M. Davis, *Nella Larsen, Novelist of the Harlem Renaissance: A Woman's Life Unveiled* (Baton Rouge: Louisiana State University Press, 1994), 325; and Gloria T. Hull, *Color, Sex, and Poetry: Three Women Writers of the Harlem Renaissance* (Bloomington: Indiana University Press, 1987), 95–97, 136–47.

25   Gates, "The Black Man's Burden," 233.

26   Johnson, *Along This Way,* 239.

5   "Queer to Myself As I Am to You": Jean Toomer, Racial Disidentification, and Queer Reading

1   William Stanley Braithwaite, "The Negro in American Literature," in *The New Negro,* ed. Alain Locke (New York: Albert and Charles Boni, 1925), 44.

2   Sherwood Anderson to Jean Toomer, 22 December 1922, reprinted in Jean Toomer, *Cane,* ed. Darwin Turner (New York: W. W. Norton, 1988), 160.

3   Jean Toomer, *The Wayward and the Seeking: A Collection of Writings by Jean Toomer,* ed. Darwin T. Turner (Washington, D.C.: Howard University Press, 1980), 127. See also Jean Toomer to Horace Liveright, 5 September 1923, reprinted in Toomer, *Cane,* 157.

4   Jean Toomer to James Weldon Johnson, 11 July 1930, reprinted in *A Jean Toomer Reader: Selected Unpublished Writings,* ed. Frederik L. Rusch (New York: Oxford University Press, 1993), 106.

5   Alice Walker, "The Divided Life of Jean Toomer," *New York Times Book Review,* 13 June 1980, 16.

6   Pinchback, whose father was a white farmer and his mother a freed slave, was elected to the United States Senate from Louisiana during Reconstruction and was at one time the acting governor of Louisiana. He was also a member of the American Citizens' Equal Rights Association of Louisiana ("Introduction," in *The Thin Disguise: Turning Point in Negro History,* ed. Otto Olsen [New York: Humanities Press, 1967], 10; "Introduction," *A Jean Toomer Reader,* xiv).

7   Arna Bontemps, "The Negro Renaissance: Jean Toomer and the Harlem Writers of the 1920s," in *Anger, and Beyond: The Negro Writer in the United States,* ed. Herbert Hill (New York: Harper and Row, 1966), 27.

8   Robert Hayden, *Kaleidoscope: Poems by American Negro Poets* (New York: Harcourt, Brace and World, 1967), 50.

9   Henry Louis Gates Jr., "The Same Difference: Reading Jean Toomer, 1923–1982," in *Figures in Black: Words, Signs, and the "Racial" Self* (New York: Oxford University Press, 1987), 202.

10   Ibid., 205.

11   The question of Toomer's literary lineages is vexed and complex, one that I will touch on hereafter. Rudolph P. Byrd has complicated the common inclusion of Toomer with other figures of the so-called Harlem Renaissance. He notes that Toomer's "literary world" included not African American writers such as Hughes and Cullen but rather, according to Toomer himself, Waldo Frank, Gorham Munson, Kenneth Burke, Hart Crane, Matthew Josephson, Malcolm Cowley, Paul Rosenfeld, Van Wyck Brooks, and Robert Littell, and journals such as *Broom,* the *Dial,* and *New Republic.* See Rudolph P. Byrd, "Jean Toomer and the Writers of the Harlem Renaissance: Was He There with Them?" in *The Harlem Renaissance: Revaluations,* ed. Amritjit Singh, William S. Shiver, and Stanley Brodwin (New York: Garland, 1989), 213.

12   Gates, "The Same Difference," 206.

13   Ibid.

14 On the figure of the tragic mulatto, see the classic discussion by Ster-
    ling Brown, "Negro Character as Seen by White Authors," *Journal of Negro
    Education* 2 (January 1933): 180–201, reprinted in *Dark Symphony: Negro
    Literature in America,* ed. James A. Emanuel and Theodore L. Gross (New
    York: Free Press, 1968), 139–71. For more recent discussions, see Hazel V.
    Carby, *Reconstructing Womanhood: The Emergence of the Afro-American Woman
    Novelist* (New York: Oxford University Press, 1987), 73, 88–91; Werner
    Sollors, " 'Never Was Born': The Mulatto, an American Tragedy?" *Massa-
    chusetts Review* 27 (summer 1986): 293–316; Susan Gillman, "The Mulatto,
    Tragic or Triumphant? The Nineteenth-Century American Race Melo-
    drama," in *The Culture of Sentiment: Race, Gender, and Sentimentality in
    Nineteenth-Century America,* ed. Shirley Samuels (New York: Oxford Uni-
    versity Press, 1992), 221–43; Judith Berzon, *Neither White nor Black: The
    Mulatto Character in American Fiction* (New York: New York University
    Press, 1978), 99–116; Barbara Christian, *Black Women Novelists: The Devel-
    opment of a Tradition, 1892–1976* (Westport, Conn.: Greenwood Press, 1980),
    22–23; John G. Mencke, *Mulattoes and Race Mixture: American Attitudes and
    Images, 1865–1918* (Ann Arbor, Mich.: UMI Research Press, 1979), 144–49,
    199–204; and Anna Shannon Elfenbein, *Women on the Color Line; Evolv-
    ing Stereotypes and the Writings of George Washington Cable, Grace King, Kate
    Chopin* (Charlottesville: University Press of Virginia, 1989), 1–12.

15 Jean Toomer, "Not Typically American," in *A Jean Toomer Reader,* 99;
    Toomer, letter to James Weldon Johnson, 11 July 1930.

16 Gates, "The Same Difference," 207.

17 Ibid., 208.

18 In a discussion of Isaac Julien's *Looking for Langston,* for instance, Gates
    problematizes the homophobia that he calls "an almost obsessive motif
    that runs through the major authors of the Black Aesthetic and the Black
    Power movements." See Henry Louis Gates Jr., "The Black Man's Bur-
    den," in *Fear of a Queer Planet: Queer Politics and Social Theory,* ed. Michael
    Warner (Minneapolis: University of Minnesota Press, 1993), 234.

19 Jean Toomer Papers, James Weldon Johnson Memorial Collection, box 17,
    folder 485, Beinecke Rare Book and Manuscript Library, Yale University,
    New Haven, Conn.

20 See, for instance, Lauren Berlant and Michael Warner, "What Does Queer
    Theory Teach Us about X?" *PMLA* 110, no. 3 (May 1995): 343–49; Lisa
    Duggan, "The Discipline Problem: Queer Theory Meets Lesbian and Gay
    History," *GLQ* 2 (1995): 179–91; Donna Penn, "Queer: Theorizing Politics
    and History," *Radical History Review* 62 (spring 1995): 24–43; Eve Sedg-
    wick, "Queer and Now," *Tendencies* (Durham, N.C.: Duke University Press,

1993); Martha Umphrey, "The Trouble with Harry Thaw," *Radical History Review* 62 (spring 1995): 8–23.

21 Others have noted a need to take up similar questions about the role of race and ethnicity in queer politics and theory. See, for instance, Mab Segrest, "A Bridge, not a Wedge," from *Memoirs of a Race Traitor* (Boston: South End Press, 1994), 229–46; Ruth Goldman, "Who Is That *Queer* Queer? Exploring Norms around Sexuality, Race, and Class in Queer Theory," in *Queer Studies: A Lesbian, Gay, Bisexual, and Transgender Anthology,* ed. Brett Beemyn and Mickey Eliason (New York: New York University Press, 1996), 169–82.

22 Sedgwick, "Queer and Now," 8–9.

23 Judith Butler, *Bodies That Matter: On the Discursive Limits of "Sex"* (New York: Routledge, 1993), 229.

24 Sedgwick, "Queer and Now," 8.

25 Toomer, *Cane,* 92. Hereafter cited in the text.

26 Implying the questionable sexuality of Kabnis, Arthur P. Davis in his *From the Dark Tower: Afro-American Writers, 1900–1960* (Washington, D.C.: Howard University Press, 1974) has described Kabnis as "a complex and mixed-up soul. A Northern, educated, light-skinned Negro . . . a coward, a drunkard, a sexual neuter, and a misguided dreamer" (48).

27 See Eve Kosofsky Sedgwick's discussion of "homosexual panic" and its literary representation in *Epistemology of the Closet* (Berkeley: University of California Press, 1990), 18–22, 182–212.

28 Lauren Berlant has recently distinguished between these two components of desire in a discussion of Nella Larsen's *Passing:* "There may be a difference between wanting someone sexually and wanting someone's body: and I wonder whether Irene's xenophilia isn't indeed a desire to occupy, to experience the privileges of Clare's body, not to love or make love to her, but rather to wear her way of wearing her body, like a prosthesis, or a fetish" (Lauren Berlant, "National Brands/National Body: *Imitation of Life,*" in *Comparative American Identities: Race, Sex, and Nationality in the Modern Text,* ed. Hortense Spillers [New York: Routledge, 1991], 111).

29 Jean Toomer to Waldo Frank, n.d. [late 1922 or early 1923], Toomer's italics; reprinted in *A Jean Toomer Reader,* 25.

30 Jean Toomer, *Outline of an Autobiography,* quoted in John Chandler Griffin, "Jean Toomer: American Writer (A Biography)" (Ph.D. diss., University of South Carolina, 1976), 87.

31 George Chauncey, *Gay New York: Gender, Urban Culture, and the Making of the Gay Male World, 1890–1940* (New York: Basic Books, 1994), 15–16, Chauncey's italics.

32   Ibid., 106.

33   Deborah McDowell, introduction to *"Quicksand" and "Passing,"* by Nella
      Larsen (New Brunswick, N.J.: Rutgers University Press, 1986), ix–xxxv.
      For another useful approach to the question of sexual and racial identifi-
      cation, see Berlant, "National Brands/National Body," 110–40.

34   Judith Butler, "Passing, Queering: Nella Larsen's Psychoanalytic Chal-
      lenge," in her *Bodies That Matter,* 176. Butler differs from Chauncey in her
      understanding of the meanings of "queer" in the historical context of the
      1920s, stating that "at the time, it seems, 'queer' did not yet mean homo-
      sexual, but it did encompass an array of meanings associated with the
      deviation from normalcy which might well include the sexual" (176).

35   Toomer, "Withered Skin of Berries," reprinted in *The Wayward and the
      Seeking,* 139–65. Hereafter cited in the text.

36   Peter Christensen, "Sexuality and Liberation in Jean Toomer's 'Withered
      Skin of Berries,'" *Callaloo* 11, no. 3 (summer 1988): 619.

37   Throughout Toomer's writing, he seems to call Native Americans "Indi-
      ans," and he refers to South Asian Indians as "Hindu."

38   This language also echoes Bona's description of Paul as "an autumn leaf"
      in "Bona and Paul" (72).

39   Christensen, "Sexuality and Liberation," 619.

40   Jean Toomer, "Sheik and Anti-Sheik," n.d., n.p., MS 1, series 2, box 58,
      folder 1372, James Weldon Johnson Collection, Beinecke Rare Book and
      Manuscript Library, Yale University, New Haven, Conn. The manuscript
      exists in three incomplete and undated versions. It is possible to specu-
      late that "Sheik and Anti-Sheik" was written in the 1920s, based on its
      being set, like "Withered Skin of Berries," in Washington, D.C. In a let-
      ter to Horace Liveright dated March 1923, Toomer discusses three pieces
      that he intended to bring together in a second volume after *Cane:* "two
      pieces that approximate Kabnis in length and scope," and "another long
      story forming in my mind." In Toomer's words, "The melieu [*sic*] is con-
      stantly that of Washington. The characters are dynamic, lyric, complex"
      (Jean Toomer, letter to Horace Liveright, March 1923, reprinted in Norton
      Critical Edition of *Cane,* 157). Nellie McKay, in *Jean Toomer, Artist: A Study
      of His Literary Life and Work, 1894–1936* (Chapel Hill: University of North
      Carolina Press, 1984), suggests that the play *Natalie Mann* was one of these
      pieces (84). Turner suggests that the two pieces were "Withered Skin of
      Berries" and *Natalie Mann* (Norton Critical Edition of *Cane,* 157). Chris-
      tensen claims that *Balo* and "Withered Skin of Berries" were the other
      two pieces (Christensen, "Sexuality and Liberation," 616). *Balo,* however,
      was set in Georgia, and given Toomer's statement that Washington was

the setting of these three pieces, it may be that "Sheik and Anti-Sheik" was the third one in mind, dating it to the same period, around 1923. In addition, taking into account popular cultural references to the word and image of "sheik," which I will discuss, it seems likely that this story dates from the early to mid-1920s.

41 See Sedgwick's *Between Men* for a discussion of the ways that homoerotic bonds are secured through the exchange of women.

42 Toomer, "Sheik and Anti-Sheik," n.p.

43 I have retained Toomer's practice of omitting apostrophes and contractions because they are characteristic throughout his writing.

44 Toomer, "Sheik and Anti-Sheik," n.p. The manuscript contains a number of errors that I have corrected in quoting this material. Where Toomer's revisions have significantly changed the meaning of the passage, I have included them.

45 Toomer, "Sheik and Anti-Sheik," n.p.

46 Ibid. "Kuppenheimer" and "J and M" were brand names of men's clothing and shoes. Based on a 1912–1913 catalog, the House of Kuppenheimer, a Chicago men's clothing company, seems to have marketed its line of men's suits and coats through images of white upper-class men ("The Hub, Representing the House of Kuppenheimer, Chicago," pamphlet, box 6, "Clothing: Men's and Women's Coats," Romaine Trade Catalog Collection, Davidson Library, University of California, Santa Barbara).

47 My discussion here draws on the notion of the female spectator, as developed in discussions of the gendered gaze within feminist film theory, particularly Laura Mulvey, "Visual Pleasure and Narrative Cinema," *Screen* 16 (1975): 6–18; and responses to this essay, including Mary Ann Doane, "Film and the Masquerade: Theorizing the Female Spectator," *Screen* 23 (1982): 74–87; and Teresa de Lauretis, *Alice Doesn't: Feminism, Semiotics, and the Cinema* (Bloomington: Indiana University Press, 1984), among others.

48 Toomer, "Sheik and Anti-Sheik," n.p.

49 Ibid.

50 The film was based on a best-selling novel by E. M. Hull (pseudonym for Edith Maud Winstanley) published in England in 1919 and in the United States in 1921. According to Patricia Raub, *The Sheik* was one of the few novels to be listed on the American best-seller list two years in a row, in 1921 and 1922. See Patricia Raub, "Issues of Passion and Power in E. M. Hull's *The Sheik*," *Women's Studies* 21 (1992): 120.

Valentino himself was aware of the social scene associated with the "New Negro" movement of the 1920s. As Langston Hughes recalls in his autobiography *The Big Sea*, "One night as one of Carl Van Vechten's parties was drawing to a close, Rudolph Valentino called, saying that he was on his way. That was the only time I have ever seen the genial Van Vechten hospitality waver. He told Mr. Valentino the party was over. It seems that our host was slightly perturbed at the thought of so celebrated a guest coming into a party that had passed its peak. Besides, he told the rest of us, movie stars usually expected a lot of attention—and it was too late in the evening for such extended solicitude now" (*The Big Sea: An Autobiography* [1940; reprint, New York: Thunder's Mouth Press, 1986], 253).

51   See Raub, "Passion and Power," 120. The *Oxford English Dictionary* cites a 1925 usage of the word to mean "a type of strong, romantic lover; a lady-killer."

52   See Claude McKay, "Little Sheik," in *Gingertown* (New York: Harper and Bros., 1932; reprint, Freeport, N.Y.: Books for Libraries Press, 1972); and Frank Norris, "Son of a Sheik," in *The Third Circle* (1909; reprint, New York: Doubleday, Doran, 1928).

53   Gaylyn Studlar, "Discourses of Gender and Ethnicity: The Construction and De(con)struction of Rudolph Valentino as Other," *Film Criticism* 13, no. 2 (winter 1989): 24.

54   Ibid.

55   Ibid., 26. Studlar is quoting Janice Radway, *Reading the Romance: Women, Patriarchy, and Popular Culture* (Chapel Hill: University of North Carolina Press, 1984), 147.

56   Quoted in Studlar, "Discourses of Gender and Ethnicity," 30. The original interview appeared in J. K. Winkler, "I'm Tired of Being a Sheik," *Colliers*, January 1926, 28.

57   Miriam Hansen, *Babel and Babylon: Spectatorship in American Silent Film* (Cambridge: Harvard University Press, 1991), 254–55. Reflecting the general tendency of feminist film critics, Hansen and Studlar do not explicitly consider the race of the historical audiences and theoretical spectators to which their studies refer. Based on their generalizations, as well as the historical effects of segregation on movie audiences, their "female spectator" implicitly seems to be positioned as white.

58   Ibid., 268.

59   Quoted in Kenneth Anger, "Rudy's Rep," in *Hollywood Babylon* (San Francisco: Straight Arrow Books, 1975), 108. The original editorial appeared in the *Chicago Tribune*, 18 July 1926.

60   Kenneth Anger, "Valentino Remembered, Valentino Discovered," in *There Is a New Star in Heaven*, ed. Eva Orbanz (Berlin: Volker Speiss, 1979), 19–22.

61   Cynthia Earl Kerman and Richard Eldridge, *The Lives of Jean Toomer: A*

Hunger for Wholeness (Baton Rouge: Louisiana State University Press, 1987), 313.

62   Charles R. Larson, *Invisible Darkness: Jean Toomer and Nella Larsen* (Iowa City: University of Iowa Press, 1993), 160.

63   Ibid. This biography offers problematic treatments of both Toomer and Larsen and tends to demonize Toomer and construct Larsen as a martyr. For a fuller and more balanced biography of Larsen, see Thadious M. Davis, *Nella Larsen, Novelist of the Harlem Renaissance: A Woman's Life Unveiled* (Baton Rouge: Louisiana State University Press, 1994).

64   Griffin, "Jean Toomer," 321 n. 53.

65   Quoted in *The Wayward and the Seeking*, 42.

66   Ibid., 41–42.

67   Ibid., 45.

68   Toomer, "Outline of the Story of the Autobiography," quoted in Mark Helbling, "Jean Toomer and Waldo Frank: A Creative Friendship," in *Jean Toomer: A Critical Evaluation*, ed. Therman B. O'Daniel (Washington, D.C.: Howard University Press, 1988), 85.

69   Toomer, *Outline of an Autobiography*, quoted in Griffin, "Jean Toomer," 84.

70   Ibid.

71   Helbling, "Jean Toomer and Waldo Frank," 85. Kerman and Eldridge have similarly characterized their relationship as "spiritual brotherhood" (*The Lives of Jean Toomer*, 361).

72   Quoted in Charles Scruggs, "Jean Toomer: Fugitive," *American Literature* 47 (March 1975): 90. Scruggs notes that Frank's superficial response "indicates that he was incapable of understanding Toomer's agony. Going south as a Negro was not a game for Toomer; it meant confronting that blank spot in his identity" (90).

Frank gives a brief account of this trip in *Memoirs of Waldo Frank*, ed. Alan Trachtenberg (Amherst: University of Massachusetts Press, 1973), 104–7. Frank's experiences parallel the similar trek into the South in racial disguise three decades later by John Howard Griffin, author of *Black Like Me*. Like the naively racist Griffin, Frank seems to have undergone an identification that he found alarming: "My place on earth had frighteningly shifted! . . . I felt *with* the Negro. This empathy was startling. Lying in dark sleep I would dream I was a Negro, would spring from sleep reaching for my clothes on the chair beside the bed, to finger them, to smell them . . . in proof I was white and myself" (105). Frank's description of his fear of the disintegration of his white identity reverberates with the terror of identification that characterizes "homosexual panic." Interestingly,

Frank's clothes, not his consciousness or physical characteristics, offer him sensory evidence of his "true" racial identity.

73   Waldo Frank to Jean Toomer, n.d., ca. 1923, quoted in the Norton Critical Edition of *Cane*, ed. Darwin Turner, 160.

74   Letter from Jean Toomer to Gorham Munson, 31 October 1922. Quoted in *A Jean Toomer Reader*, 19–20.

75   See Kerman and Eldridge, *The Lives of Jean Toomer*, 112–16.

76   For further accounts of Toomer's involvement with Gurdjieff, see Kerman and Eldridge, *The Lives of Jean Toomer*, 119–207; and Robert B. Jones, *Jean Toomer and the Prison-House of Thought: A Phenomenology of the Spirit* (Amherst: University of Massachusetts Press, 1993), especially chapter 3, "Landscapes of the Self: Art and Gurdjieffian Idealism." For a more anecdotal account, see Gorham Munson, "A Weekend at the Château du Prieuré," *Southern Review* 6 (April 1970): 397–407.

77   Quoted in Griffin, "Jean Toomer," 283–84.

78   Jean Toomer, "Incredible Journey, Draft Fragments," box 18, folder 487, n.d., n.p., Jean Toomer Papers, James Weldon Johnson Collection, Beinecke Rare Book and Manuscript Library, Yale University, New Haven, Conn..

79   Ibid.

80   Berlant, "National Brands/National Body," 112.

81   Ibid.

82   George B. Hutchinson, "Jean Toomer and the 'New Negroes' of Washington," *American Literature* 63, no. 4 (1991): 687.

83   Umphrey, "The Trouble with Harry Thaw," 19.

Conclusion

I owe special thanks to Kristin Bergen and Regina Kunzel for conversations that helped me develop my discussion in this chapter.

1   See, for example, Natalie Angier, "Report Suggests Homosexuality Is Linked to Genes," *New York Times*, 16 July 1993, A1, A12; and Natalie Angier, "Zone of Brain Linked to Men's Sexual Orientation," *New York Times*, 30 August 1991, A1, D8. See also Simon LeVay, *The Sexual Brain* (Cambridge, Mass.: Harvard University Press, 1993).

2   See U.S. Census Bureau, "Conducting a Census," available at http://www.census.gov/dmd/www/genfaq.htm. Although this decision appears to respond to activists' call for acknowledgment of biracial and multiracial identities, the actual tabulation of the data effectively reverts to previous practices of limiting each person to one racial category. Through "bridg-

ing," a process used in comparing data, multiple answers will be reassigned to a single racial category corresponding to the largest of the nonwhite groups selected by the respondent. See Office of Management and Budget, "Draft Provisional Guidance on the Implementation of the 1997 Standards for the Collection of Federal Data on Race and Ethnicity," February 17, 1999 (available at http://www.multiracial.com/government/RACE.PDF). For an analysis critical of these procedures, see Susan Graham and James A. Landrith, Jr., "Blood Pressure" (available at http://www.multiracial.com/news/bloodpressure.html).

3 Tom Morganthau, "What Color Is Black?" *Newsweek,* 13 February 1995, 62.

4 Quoted in Lawrence Wright, "One Drop of Blood," *New Yorker,* 24 July 1994, 47.

5 Ivan Light and Cathie Lee, "And Just Who Do You Think You Aren't?" *Society* 34, no. 6 (September–October 1997): 28.

6 Susan Stryker, "The Transgender Issue: An Introduction," *GLQ* 4, no. 2 (1998): 149.

7 Leslie Feinberg, *Stone Butch Blues: A Novel* (Ithaca, N.Y.: Firebrand, 1993), 275. Hereafter cited in the text.

8 See Leslie Feinberg, *Transgender Warriors: Making History from Joan of Arc to RuPaul* (Boston: Beacon Press, 1996); and *Outlaw,* dir. Alisa Lebow, Docu-Drag Productions, 1994.

9 On the enduring power of the captivity narrative to shape cultural narratives of white women's relationships to "dark" peoples, see Christopher Castiglia, *Bound and Determined: Captivity, Culture-Crossing, and White Womanhood from Mary Rowlandson to Patty Hearst* (Chicago: University of Chicago Press, 1996).

10 In *Transgender Warriors* and *Outlaw,* Feinberg again uses Native American culture as the site of an affirmative sense of her own identity as transgendered. She narrates a story in which she visits the Museum of the American Indian in New York, where she finds a display of "beautiful thumb-sized clay figures" that represent "berdache" people. To Feinberg, these figures are "my first clue that trans people have not always been hated" (*Transgender Warriors,* 21).

11 In keeping with Feinberg's usage in the text, I refer to Ed with the pronouns "she" and "her."

12 The quote appears on p. 178 of *Stone Butch Blues.* The original text occurs in W. E. B. Du Bois, *The Souls of Black Folk* (1903; reprint, New York: Penguin, 1989), 5.

13 It is worth remembering, too, that Jess is marked as Jewish at various points in the text. Thus this moment of potential assimilation to a normative white masculinity may participate in a process akin to that outlined by Michael Rogin in *Blackface, White Noise: Jewish Immigrants in the Hollywood Melting Pot* (Berkeley: University of California Press, 1996).

Bibliography

Manuscript and Archival Collections

Film Studies Center. Museum of Modern Art, New York.

International Museum of Photography at George Eastman House. Rochester, New York.

Margaret Herrick Library. Academy of Motion Picture Arts and Sciences, Los Angeles.

Motion Picture, Broadcasting, and Recorded Sound Division. Library of Congress, Washington, D.C.

Robinson Locke Collection. Billy Rose Theatre Collection. New York Public Library, New York.

Romaine Trade Catalog Collection. Davidson Library, University of California, Santa Barbara.

Toomer, Jean. Papers. James Weldon Johnson Memorial Collection. Beinecke Rare Book and Manuscript Library, Yale University.

Primary and Secondary Sources

Abelove, Henry. "Freud, Male Homosexuality, and the Americans." In *The Lesbian and Gay Studies Reader,* ed. Henry Abelove, Michèle Aina Barale, and David M. Halperin, 381–93. New York: Routledge, 1993.

———. "Some Speculations on the History of 'Sexual Intercourse' during the 'Long Eighteenth Century' in England." *Genders* 6 (1989): 125–30.

"The Adventures of a Near-White." *Independent* 75 (14 August 1913): 373–76.

Allen, Robert C. *Horrible Prettiness: Burlesque and American Culture.* Chapel Hill: University of North Carolina Press, 1991.

———. *Vaudeville and Film, 1895–1915: A Study in Media Interaction.* Ph.D. diss., University of Iowa, 1977. Reprint, New York: Arno, 1980.

Althusser, Louis. "Ideology and Ideological State Apparatuses (Notes towards an Investigation)." In *Lenin and Philosophy and Other Essays,* Trans. Ben Brewster, 121–73. New York: Monthly Review Press, 1971.

Ammons, Elizabeth. *Conflicting Stories: American Women Writers at the Turn into the Twentieth Century.* New York: Oxford University Press, 1991.

Anger, Kenneth. *Hollywood Babylon*. San Francisco: Straight Arrow Books, 1975. Reprint, New York: Dell, 1981.

———. "Valentino Remembered, Valentino Discovered." In *There Is a New Star in Heaven,* ed. Eva Orbanz, 19–22. Berlin: Volker Speiss, 1979.

Angier, Natalie. "Report Suggests Homosexuality is Linked to Genes." *New York Times,* 16 July 1993, A1, A12.

———. "Zone of Brain Linked to Men's Sexual Orientation." *New York Times,* 30 August 1991, A1, D8.

"Archibald Clavering Gunter." *Bookman* 16 (October 1902): 103–6.

Baker, Houston. *Black Studies, Rap, and the Academy.* Chicago: University of Chicago Press, 1993.

———. *Modernism and the Harlem Renaissance.* Chicago: University of Chicago Press, 1987.

———. *Workings of the Spirit: The Poetics of Afro-American Women's Writing.* Chicago: University of Chicago Press, 1991.

Baker, Kathryn Hinojosa. "Delinquent Desire: Race, Sex, and Ritual in Reform Schools for Girls." *Discourse* 15. no. 1 (fall 1992): 49–68.

Baker, Paula. "The Domestication of Politics: Women and American Political Society, 1780–1920." *American Historical Review* 89 (June 1984): 620–47.

Baker, Ray Stannard. *Following the Color Line.* New York: Doubleday, Page, 1908.

———. "The Tragedy of the Mulatto." *American Magazine* 65 (1907–1908): 582–98.

Balio, Tino. *The American Film Industry.* Rev. ed. Madison: University of Wisconsin Press, 1985.

"Banjo and Bones." *Saturday Review* 57 (1884): 739–40.

Banton, Michael. *The Idea of Race.* London: Tavistock, 1977.

Bardolph, Richard, ed. *The Civil Rights Record: Black Americans and the Law, 1849–1970.* New York: Thomas Y. Crowell, 1970.

Barkan, Elazar. *The Retreat of Scientific Racism: Changing Concepts of Race in Britain and the United States between the World Wars.* New York: Cambridge University Press, 1992.

Barnestone, Willis. *Sappho: Lyrics in the Original Greek.* New York: New York University Press, 1965.

Bartlett, Neil. *Who Was That Man? A Present for Mr. Oscar Wilde.* London: Serpent's Tail, 1988.

Bederman, Gail. "'Civilization,' the Decline of Middle-Class Manliness, and Ida B. Wells's Antilynching Campaign (1892–1894)." *Radical History Review* 52 (1992): 5–30.

———. *Manliness and Civilization: A Cultural History of Gender and Race in the United States, 1880–1917.* Chicago: University of Chicago Press, 1995.

Beer, Gillian. *Darwin's Plots: Evolutionary Narrative in Darwin, George Eliot, and Nineteenth-Century Fiction.* Boston: Routledge and Kegan Paul, 1983.

Berlant, Lauren. "National Brands/National Body: *Imitation of Life.*" In *Comparative American Identities: Race, Sex, and Nationality in the Modern Text,* ed. Hortense Spillers, 110–40. New York: Routledge, 1991.

Berlant, Lauren, and Michael Warner. "What Does Queer Theory Teach Us about X?" *PMLA* 110, no. 3 (May 1995): 343–49.

Bertsch, Marguerite. *How to Write for Moving Pictures: A Manual of Instruction and Information.* New York: George H. Doran, 1917.

Berzon, Judith. *Neither White nor Black: The Mulatto Character in American Fiction.* New York: New York University Press, 1978.

Bhabha, Homi K. "The 'Other' Question: The Stereotype and Colonial Discourse." *Screen* 24, no. 6 (winter 1983): 18–36.

Billings, Dwight B., and Thomas Urban. "The Socio-Medical Construction of Transsexualism: An Interpretation and Critique." *Social Problems* 29 (February 1982): 266–82.

Birken, Lawrence. *Consuming Desire: Sexual Science and the Emergence of a Culture of Abundance, 1871–1914.* Ithaca, N.Y.: Cornell University Press, 1988.

Blackmer, Corinne. "African Masks and the Arts of Passing in Gertrude Stein's 'Melanctha' and Nella Larsen's *Passing.*" *Journal of the History of Sexuality* 4, no. 2 (1993): 230–63.

Blackton, J. Stuart. "Yesterdays of Vitagraph." *Photoplay* (July 1919): 28–33.

Bogdan, Robert. *Freak Show: Presenting Human Oddities for Amusement and Profit.* Chicago: University of Chicago Press, 1988.

Bogle, Donald. *Blacks in American Films and Television: An Encyclopedia.* New York: Garland, 1988. Reprint, New York: Fireside Books, 1989.

Bontemps, Arna. "The Negro Renaissance: Jean Toomer and the Harlem Writers of the 1920's." In *Anger and Beyond: The Negro Writer in the United States,* ed. Herbert Hill, 20–36. New York: Harper and Row, 1966.

Bordwell, David, Janet Staiger, and Kristin Thompson. *The Classical Hollywood Cinema: Film Style and Mode of Production to 1960.* New York: Columbia University Press, 1985.

Bowser, Eileen. *The Transformation of Cinema.* New York: Scribner, 1990.

Braithwaite, William Stanley. "The Negro in American Literature." In *The New Negro,* ed. Alain Locke, 29–44. New York: Albert and Charles Boni, 1925.

Brown, Sterling. "Negro Character as Seen by White Authors." *Journal of Negro Education* 2 (January 1933): 179–203. Reprinted in *Dark Symphony: Negro Literature in America,* ed. James A. Emanuel and Theodore L. Gross, 139–71. New York: Free Press, 1968.

Browne, F. W. Stella. "Studies in Feminine Inversion." *Journal of Sexology and Psychanalysis* 1 (1923): 51–58.

Browne, Nick. "Race: The Political Unconscious of American Film." *East-West Film Journal* 6 (January 1992): 5–16.

Bruce, Dickson D., Jr. *Black American Writing from the Nadir: The Evolution of a Literary Tradition, 1877–1915.* Baton Rouge: Louisiana State University Press, 1989.

Bruce, J[ohn] E. "Some Famous Negroes." *Voice of the Negro* 2 (December 1905): 876–78.

Burma, John G. "The Measurement of 'Passing.'" *American Journal of Sociology* 52 (July 1946): 18–22.

Butler, Judith. *Bodies That Matter: On the Discursive Limits of "Sex."* New York: Routledge, 1993.

———. *Gender Trouble: Feminism and the Subversion of Identity.* New York: Routledge, 1990.

Byrd, Rudolph P. "Jean Toomer and the Writers of the Harlem Renaissance: Was He There with Them?" In *The Harlem Renaissance: Revaluations,* ed. Amritjit Singh, William S. Shiver, and Stanley Brodwin. New York: Garland, 1989.

Carbine, Mary. "'The Finest outside the Loop': Motion Picture Exhibition in Chicago's Black Metropolis, 1905–1928." *Camera Obscura* 23 (May 1990): 9–41.

Carby, Hazel. "'It Jus Be's Dat Way Sometime': The Sexual Politics of Women's Blues." In *Unequal Sisters: A Multicultural Reader in U.S. Women's History,* ed. Ellen Carol DuBois and Vicki L. Ruiz, 238–49. New York: Routledge, 1990.

———. "'On the Threshold of Woman's Era': Lynching, Empire, and Sexuality in Black Feminist Theory." *Critical Inquiry* 12 (autumn 1985): 262–77.

———. *Reconstructing Womanhood: The Emergence of the Afro-American Woman Novelist.* New York: Oxford University Press, 1987.

Carlston, Erin G. "'A Finer Differentiation': Female Homosexuality and the American Medical Community, 1926–1940." In *Science and Homosexualities,* ed. Vernon A. Rosario, 177–96. New York: Routledge, 1997.

Carpenter, Edward. "The Intermediate Sex." In *Love's Coming-of-Age,* 12th enl. ed., 130–49. London: George Allen and Unwin, 1923.

———. *The Intermediate Sex: A Study of Some Transitional Types of Men and Women.* 5th ed. London: George Allen and Unwin, 1918.

———. *Intermediate Types among the Primitive Folk: A Study in Social Evolution.* 2d ed. London: George Allen and Unwin, 1919.

———. *Selected Writings.* vol. 1, *Sex.* London: GMP, 1984.

Castiglia, Christopher. *Bound and Determined: Captivity, Culture-Crossing, and*

White Womanhood from Mary Rowlandson to Patty Hearst. Chicago: University of Chicago Press, 1996.

Cather, Willa. *Not under Forty.* New York: Knopf, 1922.

Cauldwell, D. O. "Psychopathia Transexualis." *Sexology* (December 1949): 274–80.

Charters, Ann. *Nobody: The Story of Bert Williams.* New York: Macmillan, 1970.

Chauncey, George. "Christian Brotherhood or Sexual Perversion? Homosexual Identities and the Construction of Sexual Boundaries in the World War One Era." *Journal of Social History* 19 (1985–1986): 189–211.

———. "From Sexual Inversion to Homosexuality: Medicine and the Changing Conceptualization of Female Deviance." *Salmagundi* 58–59 (fall–winter 1982): 114–46.

———. *Gay New York: Gender, Urban Culture, and the Making of the Gay Male World, 1890–1940.* New York: Basic Books, 1994.

Chesnutt, Charles. *The House Behind the Cedars.* 1900. Reprint, Athens: University of Georgia Press, 1988.

Christensen, Peter. "Sexuality and Liberation in Jean Toomer's 'Withered Skin of Berries.'" *Callaloo* 11, no. 3 (summer 1988): 616–26.

Christian, Barbara. *Black Women Novelists: The Development of a Tradition, 1892–1976.* Westport, Conn.: Greenwood Press, 1980.

Clarke, Cheryl. "Race, Homosocial Desire, and 'Mammon' in *Autobiography of an Ex-Coloured Man.*" In *Professions of Desire: Lesbian and Gay Studies in Literature,* ed. George E. Haggerty and Bonnie Zimmerman, 84–97. New York: Modern Language Association, 1995.

Cohen, Ed. "Writing Gone Wilde: Homoerotic Desire in the Closet of Representation." *PMLA* 102 (1987): 801–13.

Cohen, Philip. "Tarzan and the Jungle Bunnies: Class, Race, and Sex in Popular Culture." *New Formations* 5 (summer 1988): 25–30.

"Colored Lubin Comedies." *Moving Picture World* 16 (10 May 1913): 600.

Condict, Cornelia. Letter to the editor. *Colored American Magazine* 6 (March 1903): 398–99.

Conway, Jill. "Stereotypes of Femininity in a Theory of Sexual Evolution." *Victorian Studies* 14 (1970): 47–62.

Cooley, John. "White Writers and the Harlem Renaissance." In *The Harlem Renaissance: Revaluations,* ed. Amritjit Singh, William S. Shiver, and Stanley Brown. New York: Garland, 1989.

Cott, Nancy. "Passionlessness: An Interpretation of Victorian Sexual Ideology, 1790–1850." In *A Heritage of Her Own: Toward a New Social History of American Women,* ed. Nancy F. Cott and Elizabeth H. Pleck, 162–81. New York: Simon and Schuster, 1979.

Courtney, William Basil. "History of Vitagraph." *Motion Picture News,* 7 February 1925–11 April 1925.

Cripps, Thomas. *Slow Fade to Black: The Negro in American Film, 1900–1942.* New York: Oxford University Press, 1977.

Curtin, Kaier. *"We Can Always Call Them Bulgarians": The Emergence of Lesbians and Gay Men on the American Stage.* Boston: Alyson Publications, 1987.

Cuvier, Georges. "Extraits d'observations faites sur le cadavre d'une femme connue à Paris et à Londres sous le nom de Vénus Hottentote." *Mémoires du Musée d'histoire naturelle* 3 (1817): 259–74.

Davenport, Charles B. *State Laws Limiting Marriage Selection: Examined in Light of Eugenics.* Cold Spring Harbor, N.Y.: Eugenics Record Office, 1913.

Davidson, Arnold I. "Sex and the Emergence of Sexuality." *Critical Inquiry* 14 (autumn 1987): 16–48.

Davis, Angela. *Women, Race, and Class.* New York: Random House, 1981. Reprint, New York: Vintage, 1983.

Davis, Arthur P. *From the Dark Tower: Afro-American Writers, 1900–1960.* Washington, D.C.: Howard University Press, 1974.

Davis, F. James. *Who Is Black? One Nation's Definition.* University Park: Pennsylvania State University Press, 1991.

Davis, Susan G. "'Making Night Hideous': Christmas Revelry and Public Order in Nineteenth-Century Philadelphia." *American Quarterly* 34 (1982): 185–99.

Davis, Thadious M. *Nella Larsen, Novelist of the Harlem Renaissance: A Woman's Life Unveiled.* Baton Rouge: Louisiana State University Press, 1994.

Dearborn, Mary. *Pocahontas's Daughters: Gender and Ethnicity in American Culture.* New York: Oxford University Press, 1986.

Degler, Carl N. *Neither Black nor White: Slavery and Race Relations in Brazil and the United States.* New York: Macmillan, 1971. Reprint, Madison: University of Wisconsin Press, 1986.

DeGroot, Joanna. "'Sex' and 'Race': The Construction of Language and Image in the Nineteenth Century." In *Sexuality and Subordination: Interdisciplinary Studies of Gender in the Nineteenth Century,* ed. Susan Mendus and Jane Rendall, 89–128. New York: Routledge, 1989.

DeJean, Joan. *Fictions of Sappho, 1546–1937.* Chicago: University of Chicago Press, 1989.

de Lauretis, Teresa. *Alice Doesn't: Feminism, Semiotics and the Cinema.* Bloomington: Indiana University Press, 1984.

———. "Film and the Visible." In *How Do I Look? Queer Film and Video,* ed. Bad Object-Choices, 223–84. Seattle: Bay Press, 1991.

———. *Technologies of Gender: Essays on Theory, Film, and Fiction*. Bloomington: Indiana University Press, 1987.

D'Emilio, John. "Capitalism and Gay Identity." In *Powers of Desire: The Politics of Sexuality*, ed. Ann Snitow, Christine Stansell, and Sharon Thompson, 100–113. New York: Monthly Review Press, 1983.

———. *Sexual Politics, Sexual Communities: The Making of a Homosexual Minority in the United States, 1940–1970*. Chicago: University of Chicago Press, 1983.

D'Emilio, John, and Estelle B. Freedman. *Intimate Matters: A History of Sexuality in America*. New York: Harper and Row, 1988.

Denning, Michael. *Mechanic Accents: Dime Novels and Working-Class Culture in Nineteenth-Century America*. London: Verso, 1987.

Derr, Mark. *Some Kind of Paradise: A Chronicle of Man and the Land in Florida*. New York: William Morrow, 1989.

Diawara, Manthia. "Black Spectatorship: Problems of Identification and Resistance." *Screen* 29 (1988): 66–76.

Dickinson, Justus. "Putting One's Best Face Forward." *Green Book Magazine* (December 1914): 1013–16.

Diggs, Marylynne. "Romantic Friends or a 'Different Race of Creatures'? The Representation of Lesbian Pathology in Nineteenth-Century America." *Feminist Studies* 21, no. 2 (summer 1995): 317–40.

Di Stefano, Christine. "Who the Heck Are We? Theoretical Turns against Gender." *Frontiers* 12 (1991): 86–108.

Dixon, Melvin. *Ride Out the Wilderness: Geography and Identity in Afro-American Literature*. Urbana: University of Illinois Press, 1987.

Doane, Mary Ann. "Film and the Masquerade: Theorizing the Female Spectator." *Screen* 23 (1982): 74–87.

Docter, Richard F. *Transvestites and Transsexuals: Toward a Theory of Cross-Gender Behavior*. New York: Plenum Press, 1988.

Doty, Alexander. *Making Things Perfectly Queer: Interpreting Mass Culture*. Minneapolis: University of Minnesota Press, 1993.

Drake, St. Clair, and Horace R. Cayton. *Black Metropolis: A Study of Negro Life in a Northern City*. Rev. and enl. ed. New York: Harper and Row, 1962.

Du Bois, W. E. B. "The Conservation of Races." In *W. E. B. Du Bois Speaks: Speeches and Addresses, 1890–1919*, ed. Philip S. Foner. New York: Pathfinder, 1970.

———. *The Souls of Black Folk*. 1903. Reprint, New York: Penguin, 1989.

———, ed. *The Health and Physique of the Negro American*. Atlanta: Atlanta University Press, 1906.

Du Bois, W. E. B., and Alain Locke. "The Younger Literary Movement." *Crisis* 27 (February 1924): 161–163.

duCille, Ann. *The Coupling Convention: Sex, Text, and Tradition in Black Women's Fiction.* New York: Oxford University Press, 1993.

Duggan, Lisa. "The Discipline Problem: Queer Theory Meets Lesbian and Gay History." *GLQ* 2 (1995): 179–91.

———. "The Social Enforcement of Heterosexuality and Lesbian Resistance in the 1920s." In *Class, Race, and Sex: The Dynamics of Control,* ed. Amy Swerdlow and Hanna Lessinger. Boston: G. K. Hall, 1983.

———. "The Trials of Alice Mitchell: Sensationalism, Sexology, and the Lesbian Subject in Turn-of-the-Century America." *Signs* 18 (summer 1993): 791–814.

Dyer, Richard. *Heavenly Bodies.* London: Macmillan, 1986.

———. *White.* New York: Routledge, 1997.

———. "White." *Screen* 29 (1988): 44–64.

———, ed. *Gays and Film.* Rev. ed. New York: Zoetrope, 1984.

Dyer, Thomas G. *Theodore Roosevelt and the Idea of Race.* Baton Rouge: Louisiana State University Press, 1980.

Edwards, Paul K. *The Southern Urban Negro as a Consumer.* New York: Prentice Hall, 1932.

Elbe, Lili. *Man into Woman: An Authentic Record of a Change of Sex.* Ed. Neils Hoyer [Ernst Ludwig Harthern Jacobsen]. Trans. H. J. Stenning. New York: E. P. Dutton, 1933.

Elfenbein, Anna Shannon. *Women on the Color Line: Evolving Stereotypes and the Writings of George Washington Cable, Grace King, Kate Chopin.* Charlottesville: University Press of Virginia, 1989.

Ellis, Havelock. *Man and Woman: A Study of Human Secondary Sexual Characters.* 4th ed., rev. and enl. New York: Scribners, 1911.

———. *The Problem of Race-Regeneration.* New York: Moffat, Yard, 1911.

———. "Sexual Inversion in Women." *Alienist and Neurologist* 16 (1895): 141–58.

———. "The Sterilization of the Unfit." *Eugenics Review* (October 1909): 203–6.

———. *Studies in the Psychology of Sex.* Vol. 1, *Sexual Inversion.* 1897. London: University Press, 1900.

———. *Studies in the Psychology of Sex.* Vol. 2, *Sexual Inversion.* 3d ed. Philadelphia: F. A. Davis, 1915.

Ellison, Ralph. "Change the Joke and Slip the Yoke." In *Shadow and Act,* 45–59. 1958. Reprint, New York: Vintage, 1972.

Ellman, Richard. *Oscar Wilde.* New York: Vintage, 1987.

Elsaesser, Thomas, ed., with Adam Barker. *Early Cinema: Space, Frame, Narrative.* London: BFI, 1990.

English, W. T. "The Negro Problem from the Physician's Point of View." *Atlanta Journal-Record of Medicine* 5 (October 1903): 459–72.

———. "Racial Anatomical Peculiarities." *New York Medical Journal* 63 (1896): 500–501.

Epstein, Steven. "Gay Politics, Ethnic Identity: The Limits of Social Constructionism." *Socialist Review* 93–94 (1987): 9–54.

Ethnic Notions. Directed by Marlon Riggs. 57 min. San Francisco: California Newsreel, 1987. Videorecording.

Faderman, Lillian. "Lesbian Magazine Fiction in the Early Twentieth Century." *Journal of Popular Culture* 11 (1978): 800–817.

———. *Surpassing the Love of Men: Romantic Friendship and Love between Women from the Renaissance to the Present*. New York: William Morrow, 1981.

Farwell, Marilyn R. "Heterosexual Plots and Lesbian Subtexts: Toward a Theory of Lesbian Narrative Space." In *Lesbian Texts and Contexts: Radical Revisions*, ed. Karla Jay and Joanne Glasgow, 91–103. New York: New York University Press, 1990.

Feinberg, Leslie. *Stone Butch Blues: A Novel*. Ithaca, N.Y.: Firebrand, 1993.

———. *Transgender Warriors: Making History from Joan of Arc to RuPaul*. Boston: Beacon Press, 1996.

Fields, Barbara. "Ideology and Race in American History." In *Region, Race, and Reconstruction: Essays in Honor of C. Vann Woodward*, ed. J. Morgan Kousser and James McPherson, 143–77. New York: Oxford University Press, 1982.

———. "Slavery, Race, and Ideology in the United States of America." *New Left Review* 181 (1990): 95–118.

A Florida Enchantment. 16 mm, 5 reels, 63 min. Directed by Sidney Drew. Vitagraph, 1914.

Flower, W. H., and James Murie. "Account of the Dissection of a Bushwoman." *Journal of Anatomy and Physiology* 1 (1867): 189–208.

Fort, C. H. "Some Corroborative Facts in Regard to the Anatomical Difference between the Negro and White Races." *American Journal of Obstetrics* 10 (1877): 258–59.

Foster, Jeannette. *Sex Variant Women in Literature*. New York: Vantage, 1956. Reprint, Tallahassee, Fla.: Naiad, 1985.

Foucault, Michel. *The History of Sexuality*. Vol. 1, *An Introduction*. Trans. Robert Hurley. New York: Pantheon, 1978. Reprint, New York: Vintage, 1980.

Fout, John C., and Maura Shaw Tantillo, eds. *American Sexual Politics: Sex, Gender, and Race since the Civil War*. Chicago: University of Chicago Press, 1993.

Frank, Waldo. *Memoirs of Waldo Frank*. Ed. Alan Trachtenberg. Amherst: University of Massachusetts Press, 1973.

Frankenberg, Ruth. *White Women, Race Matters: The Social Construction of Whiteness*. Minneapolis: University of Minnesota Press, 1993.

Frazier, E. Franklin. *The Negro Family in the United States.* Rev. and abr. Chicago: University of Chicago Press, 1966.

Fredrickson, George. *The Black Image in the White Mind: The Debate on Afro-American Character and Destiny, 1817–1914.* New York: Harper and Row, 1971.

———. *White Supremacy: A Comparative Study in American and South African History.* New York: Oxford University Press, 1981.

Friedli, Lynne. " 'Passing Women'—a Study of Gender Boundaries in the Eighteenth Century." In *Sexual Underworlds of the Enlightenment,* ed. G. S. Rousseau and Roy Porter, 234–60. Manchester: Manchester University Press, 1987.

Fuss, Diana, ed. *Inside/Out: Lesbian Theories, Gay Theories.* New York: Routledge, 1991.

Gagnier, Regenia. *Idylls of the Marketplace: Oscar Wilde and the Victorian Public.* Stanford, Calif.: Stanford University Press, 1986.

Gaines, Jane. "White Privilege and Looking Relations: Race and Gender in Feminist Film Theory." *Cultural Critique* 4 (fall 1986): 59–79.

Gaines, Kevin. "Black Americans' Racial Uplift Ideology as 'Civilizing Mission': Pauline E. Hopkins on Race and Imperialism." In *Cultures of United States Imperialism,* ed. Amy Kaplan and Donald E. Pease, 433–55. Durham, N.C.: Duke University Press, 1993.

Galton, Francis. *Inquiries into Human Faculty and Its Development.* 1883. Reprint, New York: AMS Press, 1973.

Garber, Eric. "A Spectacle in Color: The Lesbian and Gay Subculture of Jazz Age Harlem." In *Hidden from History: Reclaiming the Gay and Lesbian Past,* ed. Martin Duberman, Martha Vicinus, and George Chauncey Jr., 318–31. New York: Meridian, 1989.

Garber, Marjorie. *Vested Interests: Cross-Dressing and Cultural Anxiety.* New York: Routledge, 1992.

Gates, Henry Louis, Jr. "The Black Man's Burden." In *Fear of a Queer Planet: Queer Politics and Social Theory,* ed. Michael Warner, 230–38. Minneapolis: University of Minnesota Press, 1993.

———. *Figures in Black: Words, Signs, and the "Racial" Self.* New York: Oxford University Press, 1987.

———. *The Signifying Monkey: A Theory of Afro-American Literary Criticism.* New York: Oxford University Press, 1988.

———. "The Trope of a New Negro and the Reconstruction of the Image of the Black." *Representations* 24 (1988): 129–55.

———. "Writing 'Race' and the Difference It Makes." In *"Race," Writing, and Difference,* ed. Henry Louis Gates Jr., 1–20. Chicago: University of Chicago Press, 1985.

Gayle, Addison. *The Way of the New World: The Black Novel in America.* New York: Anchor Books, 1975.

Geddes, Patrick, and J. Arthur Thomson. *The Evolution of Sex.* London: W. Scott, 1889. New York: Scribner, 1890.

"The Gentle Art of Being a Man: A Chat with Kathleen Clifford, 'The Smartest Chap in Town.'" *New York Dramatic Mirror* (4 March 1914): 23.

Gibson, Margaret. "Clitoral Corruption: Body Metaphors and American Doctors' Constructions of Female Homosexuality, 1870–1900." In *Science and Homosexualities,* ed. Vernon A. Rosario, 108–32. New York: Routledge, 1997.

Gilbert, Douglas. *American Vaudeville: Its Life and Times.* 1940. Reprint, New York: Dover, 1963.

Gilbert, Sandra M. "Costumes of the Mind: Transvestism as Metaphor in Modern Literature." In *Gender Studies: New Directions in Feminist Criticism,* ed. Judith Spector. Bowling Green, Ohio: Bowling Green State University Popular Press, 1986.

Gillman, Susan. "The Mulatto, Tragic or Triumphant? The Nineteenth-Century American Race Melodrama." In *The Culture of Sentiment: Race, Gender, and Sentimentality in Nineteenth-Century America,* ed. Shirley Samuels, 221–43. New York: Oxford University Press, 1992.

Gilman, Sander. *Difference and Pathology: Stereotypes of Sexuality, Race, and Madness.* Ithaca, N.Y.: Cornell University Press, 1985.

———. *Freud, Race, and Gender.* Princeton, N.J.: Princeton University Press, 1993.

Ginsberg, Elaine K., ed. *Passing and the Fictions of Identity.* Durham, N.C.: Duke University Press, 1996.

Goldberg, Jonathan. *Sodometries: Renaissance Texts, Modern Sexualities.* Stanford, Calif.: Stanford University Press, 1992.

Goldman, Ruth. "Who Is That *Queer* Queer? Exploring Norms around Sexuality, Race, and Class in Queer Theory." In *Queer Studies: A Lesbian, Gay, Bisexual, and Transgender Anthology,* ed. Brett Beemyn and Mickey Eliason, 169–82. New York: New York University Press, 1996.

Gomery, Douglas. *Shared Pleasures: A History of Movie Presentation in the United States.* Madison: University of Wisconsin Press, 1992.

Gomez, Jewelle. "Repeat after Me: We Are Different, We Are the Same." *New York University Review of Law and Social Change* 14 (1986): 935–41.

Gossett, Thomas F. *Race: The History of an Idea in America.* Dallas: Southern Methodist University Press, 1963.

Gould, Stephen Jay. *The Flamingo's Smile.* New York: W. W. Norton, 1985.

———. *The Mismeasure of Man.* New York: W. W. Norton, 1981.

Griffin, John Chandler. "Jean Toomer: American Writer (A Biography)." Ph.D. diss., University of South Carolina, 1976.

Grosskurth, Phyllis. *Havelock Ellis: A Biography.* New York: Knopf, 1980.

Gruesser, John Cullen, ed. *The Unruly Voice: Rediscovering Pauline Elizabeth Hopkins.* Urbana: University of Illinois Press, 1996.

Gubar, Susan. "Sapphistries." *Signs* 10 (autumn 1984): 43–62.

Gunning, Tom. "The Cinema of Attractions: Early Film, Its Spectator, and the Avant-Garde." *Wide Angle* 8 (1986): 63–70. Reprinted in *Early Cinema: Space, Frame, Narrative,* ed. Thomas Elsaesser with Adam Barker, 56–62. London: BFI, 1990.

———. "Take This Book and Eat It: Burlesque and the Comedy of Signs in Vitagraph's 'Goodness Gracious.'" In *The Slapstick Symposium,* ed. Eileen Bowser. New York: Museum of Modern Art, 1988.

———. "Weaving a Narrative: Style and Economic Background in Griffith's Biograph Films." In *Early Cinema: Space, Frame, Narrative,* ed. Thomas Elsaesser, 336–47. London: BFI, 1990.

Gunter, Archibald C. "Authors as Publishers." *The Writer: A Monthly Magazine to Interest and Help All Literary Workers* 14 (October 1901): 145–46.

Gunter, Archibald Clavering, and Fergus Redmond. *A Florida Enchantment: A Novel.* New York: Hurst, 1891.

"*Gunter's Magazine* Announced by Home Publishing Company." *Publisher's Weekly* 66 (24 December 1904): 1704–5.

Gutman, Herbert. *The Black Family in Slavery and Freedom, 1750–1925.* New York: Pantheon, 1976.

Guy-Blaché, Alice. "Woman's Place in Photoplay Production." *Moving Picture World* (11 July 1914). Reprinted in *Women and the Cinema: A Critical Anthology,* ed. Karyn Kay and Gerald Peary, 337–40. New York: Dutton, 1977.

Habegger, Alfred. *Gender, Fantasy, and Realism in American Literature.* New York: Columbia University Press, 1982.

Hall, Charles Winslow. "Fascinating Bible Stories 4: Hagar and Ishmael." *Colored American Magazine* 2 (February 1901): 302–6.

Hall, Jacquelyn Dowd. "The Mind That Burns in Each Body." In *Powers of Desire: The Politics of Sexuality,* ed. Ann Snitow, Christine Stansell, and Sharon Thompson, 328–49. New York: Monthly Review Press, 1983.

———. *Revolt against Chivalry: Jessie Daniel Ames and the Women's Campaign against Lynching.* New York: Columbia University Press, 1979.

Hall, Stuart. "New Ethnicities." In *Black Film/British Cinema,* ed. Kobena Mercer, 27–31. London: ICA, 1988.

———. "Race, Articulation, and Societies Structured in Dominance." In *Sociological Theories: Race and Colonialism.* Paris: UNESCO, 1980.

Haller, John S., Jr. *Outcasts from Evolution: Scientific Attitudes of Racial Inferiority, 1859-1900*. Urbana: University of Illinois Press, 1971.

Haller, Mark H. *Eugenics: Hereditarian Attitudes in American Thought*. New Brunswick, N.J.: Rutgers University Press, 1963.

Halley, Janet. "The Politics of the Closet: Towards Equal Protection for Gay, Lesbian, and Bisexual Identity." *UCLA Law Review* 36 (1989): 915-76.

Halperin, David. "Is There a History of Sexuality?" In *The Lesbian and Gay Studies Reader*, ed. Henry Abelove, Michèle Aina Barale, and David M. Halperin, 416-31. New York: Routledge, 1993.

————. *One Hundred Years of Homosexuality: And Other Essays on Greek Love*. New York: Routledge, 1990.

Hansen, Miriam. *Babel and Babylon: Spectatorship in American Silent Film*. Cambridge: Harvard University Press, 1991.

Harper, Phillip Brian. *Are We Not Men? Masculine Anxiety and the Problem of African-American Identity*. New York: Oxford University Press, 1996.

Harris, M. A. ("Spike"). *A Negro History Tour of Manhattan*. New York: Greenwood, 1968.

Harris, Neil. *Humbug: The Art of P. T. Barnum*. Chicago: University of Chicago Press, 1973.

Harris, Trudier. *Exorcising Blackness: Historical and Literary Lynching and Burning Rituals*. Bloomington: Indiana University Press, 1984.

Hayden, Robert. *Kaleidoscope: Poems by American Negro Poets*. New York: Harcourt, Brace and World, 1967.

Helbling, Mark. "Jean Toomer and Waldo Frank: A Creative Friendship." In *Jean Toomer: A Critical Evaluation*, ed. Therman B. O'Daniel, 85-97. Washington, D.C.: Howard University Press, 1988.

Herrmann, Anne. "'Passing' Women, Performing Men." *Michigan Quarterly Review* 30 (1991): 60-71.

Herskovits, Melville J. *The American Negro: A Study in Racial Crossing*. New York: Knopf, 1928.

Higashi, Sumiko. *Virgins, Vamps, and Flappers*. Montreal: Eden Press Women's Publications, 1978.

Higginson, Thomas Wentworth. "Sappho." *Atlantic Monthly* 28 (July 1871): 83-93.

Higham, John. *Strangers in the Land: Patterns of American Nativism, 1860-1925*. New Brunswick, N.J.: Rutgers University Press, 1955. Reprint, New York: Atheneum, 1963.

hooks, bell. *Ain't I a Woman: Black Women and Feminism*. Boston: South End Press, 1981.

————. *Black Looks: Race and Representation*. Boston: South End Press, 1992.

―――. *Talking Back: Thinking Feminist, Thinking Black.* Boston: South End Press, 1989.

Hopkins, Pauline E. "Club Life among Colored Women." *Colored American Magazine* 5 (August 1902): 273–77.

―――. *Contending Forces: A Romance Illustrative of Negro Life North and South.* Edited and with an introduction by Richard Yarborough. 1900. Reprint, New York: Oxford University Press, 1988.

―――. "A Dash for Liberty." *Colored American Magazine* 3 (August 1901): 243–47.

―――. *Hagar's Daughter: A Story of Southern Caste Prejudice.* In *The Magazine Novels of Pauline Hopkins,* edited and with an introduction by Hazel V. Carby, 3–284. New York: Oxford University Press, 1988. First published in *Colored American Magazine,* March 1901-March 1902.

―――. *Of One Blood; or, the Hidden Self.* In *The Magazine Novels of Pauline Hopkins,* edited and with an introduction by Hazel V. Carby, 441–621. New York: Oxford University Press, 1988. First published in *Colored American Magazine,* November 1902-November 1903.

―――. Reply to Condict. *Colored American Magazine* 6 (March 1903): 399.

―――. *Winona: A Tale of Negro Life in the South and Southwest.* In *The Magazine Novels of Pauline Hopkins,* edited and with an introduction by Hazel V. Carby, 287–437. New York: Oxford University Press, 1988. First published in *Colored American Magazine,* May–October 1902.

Howells, William Dean. "At a Dime Museum." In *Literature and Life: Studies,* 193–201. New York: Harper and Brothers, 1902.

Hrdlicka, Ales. "Physical Differences between White and Colored Children." *American Anthropologist* 11 (1898): 347–50.

Hughes, Langston. *The Big Sea: An Autobiography.* 1940. Reprint, New York: Thunder's Mouth Press, 1986.

―――. "The Twenties: Harlem and Its Negritude." *African Forum* 1 (spring 1966): 11–20.

Hughes, Langston, and Milton Meltzer. *Black Magic: A Pictorial History of the Negro in American Entertainment.* Englewood Cliffs, N.J.: Prentice-Hall, 1967.

Hull, Gloria T. *Color, Sex, and Poetry: Three Women Writers of the Harlem Renaissance.* Bloomington: Indiana University Press, 1987.

Hutchinson, George B. "Jean Toomer and the 'New Negroes' of Washington." *American Literature* 63, no. 4 (1991): 683–92.

Hutton, Laurence. "The Negro on the Stage." *Harper's Magazine* 79 (1889): 131–45.

Hyatt, H. Otis. "Note on the Normal Anatomy of the Vulvo-Vaginal Orifice."
    American Journal of Obstetrics 10 (1877): 253–58.

Hyde, H. Montgomery, ed. *The Trials of Oscar Wilde.* London: William Hodge,
    1948.

Irvine, Janice. *Disorders of Desire: Sex and Gender in Modern American Sexology.*
    Philadelphia: Temple University Press, 1990.

Jackson, Peter, ed. *Race and Racism: Essays in Social Geography.* Boston: Allen and
    Unwin, 1987.

Jacobs, Harriet A. *Incidents in the Life of a Slave Girl, Written by Herself.* Edited
    and with an introduction by Jean Fagan Yellin. 1861. Reprint, Cambridge:
    Harvard University Press, 1987.

Jacobus, Mary, Evelyn Fox Keller, and Sally Shuttleworth, eds. *Body/Politics:*
    Women and the Discourses of Science. New York: Routledge, 1990.

J.A.M.A. "The Legal Status of the Homosexual." *Journal of Sexology and Psych-*
    analyis 1 (1923): 110–12.

Jameson, Fredric. "Magical Narratives: Romance as Genre." *New Literary History*
    7 (1975): 135–63.

———. *The Political Unconscious: Narrative as a Socially Symbolic Act.* Ithaca, N.Y.:
    Cornell University Press, 1981.

JanMohamed, Abdul R. "Sexuality on/of the Racial Border: Foucault, Wright,
    and the Articulation of 'Racialized Sexuality.'" In *Discourses of Sexuality:*
    From Aristotle to AIDS, ed. Domna C. Stanton, 94–116. Ann Arbor: Uni-
    versity of Michigan Press, 1992.

Jenkins, Henry. *What Made Pistachio Nuts? Early Sound Comedy and the Vaudeville*
    Aesthetic. New York: Columbia University Press, 1992.

Johnson, Abby Arthur, and Ronald M. Johnson. "Away from Accommodation:
    Radical Editors and Protest Journalism, 1900–1910." *Journal of Negro His-*
    tory 62 (1977): 325–38.

Johnson, Barbara. *The Critical Difference: Essays in the Contemporary Rhetoric of*
    Reading. Baltimore: Johns Hopkins University Press, 1980.

Johnson, James Weldon. *Along This Way: The Autobiography of James Weldon John-*
    son. New York: Viking Penguin, 1933. Reprint, with an introduction by
    Sondra Kathryn Wilson, New York: Penguin, 1990.

———. *The Autobiography of an Ex-Coloured Man.* New York: Knopf, 1927. Re-
    print, New York: Vintage Books, 1989.

———. *Black Manhattan.* 1930. Reprint, with a new preface by Allan H. Spear,
    New York: Atheneum, 1969.

Johnson, Joseph Taber. "On some of the apparent peculiarities of parturition in
    the Negro race, with remarks on race pelves in general." *American Journal*
    of Obstetrics 8 (1875): 88–123.

Johnson, Julian. "The Story of Storey." *Photoplay Magazine* (January 1920): 114.

Jones, Robert B. *Jean Toomer and the Prison-House of Thought: A Phenomenology of the Spirit.* Amherst: University of Massachusetts Press, 1993.

Jordanova, Ludmilla. *Sexual Visions: Images of Gender in Science and Medicine between the Eighteenth and Twentieth Centuries.* Madison: University of Wisconsin Press, 1989.

Kaplan, Amy. *The Social Construction of American Realism.* Chicago: University of Chicago Press, 1988.

Kaplan, Amy, and Donald E. Pease, eds. *Cultures of United States Imperialism.* Durham, N.C.: Duke University Press, 1993.

Katz, Jonathan. *Gay American History: Lesbians and Gay Men in the USA: A Documentary.* New York: Crowell, 1976. Reprint, New York: Harper and Row, 1985.

———. *Gay/Lesbian Almanac: A New Documentary.* New York: Harper and Row, 1983.

———. "The Invention of Heterosexuality." *Socialist Review* 20 (1990): 7–34.

Katzman, David. *Seven Days a Week: Women and Domestic Service in Industrializing America.* New York: Oxford University Press, 1978.

Keller, Evelyn Fox. *Reflections on Gender and Science.* New Haven: Yale University Press, 1985.

Kellner, Bruce. *Carl Van Vechten and the Irreverent Decades.* Norman: University of Oklahoma Press, 1968.

Kerman, Cynthia Earl, and Richard Eldridge. *The Lives of Jean Toomer: A Hunger for Wholeness.* Baton Rouge: Louisiana State University Press, 1987.

Kiernan, James G. "Bisexuality." *Urologic and Cutaneous Review* 18 (1914): 372–76.

———. "Classification of Homosexuality." *Urologic and Cutaneous Review* 20 (1916): 348–50.

———. "Increase of American Inversion." *Urologic and Cutaneous Review* 20 (1916): 44–46.

———. "Inversion and Dreams." *Urologic and Cutaneous Review* 19 (June 1915): 350–352.

———. "Invert Marriages." *Urologic and Cutaneous Review* 18 (1914): 550.

———. "The Neutral Sex." *Urologic and Cutaneous Review* 21 (1917): 164–65.

———. "Race and Insanity." *Journal of Nervous and Mental Diseases* 12 (1885): 174–75, 290–93.

Klotman, Phyllis. " 'Tearing a Hole in History': Lynching as Theme and Motif." *Black American Literature Forum* 19 (1985): 55–63.

Koestenbaum, Wayne. *Double Talk: The Erotics of Male Literary Collaboration.* New York: Routledge, 1989.

Koppelman, Andrew. "The Miscegenation Analogy: Sodomy Law as Sex Discrimination." *Yale Law Journal* 98 (November 1988): 145–64.

———. "The Miscegenation Precedents." In *Same-Sex Marriage: Pro and Con*, ed. Andrew Sullivan, 335–42. New York: Vintage, 1997.

Krafft-Ebing, Richard von. "Perversion of the Sexual Instinct—Report of Cases." Trans. H. M. Jewett. *Alienist and Neurologist* 9, no. 4 (October 1888): 565–81.

———. *Psychopathia Sexualis, with Especial Reference to Contrary Sexual Instinct.* 12th ed. Trans. Franklin S. Klaf. New York: Stein and Day, 1965.

Kramer, Peter. "Vitagraph, Slapstick, and Early Cinema." *Screen* 29, no. 2 (1988): 9–104.

Kutzinski, Vera M. "Unseasonal Flowers: Nature and History in Plácido and Jean Toomer." *Yale Journal of Criticism* 3 (1990): 153–79.

Laqueur, Thomas. *Making Sex: Body and Gender from the Greeks to Freud.* Cambridge: Harvard University Press, 1990.

Larson, Charles R. *Invisible Darkness: Jean Toomer and Nella Larsen.* Iowa City: University of Iowa Press, 1993.

Lauritzen, Einar, and Gunnar Lundquist, eds. *American Film Index, 1908–1915.* Stockholm, Sweden: Film-Index, 1976.

Law, Sylvia A. "Homosexuality and the Social Meaning of Gender." *Wisconsin Law Review* 2 (1988): 187–235.

Leab, Daniel J. *From Sambo to Superspade: The Black Experience in Motion Pictures.* Boston: Houghton Mifflin, 1975.

Leach, William. "Transformations in a Culture of Consumption: Women and Department Stores, 1890–1925." *Journal of American History* 71, no. 2 (September 1984): 319–42.

Leonard, William Torbert. *Masquerade in Black.* Metuchen, N.J.: Scarecrow Press, 1986.

LeVay, Simon. *The Sexual Brain.* Cambridge: Harvard University Press, 1993.

Levine, George. *Darwin and the Novelists: Patterns of Science in Victorian Fiction.* Cambridge: Harvard University Press, 1988.

Levy, Anita. *Other Women: The Writing of Class, Race, and Gender, 1832–1898.* Princeton: Princeton University Press, 1991.

Lichtenstein, Perry M. "The 'Fairy' and the Lady Lover." *Medical Review of Reviews* 27 (1921): 369–74.

Logan, Rayford. *The Betrayal of the Negro, from Rutherford B. Hayes to Woodrow Wilson.* New York: Collier, 1965.

Lothstein, Leslie Martin. *Female-to-Male Transsexualism: Historical, Clinical, and Theoretical Issues.* Boston: Routledge and Kegan Paul, 1983.

Lott, Eric. *Love and Theft: Blackface Minstrelsy and the American Working Class.* New York: Oxford University Press, 1993.

Maitland, Sara. *Vesta Tilley.* London: Virago, 1986.

Marks, Carole. *Farewell—We're Good and Gone: The Great Black Migration.* Bloomington: Indiana University Press, 1989.

Marks, Elaine. "Lesbian Intertextuality." In *Homosexualities and French Literature,* ed. George Stambolian and Elaine Marks, 353–78. Ithaca, N.Y.: Cornell University Press, 1978.

Martin, Biddy. "Sexualities without Gender and Other Queer Utopias." *Diacritics* 24 (summer–fall 1994): 104–21.

May, Lary. *Screening Out the Past: The Birth of Mass Culture and the Motion Picture Industry.* New York: Oxford University Press, 1980. Reprint (with a new preface), Chicago: University of Chicago Press, 1983.

Mayne, Judith. "Lesbian Looks: Dorothy Arzner and Female Authorship." In *How Do I Look? Queer Film and Video,* ed. Bad Object-Choices, 103–43. Seattle: Bay Press, 1991.

Mayne, Xavier [Edward Irenaeus Prime Stevenson]. *The Intersexes: A History of Similisexualism as a Problem in Social Life.* 1908. Reprint, New York: Arno, 1975.

McDowell, Deborah. Introduction to *"Quicksand" and "Passing,"* by Nella Larsen. New Brunswick, N.J.: Rutgers University Press, 1986.

———. "New Directions for Black Feminist Criticism." In *The New Feminist Criticism: Essays on Women, Literature, and Theory,* ed. Elaine Showalter. New York: Pantheon, 1985.

McLean, Albert P. *American Vaudeville as Ritual.* Lexington: University of Kentucky Press, 1965.

McKay, Claude. *Gingertown.* 1932. Reprint, Freeport, N.Y.: Books for Libraries Press, 1972.

McKay, Nellie Y. *Jean Toomer, Artist: A Study of His Literary Life and Work, 1894–1936.* Chapel Hill: University of North Carolina Press, 1984.

McMurtrie, Douglas C. "A Legend of Lesbian Love among the North American Indians." *Urologic and Cutaneous Review* 18 (1914): 192–93.

———. "Sexual Inversion among Women in Spain." *Urologic and Cutaneous Review* 18 (1914): 308.

Mencke, John G. *Mulattoes and Race Mixture: American Attitudes and Images, 1865–1918.* Ann Arbor, Mich.: UMI Research Press, 1979.

Mercer, Kobena. "Traveling Theory: The Cultural Politics of Race and Representation." *Afterimage* 18 (1990): 7–9.

Mercer, Kobena, and Isaac Julien. "Race, Sexual Politics, and Black Masculinity:

A Dossier." In *Male Order: Unwrapping Masculinity,* ed. Rowena Chapman and Jonathan Rutherford, 97–164. London: Lawrence and Wishart, 1988.

Michaels, Walter Benn. "The Souls of White Folk." In *Literature and the Body: Essays on Populations and Persons,* ed. Elaine Scarry, 185–209. Baltimore: Johns Hopkins University Press, 1988.

Miller, D. A. "Anal Rope." *Representations* 32 (1990): 114–33.

———. *The Novel and the Police.* Berkeley: University of California Press, 1988.

Montagu, Ashley. *The Idea of Race.* Lincoln: University of Nebraska Press, 1965.

———. *Man's Most Dangerous Myth: The Fallacy of Race.* New York: Columbia University Press, 1942.

———. "On the Nonperception of 'Race' Differences." *Current Anthropology* 18 (1977): 743–44.

Morris, [?]. "Is Evolution Trying to Do Away with the Clitoris?" Paper presented at the meeting of the American Association of Obstetricians and Gynecologists, St. Louis, Missouri. 21 September 1892. Pamphlet, Yale University Medical Library, New Haven, Conn.

Morrison, Toni. "Jean Toomer's Art of Darkness." *Washington Post Book World,* 13 July 1980.

———. *Playing in the Dark: Whiteness and the Literary Imagination.* Cambridge: Harvard University Press, 1992.

Mosse, George L. "Nationalism and Respectability: Normal and Abnormal Sexuality in the Nineteenth Century." *Journal of Contemporary History* 17 (1982): 221–46.

Mulvey, Laura. "Visual Pleasure and Narrative Cinema." *Screen* 16 (1975): 6–18.

Mumford, Kevin. *Interzones: Black/White Sex Districts in Chicago and New York in the Early Twentieth Century.* New York: Columbia University Press, 1997.

Munson, Gorham. "A Weekend at the Château du Prieuré." *Southern Review* 6 (April 1970): 397–407.

Murray, Pauli. *States' Laws on Race and Color.* Woman's Division of Christian Service, 1951.

Musser, Charles. *Before the Nickelodeon: Edwin S. Porter and the Edison Manufacturing Company.* Berkeley: University of California Press, 1991.

———. *The Emergence of Cinema: The American Screen to 1907.* New York: Scribner, 1990.

Myrdal, Gunnar. "Crossing the Color Line." In *An American Dilemma: The Negro Problem and Modern Democracy,* 683–88. New York: Harper, 1944.

Nelson, Richard Alan. "Movie Mecca of the South: Jacksonville, Florida, as an Early Rival to Hollywood." *Journal of Popular Film and Television* 8 (fall 1980): 38–51.

Newby, Idus A. *Jim Crow's Defense: Anti-Negro Thought in America, 1900–1930*. Baton Rouge: Louisiana State University Press, 1965.

Newton, Esther. *Mother Camp: Female Impersonators in America*. Chicago: University of Chicago Press, 1972.

———. "The Mythic Mannish Lesbian: Radclyffe Hall and the New Woman." *Signs* 9, no. 4 (summer 1984): 557–75.

Noble, Jeanne. *Beautiful Also, Are the Souls of My Black Sisters: A History of the Black Woman in America*. Englewood Cliffs, N.J.: Prentice-Hall, 1978.

Noble, Peter. *The Negro in Films*. New York: Arno Press, 1970.

Nochlin, Linda. "The Imaginary Orient." *Art in America* 71 (May 1983): 118–31, 186–91.

Norden, Martin. "Women in the Early Film Industry." *Wide Angle* 6 (1984): 68–75.

Norris, Frank. *The Third Circle*. 1909. Reprint, New York: Doubleday, Doran, 1928.

O'Daniel, Therman B., ed. *Jean Toomer: A Critical Evaluation*. Washington, D.C.: Howard University Press, 1988.

Olsen, Otto. *The Thin Disguise: Turning Point in Negro History*. New York: AIMS, 1967.

Omi, Michael, and Howard Winant. *Racial Formation in the United States: From the 1960s to the 1980s*. New York: Routledge, 1986.

Oscar Wilde: Three Times Tried. London: Ferrestone Press, n.d.

Otis, Margaret. "A Perversion Not Commonly Noted." *Journal of Abnormal Psychology* 8 (June–July 1913): 113–16.

Outlaw, Lucius. "Towards a Critical Theory of Race." In *Anatomy of Racism*, ed. David Theo Goldberg. Minneapolis: University of Minnesota Press, 1990.

Padgug, Robert. "Sexual Matters: Rethinking Sexuality in History." *Radical History Review* 20 (spring–summer 1979): 3–23.

Parish, James Robert. *Gays and Lesbians in Mainstream Cinema: Plots, Critiques, Casts, and Credits for 272 Theatrical and Made-for-Television Hollywood Releases*. Jefferson, N.C.: McFarland, 1993.

Parsons, Alice Beal. "Toomer and Frank." *The World Tomorrow* 7 (March 1924): 96.

Pascoe, Peggy. "Race, Gender, and Intercultural Relations: The Case of Interracial Marriage." *Frontiers* 12 (1991): 5–18.

"Passes for White to Get Living Wages." *Chicago Defender,* 15 August 1914.

Peiss, Kathy. *Cheap Amusements: Working Women and Leisure in Turn-of-the-Century New York*. Philadelphia: Temple University Press, 1986.

Penn, Donna. "Queer: Theorizing Politics and History." *Radical History Review* 62 (spring 1995): 24–43.

Poovey, Mary. *Uneven Developments: The Ideological Work of Gender in Mid-Victorian England.* Chicago: University of Chicago Press, 1988.

Prince, Morton. "Sexual Perversion or Vice? A Pathological and Therapeutic Inquiry." In *Psychotherapy and Multiple Personality: Selected Essays.* Cambridge: Harvard University Press, 1975. First published in *Journal of Nervous and Mental Disease* 25 (April 1898): 237–56.

Quart, Barbara Koenig. *Women Directors: The Emergence of a New Cinema.* New York: Praeger, 1988.

Radway, Janice. *Reading the Romance: Women, Patriarchy, and Popular Culture.* Chapel Hill: University of North Carolina Press, 1984.

Raiskin, Judith. "Inverts and Hybrids: Lesbian Rewritings of Sexual and Racial Identities." In *The Lesbian Postmodern,* ed. Laura Doan, 156–72. New York: Columbia University Press, 1994.

Ramsey, Priscilla. "A Study of Black Identity in 'Passing' Novels of the Nineteenth and Early Twentieth Century." *Studies in Black Literature* 7 (1976): 1–7.

Raper, Arthur F. *The Tragedy of Lynching.* Chapel Hill: University of North Carolina Press, 1933.

Raub, Patricia. "Issues of Passion and Power in E. M. Hull's *The Sheik.*" *Women's Studies* 21 (1992): 119–28.

Reid, Mark A. *Redefining Black Film.* Berkeley: University of California Press, 1993.

"The Return of Burton Barnes." *Bookman* 25 (March 1907): 234–36.

Reuter, Edward Byron. *The Mulatto in the United States: Including a Study of the Role of Mixed-Blood Races throughout the World.* Boston: Gorham Press, 1918.

Rich, B. Ruby. "When Difference Is (More Than) Skin Deep." In *Queer Looks: Perspectives on Lesbian and Gay Film and Video,* ed. Martha Gever, John Greyson, and Pratibha Parmar, 318–39. New York: Routledge, 1993.

Richardson, F. H. "The Home of the Vitagraph." *Moving Picture World* 19, no. 4 (24 January 1914): 401–3.

Riley, Denise. *"Am I That Name?" Feminism and the Category of "Women" in History.* Minneapolis: University of Minnesota Press, 1988.

Robinson, Amy. "Forms of Appearance of Value: Homer Plessy and the Politics of Privacy." In *Performance and Cultural Politics,* ed. Elin Diamond, 237–61. New York: Routledge, 1996.

Robinson, Paul A. *The Modernization of Sex: Havelock Ellis, Alfred Kinsey, William Masters, and Virginia Johnson.* New York: Harper and Row, 1976.

Robinson, William. "My Views on Homosexuality." *American Journal of Urology* 10 (1914): 550–52.

Rodowick, David. *The Difficulty of Difference: Psychoanalysis, Sexual Difference, and Film Theory.* New York: Routledge, 1991.

Roediger, David R. *The Wages of Whiteness: Race and the Making of the American Working Class.* New York: Verso, 1991.

Rogin, Michael. *Blackface, White Noise: Jewish Immigrants and the Hollywood Melting Pot.* Berkeley: University of California Press, 1995.

———. "Blackface, White Noise: The Jewish Jazz Singer Finds His Voice." *Critical Inquiry* 18 (spring 1992): 417–53.

———. " 'Make My Day!' Spectacle as Amnesia in Imperial Politics [and] the Sequel." In *Cultures of United States Imperialism,* ed. Amy Kaplan and Donald E. Pease, 499–534. Durham, N.C.: Duke University Press, 1993.

———. *Ronald Reagan, the Movie: And Other Episodes in Political Demonology.* Berkeley: University of California Press, 1987.

Rollins, Judith. *Between Women: Domestics and Their Employers.* Philadelphia: Temple University Press, 1985.

Rosario, Vernon, ed. *Science and Homosexualities.* New York: Routledge, 1997.

Rose, Jacqueline. *Sexuality in the Field of Vision.* London: Verso, 1986.

Rose, Peter I. *The Subject Is Race.* New York: Oxford University Press, 1968.

Rowbotham, Sheila, and Jeffrey Weeks. *Socialism and the New Life: The Personal and Sexual Politics of Edward Carpenter and Havelock Ellis.* London: Pluto Press, 1977.

Royden, A. Maude. "Consanguineous and Mixed Marriages." *Journal of Sexology and Psychanalysis* 1 (1923): 213–17.

Rubin, Gayle. "Thinking Sex: Notes for a Radical Theory of the Politics of Sexuality." In *Pleasure and Danger,* ed. Carole Vance. Boston: Routledge and Kegan Paul, 1984.

Russo, Vito. *The Celluloid Closet: Homosexuality in the Movies.* New York: Harper and Row, 1981.

Saks, Eva. "Representing Miscegenation Law." *Raritan* 8 (fall 1988): 39–69.

Sampson, Henry T. *Blacks in Black and White: A Source Book on Black Films.* Metuchen, N.J.: Scarecrow Press, 1977.

———. *Blacks in Blackface: A Sourcebook on Early Black Musical Shows.* Metuchen, N.J.: Scarecrow Press, 1980.

———. *The Ghost Walks: A Chronological History of Blacks in Show Business, 1865–1910.* Metuchen, N.J.: Scarecrow Press, 1988.

San Francisco Lesbian and Gay History Project. " 'She Even Chewed Tobacco': A Pictorial Narrative of Passing Women in America." In *Hidden from History: Reclaiming the Gay and Lesbian Past,* ed. Martin Duberman, Martha Vicinus, and George Chauncey Jr., 183–94. New York: New American Library, 1989.

Schiebinger, Londa. *The Mind Has No Sex? Women in the Origins of Modern Science.* Cambridge: Harvard University Press, 1989.

———. *Nature's Body: Gender in the Making of Modern Science.* Boston: Beacon Press, 1993.

Scruggs, Charles. "Jean Toomer: Fugitive." *American Literature* 47 (March 1975): 84–96.

Sedgwick, Eve Kosofsky. *Between Men: English Literature and Male Homosocial Desire.* New York: Columbia University Press, 1985.

———. *Epistemology of the Closet.* Berkeley: University of California Press, 1990.

———. *Tendencies.* Durham, N.C.: Duke University Press, 1993.

Segrest, Mab. *Memoirs of a Race Traitor.* Boston: South End Press, 1994.

Seligman, C. G. "Sexual Inversion among Primitive Races." *Alienist and Neurologist* 23 (1902): 11–15.

Senelick, Laurence. "The Evolution of the Male Impersonator on the Nineteenth-Century Stage." *Essays in Theatre* 1 (1982): 31–46.

The Sexual Subject: A Screen Reader in Sexuality. New York: Routledge, 1992.

Shockley, Ann Allen. *Afro-American Women Writers, 1746–1933.* Boston: G. K. Hall, 1988.

———. "The Black Lesbian in American Literature." *Conditions: Five* 2 (autumn 1979): 133–42.

———. "Pauline Elizabeth Hopkins: A Biographical Excursion into Obscurity." *Phylon* 33 (1972): 22–26.

Showalter, Elaine. *Sexual Anarchy: Gender and Culture at the Fin de Siècle.* New York: Viking, 1990.

Simmons, Christina. "Companionate Marriage and the Lesbian Threat." *Frontiers* 4 (1979): 54–59.

Simon, Scott. "Sex Change and Cross-Dressing in the Early Silent Film." San Francisco International Lesbian and Gay Film Festival. 16–25 June 1989.

Singh, Amritjit, William Shiver, and Stanley Brodwin, eds. *The Harlem Renaissance: Revaluations.* New York: Garland, 1989.

Slide, Anthony. *The Big V: A History of the Vitagraph Company.* Metuchen, N.J.: Scarecrow Press, 1976.

———. *Early Women Directors.* New York: A. S. Barnes, 1977.

———, ed. *Selected Vaudeville Criticism.* Metuchen, N.J.: Scarecrow Press, 1988.

Smith, Albert E. *Two Reels and a Crank.* Garden City, N.Y.: Doubleday, 1952.

Smith, Valerie. "Reading the Intersection of Race and Gender in Narratives of Passing." *Diacritics* 24 (1994): 43–57.

———. *Self-Discovery and Authority in Afro-American Narrative.* Cambridge: Harvard University Press, 1987.

Smith-Rosenberg, Carroll. *Disorderly Conduct: Visions of Gender in Victorian America.* New York: Alfred A. Knopf, 1985.

———. "The Female World of Love and Ritual: Relations between Women in Nineteenth-Century America." *Signs* 1 (autumn 1975): 1–29.

Smythe, A. G. "The Position of the Hymen in the Negro Race." *American Journal of Obstetrics* 10 (1877): 638–39.

Sollors, Werner. " 'Never Was Born': The Mulatto, an American Tragedy?" *Massachusetts Review* 27 (summer 1986): 293–316.

Spelman, Elizabeth V. *Inessential Woman: Problems of Exclusion in Feminist Thought.* Boston: Beacon Press, 1988.

Spillers, Hortense. *Comparative American Identities: Race, Sex, and Nationality in the Modern Text.* New York: Routledge, 1991.

Stepan, Nancy. *The Idea of Race in Science: Great Britain, 1800–1960.* Hamden, Conn.: Archon Books, 1982.

———. "Race and Gender: The Role of Analogy in Science." In *Anatomy of Racism,* ed. David Theo Goldberg, 38–57. Minneapolis: University of Minnesota Press, 1990.

Stepan, Nancy Leys, and Sander Gilman. "Appropriating the Idioms of Science: The Rejection of Scientific Racism." In *The Bounds of Race: Perspectives on Hegemony and Resistance,* ed. Dominick LaCapra, 72–103. Ithaca, N.Y.: Cornell University Press, 1991.

Stepto, Robert B. *From behind the Veil: A Study of Afro-American Narrative.* Chicago: University of Illinois Press, 1979.

Stocking, George W., Jr. *Race, Culture, and Evolution: Essays in the History of Anthropology.* Chicago: University of Chicago Press, 1982.

Stoddard, Thomas B., E. Carrington Boggan, Marilyn G. Haft, Charles Lister, and John P. Rupp, eds. *The Rights of Gay People.* 1975. Reprint, New York: Bantam Books, 1983.

Stoler, Ann Laura. *Race and the Education of Desire: Foucault's History of Sexuality and the Colonial Order of Things.* Durham, N.C.: Duke University Press, 1995.

Storey, Edith. "My Theories of Physical Culture." *Physical Culture* (September 1916): 76–78.

Stryker, Susan. "The Transgender Issue: An Introduction." *GLQ* 4, no. 2 (1998): 145–48.

Studlar, Gaylyn. "Discourses of Gender and Ethnicity: The Construction and De(con)struction of Rudolph Valentino as Other." *Film Criticism* 13 no. 2 (winter 1989): 18–35.

Sundquist, Eric. "Mark Twain and Homer Plessy." *Representations* 24 (fall 1988): 102–28.

Swerdlow, Amy, and Hannah Lessinger. *Class, Race, and Sex: The Dynamics of Control.* Boston: G. K. Hall, 1983.

Symonds, John Addington. *Studies of Greek Poets.* First series. New York: Harper and Brothers, 1880.

Szwed, John F. "Race and the Embodiment of Culture." *Ethnicity* 2 (March 1975): 19–33.

Tate, Claudia. "Allegories of Black Female Desire: Or, Rereading Nineteenth-Century Sentimental Narratives of Black Female Authority." In *Changing Our Own Words: Essays on Criticism, Theory, and Writing by Black Women,* ed. Cheryl Wall, 98–126. New Brunswick, N.J.: Rutgers University Press, 1989.

———. *Domestic Allegories of Political Desire: The Black Heroine's Text at the Turn of the Century.* New York: Oxford University Press, 1992.

Terry, Jennifer. "Lesbians under the Medical Gaze: Scientists Search for Re-markable Differences." *Journal of Sex Research* 27 (August 1990): 317–39.

———. "Theorizing Deviant Historiography." *Differences* 3 (summer 1991): 55–74.

Thompson, Denise. *Flaws in the Social Fabric: Homosexuals and Society in Sydney.* Boston: George Allen and Unwin, 1985.

Thurman, Wallace. "Negro Artists and the Negro." *New Republic* 52 (1927): 37–39.

Toll, Robert C. *Blacking Up: The Minstrel Show in Nineteenth Century America.* New York: Oxford University Press, 1974.

———. *On with the Show: The First Century of Show Business in America.* New York: Oxford University Press, 1976.

Tompkins, Jane. *West of Everything: The Inner Life of Westerns.* New York: Oxford University Press, 1992.

Tong, Lowell. "Comparing Mixed-Race and Same-Sex Marriage." In *On the Road to Same-Sex Marriage: A Supportive Guide to Psychological, Political, and Legal Issues,* ed. Robert P. Cabaj and David W. Purcell, 109–27. San Francisco: Josey-Bass, 1998.

Toomer, Jean. *Cane.* Edited and with an introduction by Darwin Turner. Norton Critical Edition. New York: W. W. Norton, 1988.

———. *A Jean Toomer Reader: Selected Unpublished Writings.* Ed. Frederik L. Rusch. New York: Oxford University Press, 1993.

———. *The Wayward and the Seeking: A Collection of Writings by Jean Toomer.* Ed. Darwin T. Turner. Washington, D.C.: Howard University Press, 1980.

Traub, Valerie. "The Psychomorphology of the Clitoris." *GLQ* 2 (1995): 81–113.

Tucker, Sophie. *Some of These Days: The Autobiography of Sophie Tucker.* Garden City, N.Y.: Doubleday, Doran, 1945.

Turnipseed, Edward. "Some Facts in Regard to the Anatomical Differences between the Negro and White Races." *American Journal of Obstetrics* 10 (1877): 32–33.

Ullman, Sharon. " 'The Twentieth Century Way': Female Impersonation and Sexual Practice in Turn-of-the-Century America." *Journal of the History of Sexuality* 5, no. 4 (1995): 573–600.

Umphrey, Martha. "The Trouble with Harry Thaw." *Radical History Review* 62 (spring 1995): 8–23.

Uricchio, William, and Roberta E. Pearson. *Reframing Culture: The Case of the Vitagraph Quality Films.* Princeton, N.J.: Princeton University Press, 1993.

Vance, Carol S. "Social Construction Theory: Problems in the History of Sexuality." In *Homosexuality, Which Homosexuality? International Conference on Gay and Lesbian Studies,* ed. Dennis Altman et al., 13–34. London: Gay Men's Press, 1988.

Wadlington, Walter. "The *Loving* Case: Virginia's Anti-Miscegenation Statute in Historical Perspective." *Virginia Law Review* 52 (1966): 1195–1202.

Walker, Alice. "The Divided Life of Jean Toomer." In *In Search of Our Mothers' Gardens.* San Diego: Harcourt, Brace, Jovanovich, 1984.

Walker, Lisa. "How to Recognize a Lesbian: The Cultural Politics of Looking like What You Are." *Signs* (summer 1993): 866–90.

Waller, Gregory A. "Another Audience: Black Moviegoing, 1907–1916." *Cinema Journal* 31 (winter 1992): 2–25.

Walters, Ronald G. "The Erotic South: Civilization and Sexuality in American Abolitionism." *American Quarterly* 25 (1973): 177–201.

Washington, Mary Helen. *Invented Lives: Narratives of Black Women, 1860–1960.* Garden City, N.Y.: Anchor Press, 1987.

Weeks, Jeffrey. *Coming Out: Homosexual Politics in Britain from the Nineteenth Century to the Present.* London: Quartet Books, 1977.

———. *Sex, Politics, and Society: The Regulation of Sexuality since 1800.* London: Longman, 1981.

———. *Sexuality and Its Discontents: Meanings, Myths, and Modern Sexualities.* Boston: Routledge and Kegan Paul, 1985.

Weinberg, Jonathan. " 'Boy Crazy': Carl Van Vechten's Queer Collection." *Yale Journal of Criticism* 7, no. 2 (1994): 25–49.

Weiss, Andrea. *Vampires and Violets: Lesbians in the Cinema.* London: Jonathan Cape, 1992.

Welter, Barbara. "The Cult of True Womanhood, 1820–1860." In *Dimity Convictions: The American Woman in the Nineteenth Century,* 21–41. Columbus: University of Ohio Press, 1976.

Werner, Morris Robert. *Barnum.* New York: Harcourt, Brace, 1923.

Wharton, Henry Thornton. *Sappho: Memoir, Text, Selected Renderings, and a Literal Translation.* 1885. Chicago: A. C. McClurg, 1895.

Wiegman, Robyn. *American Anatomies: Theorizing Race and Gender.* Durham, N.C.: Duke University Press, 1995.

Williamson, Joel. *New People: Miscegenation and Mulattoes in the United States.* New York: Free Press, 1980.

Wirth, Louis, and Herbert Goldhamer. "The Hybrid and the Problem of Miscegenation." In *Characteristics of the American Negro,* ed. Otto Klineberg. New York: Harper and Brothers, 1944.

Wood, J. G. "Dime Museums from a Naturalist's Point of View." *Atlantic Monthly* 55 (June 1885): 759–65.

Woodward, C. Vann. *The Strange Career of Jim Crow.* 2d rev. ed. New York: Oxford University Press, 1966.

Yeazell, Ruth Bernard. "Nature's Courtship Plot in Darwin and Ellis." *Yale Journal of Criticism* 2 (1989): 33–53.

Index

Passionlessness, ideology of: in *Contending Forces,* 93–95

Pearson, Roberta E., 194 n.11

Peiss, Kathy, 67

Penn, Donna, 212 n.20

Pinchback, Bismarck ("Uncle Bis"), 157–158

Pinchback, P. B. S., 132, 162, 211 n.6

Plessy v. Ferguson, 1, 35, 132

Polygeny, 22

Popular culture: and comparative anatomy, 25–26; and "invention" of homosexuality, 2, 39–40, 43–44; in "Sheik and Anti-Sheik," 149–156; and Vitagraph, 58–62. *See also* Burlesque; Cinema, early; Dime museum; Minstrelsy, blackface; Vaudeville

Property relations, racialized: in *The Autobiography of an Ex-Coloured Man,* 119–122; in *A Florida Enchantment,* 71–74; in *Plessy v. Ferguson,* 9, 184 n.28

Psychoanalysis: and homosexuality, 20–21; and race, 21

Psychology, 20–21, 34

Psychopathia Sexualis (Krafft-Ebing), 18, 27, 31

"Queer" (term): 142–143, 214 n.34; in "Bona and Paul," 144–145; in "Kabnis," 140–144; in *Passing,* 145–146; in Toomer's writing, 139–149, 163; in "Withered Skin of Berries," 146–149

Queer reading, 6; and Toomer, 137–140, 163–165; and Van Vechten, 127–129

Queer studies, 6

Queer theory, 136–137; and lesbian/gay history, 164–165; and race, 136–140

Race: and queer theory, 6, 136–140; scientific studies of, 9–10, 21–28, 29–31. *See also* Passing, racial; Racial ambiguity; Scientific racism; Segregation, racial

"Race," history of term, 21

Racial ambiguity, 32–33, 81, 83–84, 102–103; in *The Autobiography of an Ex-Coloured Man,* 112–114; and Toomer, 131–137, 144–145, 162–165. *See also* Passing, racial

Radway, Janice, 216 n.55

Rape: and race, 35, 36–37, 99–100, 106–110; in *Stone Butch Blues,* 170; in *Winona,* 106–110

Raub, Patricia, 154, 215 n.50

Razaf, Andy, 209 n.15

Recapitulation, 24

Redmond, Fergus, 40; *A Florida Enchantment* (novel), 40, 44, 46, 49–54, 58–61, 71–76

Reid, Mark, 195 n.26

Religion: Ellis's view of, 15; in *Winona,* 108–109

Reuter, Edward Byron: *The Mulatto in the United States,* 30

Rich, Ruby, 36

Riggs, Marlon, 208 n.9

Robinson, Amy, 184 n.28

Robinson, William, 31

Rogin, Michael, 70–71, 220 n.13

Romantic friendship: between women, 88–89. *See also* Homoeroticism, female

Russo, Vito, 41

Same-sex desire. *See* Homoeroticism, female; Homoeroticism,
interracial; Homoeroticism, male;
Homosexuality
Sappho (ancient poet), 85–87, 203
n.28, 204 n.38, 205 n.40; in *Contending Forces,* 85–89, 99–100; racial
identity of, 86–87
Schiebinger, Londa, 25, 189–190 n.54
Scientific racism, 9–10, 21–26, 29–31
Scruggs, Charles, 217 n.72
Sedgwick, Eve, 3, 20–21, 160, 209
n.10, 213 n.27; on the "closet,"
92–93, 96–97; on race, 137–139
Segregation, racial: in *The Autobiography of an Ex-Coloured Man,* 123;
and census, 167–168; and compulsory heterosexuality, 137; in early
cinema, 47–49, 52, 63–67, 68–70,
73; and homo/heterosexual definition, 1–5, 34–37; and homosexual
desire, 34–37; in Hopkins's fiction,
79–80; and masculinity, 134; and
sexuality, 134; in *Winona,* 100–101.
See also *Plessy v. Ferguson*
Segrest, Mab, 213 n.21
Senelick, Laurence, 54
Sex change: in *A Florida Enchantment,*
40–41, 43, 46, 55, 74–75; in *Stone
Butch Blues,* 174–175
Sexology: 9–10, 15–21, 39; and eugenics, 29–33; and scientific
racism, 25–29. *See also* Ellis, Havelock; Kiernan, James G.; Krafft-
Ebing, Richard von
Sexual ambiguity: and evolution,
29; and inversion, 28–29, 32–33,
37, 54–55, 91–92; and race, 27–29,
32–33, 37, 101–104; in scientific

studies, 26–29, 37; and sexual practices, 54–55. *See also* Inversion,
sexual; Transgender identity
Sexual danger, 51, 68–69, 74–75
Sexual Inversion (Ellis), 10, 15, 19–20,
25, 27–29, 31–32; and race, 25, 31–
32. See also *Studies in the Psychology
of Sex*
Sexual inversion. *See* Inversion,
sexual
Sexuality, 6; history of, 2–3, 5–7,
15–17, 164–165; vs. gender, 16–17,
54–56, 170–171. *See also* Heterosexuality, interracial; Homoeroticism, female; Homoeroticism,
interracial; Homoeroticism, male;
Homosexuality; Inversion, sexual
Sexual orientation. *See* Heterosexuality, interracial; Homoeroticism,
female; Homoeroticism, interracial; Homoeroticism, male;
Homosexuality; Inversion, sexual;
Sexuality
"Sheik" (term): history of, 153–155,
216 n.51
Sheik, The (film), 153–154
"Sheik and Anti-Sheik" (Toomer),
149–153, 155–156
Slavery: and concubinage, 119; in
Contending Forces, 81; in *A Florida
Enchantment,* 71–74; and marriage,
82–83, 202 n.21; and racial science,
22–23; in *Winona,* 107, 206–207
n.59
Slide, Anthony, 194 n.14
Smith, Albert E., 50, 52
Smith, Samuel Stanhope, 22
Smith, Valerie, 182 n.14
Smith-Rosenberg, Carroll, 88

Siobhan Somerville is Assistant Professor of English and Women's
Studies at Purdue University.

Library of Congress Cataloging-in-Publication Data
Somerville, Siobhan B.
Queering the color line : race and the invention of homosexuality
in American culture / Siobhan B. Somerville.
p.   cm. — (Series Q)
Includes bibliographical references and index.
ISBN 0-8223-2407-5 (cloth : alk. paper).
ISBN 0-8223-2443-1 (pbk. : alk. paper)
1. Gender identity—United States—History.
2. Race awareness—United States—History.
3. Homosexuality in literature.
4. Homosexuality in motion pictures.
5. Race relations in literature.
6. Race relations in motion pictures.
I. Title.   II. Series.
HQ1075.5.U6S65   2000
305.3'0973—dc21   99-33947 CIP